Understanding Service-Learning and Community Engagement

Crossing Boundaries Through Research

A Volume in
Advances in Service-Learning Research

Series Editor:
International Association for Research
on Service-Learning and Community Engagement

Advances in Service-Learning Research
International Association for Research
on Service-Learning and Community Engagement, Series Editor

Understanding Service-Learning and Community Engagement

Crossing Boundaries Through Research

edited by

Julie A. Hatcher and Robert G. Bringle
*Indiana University-
Purdue University Indianapolis*

Information Age Publishing, Inc.
Charlotte, North Carolina • www.infoagepub.com

Library of Congress Cataloging-in-Publication Data

Paperback: 978-1-61735-656-8
Hardcover: 978-1-61735-657-5
eBook: 978-1-61735-658-2

Printed in the United States of America

CONTENTS

PART I:
KEYNOTE ADDRESSES

PART II:
CULTURAL CONTEXTS FOR RESEARCH AND PRACTICE

PART III:
DISCIPLINARY CONTEXTS FOR RESEARCH AND PRACTICE

ACKNOWLEDGMENTS

We considered it a privilege to work with faculty, staff, and students from our campus, Indiana University-Purdue University Indianapolis (IUPUI), as well as staff from Indiana Campus Compact and the International Association for Research on Service-Learning and Community Engagement to plan and implement a successful conference in October 2010. We acknowledge the contributions of Barbara Moely who gave us excellent advice and guidance for both the conference and this publication. We thank the many colleagues who reviewed submissions and provided valuable feedback to the authors. Such a publication needs the attentive eye of a skilled proof reader, and we sincerely thank Kristi Combs, for her dedication to this task. Most important, we appreciate the contributions of the authors represented in this volume, for it is their dedication to community engagement and scholarship that will help to increase understanding and advance the field.

INTRODUCTION

Exploring Similarities and Differences Through Cross-Cultural Comparative Research

Julie A. Hatcher and Robert G. Bringle

This 11th volume of *Advances in Service-Learning Research* occurs at an interesting juncture in the activities and infrastructure associated with service-learning and community engagement. Over the past decade, since the first meeting of the International Association for Research on Service-Learning and Community Engagement (IARSLCE) in Berkeley, CA, in 2001, the field has indeed grown substantially. We were pleased that the conference we cohosted in Indianapolis, IN, October 2010 attracted more than 400 participants from 44 states and 13 different countries, with a total of 43 international attendees representing 9% of those in attendance. Flags from each country represented by attendees graced the stage in the historic Union Station as a reminder of the international dimensions of the field. The conference included 94 session presentations and 26 poster presentations, involving 360 presenters. This volume is comprised of nine chapters. The first two chapters are the keynote addresses given by Michael Quinn Patton and Barbara Ibrahim, each of whom inspired participants to improve the quality and explore new dimensions of service-learning research. The remaining seven chapters focus on a range of topics including international contexts and disciplinary contexts for service-learning and community engagement.

Understanding Service-Learning and Community Engagement:
Crossing Boundaries Through Research, pp. ix–xxii
Copyright © 2012 by Information Age Publishing

STATE OF THE FIELD IN THE UNITED STATES

A number of changes have occurred in the field of service-learning and community engagement in the United States over the past 10 years, and for some these changes may be signs for concern. For example, The American Association of Higher Education, an early and strong advocate for the civic engagement agenda and publisher of the *Service-Learning in the Disciplines Series*, no longer exists. A lifetime achievement award was presented at the conference to Edward Zlotkowski, editor of this important series, for his groundbreaking work with American Association of Higher Education and his tireless travels as the Johnny Appleseed of service-learning in higher education in the United States. Another loss to the field was the decision by the U.S. Department of Housing and Urban Development to no longer provide federal funds for Community Outreach Partnership Centers, a program that created strong networks between communities and campuses to address common goals. Likewise, federal funding for the Corporation for National and Community Service has been severely cut under the current budget, shrinking federal funding for programs such as Learn and Serve America and the National Service-Learning Clearinghouse. Learn and Serve America has been of critical importance to implementing service-learning into K-12 schools, within higher education, and through funding program initiatives of organizations such as the American Association of Community Colleges and national Campus Compact. In addition, evidence indicates that within the past 8 years there has been a decline in service-learning in K-12 schools, as the demands of state curriculum guidelines present a strong barrier to classroom based service-learning (Corporation for National and Community Service, 2008). Private funding through foundations has also declined as some foundations have shifted their funding priorities away from the civic agenda. And scholarly analysis of progress of institutionalizing service-learning and civic engagement over the past two decades has questioned the degree to which the depth of change associated with civic engagement has been democratic, fundamental, and systemic (Saltmarsh & Hartley, 2011). Each of these changes can be cause for concern.

Yet, in spite of these developments, there is an increasing proliferation of service-learning courses in colleges and universities in the United States (Campus Compact, 2010). As a national organization, Campus Compact works with a network of state compact organizations. Each year, new state Compacts are formed and 35 such organizations now assume leadership for convening college and university leaders, securing external funds for institutionalization, and a variety of programs that support student engagement and professional development of faculty and staff. Staff from our Center for Service and Learning collaborated with staff from

Indiana Campus Compact to host the 10th Annual IARSLCE Conference and we can readily attest to the benefits of a strong state Compact. National Campus Compact sponsors an annual research award at the IARSLCE Conference and the Thomas Ehrlich Civically Engaged Faculty Award, a national award for faculty. Another national award, the Ernest A. Lynton Award for the Scholarship of Engagement, is awarded annually by the New England Resource Center for Higher Education.

For higher education, the last decade has also generated new support for civic engagement and for research on service-learning and civic engagement by a number of organizations. The Carnegie Foundation's elective classification for community engagement provides an important recognition for campuses dedicated to this work. The classification can heighten the salience of community engagement activities as well as generate a sense of accomplishment and pride for those associated with community engagement activities. The American Association of State Colleges and Universities has energized its member campuses through the American Democracy Project, with a focus on assessing civic learning outcomes for college graduates and building new networks for administrators, professionals, and scholars. Additionally, the Association of American Colleges and Universities supports many initiatives related to civic engagement (e.g., civic learning and democratic engagement, core commitments: educating students for personal and social responsibility, civic engagement rubric) and convenes scholars for conferences focused on cultivating civic engagement in higher education and communities.

In terms of private funding, the Spencer Foundation has designated funding for research to understand civic action among youth and college students. Called *The New Civics Initiative*, this program of research seeks to understand the developmental framework of civic commitments and civic action. The Lumina Foundation, through the degree qualifications profile, advocates that civic learning is one of five critical learning domains for all types of postsecondary education. And private donors have designated funds to endow centers for service-learning and community engagement at colleges and universities across the country.

There have been new conferences, journals, and publication outlets that have emerged, with special issues of journals devoted to service-learning, community partnerships, and civic learning outcomes. Portland State University's International Institute on Partnerships attracts attendees from across the globe. Virginia Tech sponsors a summer institute, the Engagement Academy for University Leaders, as well as themed institutes on assessment, documentation, and fund raising. Our own campus has hosted the IUPUI Research Academy for the past 3 years, which also attracts scholars from the United States and abroad. The academy is an interactive 3-day summer workshop to develop skills, learn about methods and literature, develop a research project, assist professional staff who are facilitating faculty research on their campuses, and advance research related to service-learning in higher education.

In terms of K-12 education, the work of national organizations remains pivotal during this time of reported decline in service-learning in American schools (Corporation for National and Community Service, 2008). The National Youth Leadership Council, a catalyst for service-learning for the past 25 years, has partnered with the State Farm Company Foundation to produce annual reports for each of the past 7 years to capture the state of service-learning in K-12 schools for educators, researchers, and policy makers. Each of these "Growing to Greatness" reports captures current statistics, presents relevant research, and provides a valuable summary of information related to service-learning among youth. The annual National Youth Leadership Council conference serves as a convening of scholars and practitioners. For the 2010 IARSLCE Conference, we partnered with Dr. Kathy Sikes, executive administrative director of the International Center for Service-Learning Teacher Education which is hosted at Duke University, to convene their second membership meeting at the IARSLCE conference. As a relatively new organization, International Center for Service-Learning Teacher Education hosts conferences to advance scholarship and research world-wide on the role of teachers in K-12 service-learning.

VIEW OF THE FIELD IN INTERNATIONAL CONTEXTS

Internationally, the field has also seen significant growth in a number of geographic areas in the past decade (Watson, 2007). Membership organizations now exist to convene scholars and practitioners in networks across the globe. Examples of these membership organizations include the Australian Universities Community Engagement Alliance (begun in 2004), the Canadian Alliance of Community Service-learning (begun in 2004), the Latin American Center for Service-learning (begun in 2007), the Campus Engage Network for the Promotion of Civic Engagement in Irish Higher Education (begun in 2007), and the Ma'an Arab University Alliance for Civic Engagement (begun in 2008). In Asia, the United Board for Christian Higher Education, the Service-learning Asia Network, and the Asian-Talloires Network of Engaged Universities (begun in 2010) have each supported conferences and forums on service-learning and community engagement. Case studies and reports that capture the growth of service-learning in a particular region are emerging (e.g., Annette, 2005; Badat, 2003; McIlrath, Farrel, Hughes, Lillis, & Lyons, 2007) and these will assist in understanding patterns and variables that shape practice and inform research. In terms of K-12 education, The International Baccalaureate Program now integrates service as a key component of this highly regarded degree.

CONFERENCE THEME

The 2010 IARSLCE conference theme, "International Perspectives: Crossing Boundaries Through Research," was chosen to highlight ways that research can cross all kinds of boundaries: cultural boundaries, disciplinary boundaries, epistemological boundaries, national boundaries, as well as economic and social boundaries in domestic settings. Our key goal, however, was to have a more explicit international focus to the conference program and to increase participation and boundary crossing with international colleagues. We have both had opportunities to collaborate with international colleagues, through projects such as the Community Higher Education Service Project in South Africa, through emerging networks of practitioners and scholars (e.g., in the Arab region, Ireland, Mexico, Macedonia, Asia), and through participation in Fulbright funded program in Kenya. Additionally, with the work of faculty and staff at IUPUI, we have seen the reach and felt the rewards of working with service-learning colleagues from Australia, China, Congo, Czechoslovakia, Dominican Republic, Germany, Greece, Indonesia, Macedonia, Mexico, and Thailand. In collaboration with the International Center of Indianapolis, we host guests and teams of visitors through the International Visitor Leadership Program, an initiative of the U.S. Department of State Bureau of Educational and Cultural Affairs.

Our conceptualization of civic engagement is always refined and improved when we collaborate on projects with international colleagues, debate contestable terms and assumptions, explore issues of language and cultural traditions, and learn from others about the complexity of this work within and across diverse cultural, political, and educational contexts. Cross-cultural perspectives are invaluable to understanding and improving both research and practice in service-learning and community engagement.

The call for proposals for the conference stated that service-learning is valued as an active learning strategy across the globe; however, little is known about the ways that service-learning is similar or different in varied contexts. Understanding service-learning and community engagement from diverse cultural perspectives and comparative research will improve practice. Questions such as the following were suggested in the call for proposals:

- How do different understandings of citizenship, civil society, and engagement influence and shape research on service-learning and community engagement in K-12 and higher education?
- Is the American, westernized concept of service-learning transferable to other contexts? And, if not, what conceptual models frame service-learning research in other national contexts?
- How does research assist in crossing boundaries between campus and community partners, between faculty and students, between disciplines, or between and across cultural contexts?
- How can the United Nations Millennium Development Goals (United Nations, 2010) inform outcome measures for research on service-learning or community engagement?

Unfortunately, many of these questions remained unanswered with little new insight generated from the conference presentations or papers. The majority of sessions focused on the U.S. context, with the emphasis on college student learning outcomes. Little mention of the United Nations Millennium Development Goals was made in terms of community impact and outcomes of service-learning and community engagement. Cross-cultural comparisons were rarely framed by theoretical analysis and were too frequently presented by American researchers. This is in spite of the widespread and growing interest in service-learning and community engagement across the globe.

ADVANCING CROSS-CULTURAL COMPARATIVE RESEARCH

As a response to this gap in the research on service-learning in global contexts (Giles, 2010), the following analytical framework is offered as a basis from which future cross-national and cross-cultural research can be conducted. This framework has emerged from the review of literature (e.g., Bawden, 2000), conversations and presentations with colleagues at international conferences (Bringle, Hatcher, McIlrath, Elshimi, 2010; Thomson, Smith-Tolken, Naidoo, & Bringle, 2008), and scholarship to date (Hatcher & Erasmus, 2008; Thomson, Smith-Tolken, Naidoo, & Bringle, 2011)

Three levels of analysis are posited to compare and contrast service-learning and community engagement: macrolevel, mesolevel, and microlevel analysis. The macrolevel of analysis includes systemic, national, or cultural factors that influence institutions of education in a designated category. This might be at the national level (e.g., all institutions of higher education in South Africa), but it could also be useful for all institutions within a particular religious context, or some other systemic level of analysis that creates some degree of commonality across institutions. These macrolevel factors would include the cultural, educational, and political contexts of a nation, region, or type of university as well as significant events in the history and philosophy of education (Hatcher & Erasmus, 2008). The nature of social stratification in society would also be relevant to understanding the dynamics between various groups. In addition, the civic and philanthropic traditions would be important to understanding motives for civic and community involvement, the nature and patterns of prosocial behaviors, and the normative aspirations for life-long civic habits and engagement.

Each of these macrolevel factors influences the terms, language, and practices that are associated with service-learning and civic engagement (Thomson et al., 2011). Thus, each of these macrolevel factors also influences research. For example questions such as the following would fall within the macrolevel of analysis: Is there a national policy initiative that supports community engagement, a transformational role for higher education, or civic learning outcomes for students? What is the philosophy of education that guides teaching and learning? Is assessment of learning and accountability formalized by the government or a third-party organization? What is the nature of civil society? Is *democratic* an appropriate description of the principles valued within society? Does *civic* have meaning in this context? Is the term *service-learning* a problematic term or an acceptable term? What are the philanthropic traditions and norms for volunteering?

The mesolevel of analysis is viewed as encompassing factors that are operating at the institutional level (e.g., intraorganizational factors at a particular university), across institutions, and interorganizational relationships (e.g., schools, universities, nongovernmental organizations, local government, foundations). Furco and Holland (in press) identify the types of institutional factors that shape the nature of service-learning and civic engagement in higher education and a research agenda for studying them. For example, each institution has its own particular mission that shapes what is valued, what is strategically supported, what is relevant to its constituencies.

A comparative analysis of community engagement at institutions in different nations will need to consider these types of mesolevel factors in developing an understanding of what is happening, why, and with what results as well as macrolevel factors. For example, at faith-based institutions, the learning objectives for students will be different from those institutions with an emphasis on technical preparation of students for professions. Questions such as the following would fall within the mesolevel of analysis: How is community engagement evident in the mission of institutions of higher education in different national contexts? What types of nonprofit or nongovernmental organizations exist in the immediate community? What is the capacity of organizations and K-12 schools to host and manage service-learners? Does local government assume an important role in supporting and managing educational partnerships? Are there foundations, or similar entities, that provide financial support for community engagement? To what extent do businesses and corporations support community engagement and service-learning?

At the microlevel of analysis, factors are included that are particular to individual actors as well as a particular service-learning course, a particular set of courses (e.g., all business courses at an institution), or a particular program (Bringle & Tonkin, 2004). There are a variety of individuals who assume various roles in community engagement; these roles and the relationships between and among them are likely to vary across cultural and national contexts. The SOFAR model (Bringle, Clayton & Price, 2009) identifies students, organizational staff, faculty, administrators, and residents in the community as key individuals involved in service-learning in higher education. Each of the relationships between these individuals and roles creates a number of variables that has implications for both practice and research. There are a number of practical issues faced in the design of the course, its operations, and the development of partnerships with the community. In addition, research on the relationships among these various players lead to vary interesting findings about how higher education relates to its communities and the outcomes that result for persons in each group.

Microlevel issues relevant to cross-cultural research may include comparing student outcomes, faculty motivations, or community benefits. Course-specific or program-specific issues are also important variables to consider. For example: Are there issues related to travel, safety, or communication at the service site that create different challenges across settings? Is there institutional funding for the project and the capacity to produce deliverables to a community partner? In what ways do structural issues associated with a service-learning course (e.g., credit hours, contact hours, course policies, reflection activities) vary across contexts? Can faculty receive stipends or course-release time to develop service-learning courses? Is a memorandum of understanding between educators and staff at the community organizations necessary or required? Is a learning contract used with students? What are the assessment criteria and how is the evaluation conducted? How are academic, civic, and community outcomes influenced by course specific factors? Any cross-cultural or cross-national research that focuses on courses or programs at this microlevel will also have to take into account the mesolevel and macrolevel factors.

IMPLICATIONS FOR PRACTICE AND RESEARCH

In addition to this analytical framework for cross-cultural comparative research, we offer a number of implications for both practice and research to increase cross-cultural understanding. In terms of practice, we recommend that scholars work with international colleagues and intentionally cross national, cultural, and other relevant boundaries to increase understanding through research projects. Specific steps might include:

- collaborating on conference presentations, which can help develop a working relationship among colleagues and a research agenda;
- seeking funds for travel stipends to visit international sites (e.g., Fulbright grants, campus travel funds, Rotary Club) to build relationships with colleagues and gain first-hand experience of cultural contexts and differences;
- writing grant proposals for joint projects and research as a way to identify and clarify common objectives and provide support for research; and
- building networks with other faculty and staff with international interests or responsibilities (e.g., international programs, study abroad, Title VI Area Studies Resource Centers) as well as teachers and community partners through international centers, sister city programs, or service organizations (e.g., Kiwanis International, Rotary Club), which can enrich these programs through service-learning and community engagement activities.

In terms of future research, we have some ambitious aspirations. There are many areas of scholarship related to community engagement and community outcomes that have grown over the past 2 decades. One important area of study is focused on an emerging set of activities that are present within and strengthen the third sector of society (e.g., civic service, nonprofit organizations, volunteering, civil society). Research on service-learning and community engagement aligns well with this area of research. The goals of service-learning include cultivating civic-learning outcomes and social responsibility among participants and strengthening communities and community organizations through the active involvement of students, graduates, faculty, teachers, and staff. Virginia Hodgkinson (2004), a noted and pioneering scholar in the field of philanthropy and nonprofit studies, summarized the following steps as critical to building a research agenda in a new field:

1. Collecting good data
2. Agreeing upon clear definitions
3. Creating good bibliographies
4. Theory building
5. Mapping the terrain
6. Building a community of scholars
7. Providing conference opportunities

We affirm the importance of each of these seven steps for understanding service-learning and community engagement and highlight two that are necessary to understand service-learning from a cross-cultural perspective.

First, much like the comparative work that has been done in mapping the third sector internationally over the past 15 years through the Johns Hopkins Comparative Nonprofit Sector project, it is time to create a good parallel data base of service-learning across the globe. The Comparative Nonprofit Sector project is "the largest systematic effort ever undertaken to analyze the scope, structure, financing, and impact of the nonprofit activity throughout the world in order to improve our knowledge and enrich our theoretical understanding of this sector and to provide a sounder basis for both public and private action toward it" (Johns Hopkins Institute for Policy Studies, 2011). Scholars were convened to come to consensus on definitional issues and on strategies to gather evidence to document the size and scope of the third sector. In-country scholars and research teams used the same protocol to gather information. To date, data that has been collected from 46 countries is used in research, publications, and books (e.g., Salamon, Wojciech Sokolowski, & Associates 2004) to advance understanding of the various conditions that support the development of the nonprofit sector. A similar strategy could be used to convene scholars from across the globe to generate consensus on a template of information to collect data on service-learning at the macro-, meso-, and microlevel of analysis. In-country scholars would be identified to form research teams to collect data on the size and scope of service-learning and create a researchable data base for scholars to use for comparative analysis.

In addition, describing the developments of service-learning in international contexts is necessary to understanding the conditions that support its growth. Following a model used by scholars at the Center for Social Development at Washington University in St. Louis to understand civic service in its various forms across the world (McBride & Sherraden, 2007), a similar compilation of portraits of service-learning could be produced. Using factors at the macro-, meso-, and microlevel of analysis, a common template would be developed by a group of scholars from various regional networks. This template would create a common framework used to describe and portray service-learning in national contexts. Patterns would undoubtedly emerge that could inform further research as well as public policy. Both of these two projects would (a) provide systematic qualitative and quantitative data to advance comparative research, (b) strengthen social networks and ties with colleagues across the globe, and (c) help to overcome "parochial bias" which is "one of the biggest challenges facing the researcher in this field" (Tonkin, 2011, p.193).

CONCLUSION

From the presentations at the conference, and the chapters in this current volume, we are confident in saying that the field of service-learning and community engagement is firmly established, yet the field has further work on the horizon in order to maintain its strength and legitimacy. Substantial research is in order to understand how service-learning is similar or different across the globe.

This is likely to be the last volume in the *Advances in Service-Learning Research* series, which began more than a decade ago by IARSLCE and in partnership with Information Age Publishing. Each volume is comprised of peer-reviewed papers presented at the annual conference. The intention of the series was to bring together the K-12 research on service-learning, both domestic and international, with the higher education research on service-learning and community engagement. By design, the work in the two educational sectors can inform each other in terms of theory, instrumentation, methodology as well as developmental issues for students. The series is designed to describe key research issues in the field, through discussions of methodological changes, presentation of research agendas, and a call for more and better research. In this regard, the volume is not just about presenting study findings, but also includes chapters focused on service-learning research more broadly and theoretical perspectives that can guide future research.

Strategically, the executive board of IARSLCE recognizes the need for a peer-reviewed journal. Beginning in January 2012, IARSLCE will adopt a new journal format for publishing research to advance the field, still in partnership with Information Age. The journal will welcome scholarship and research from across the globe to increase understanding of service-learning and community engagement in a variety of contexts. The new journal will better serve the field and the mission of IARSLCE as it continues to encourage and disseminate high quality international research on community engagement and service-learning. Cathy Burak and Alan

Melchior (Brandeis University) have been selected to be the editors of the new journal.

A second new publication from IARSLCE is an innovative, web-based approach to conference proceedings. The proceedings will be available on the association's webpage approximately a month prior to the annual conference and will include information on the accepted proposals as a means of informing potential registrants and of supporting attendees in planning their participation at the conference. After the conference, the Proceedings will be further developed to include a scholarly publication of extended abstracts and links to associated resources. The publication is intended to increase the public visibility of research related to service-learning and community engagement and to facilitate communication among researchers and practitioner-scholars. The proceedings is cocreated and produced by a group of editorial fellows, members of the association's Graduate Student Network, as part of the Graduate Student Network's leadership in advancing and supporting research. The group will be initially led by Senior Editorial Fellow Barbara Harrison (Brock University, Canada) and mentored by editors Billy O'Steen (University of Canterbury, Christchurch, New Zealand) and Patti Clayton (PHC Ventures, IUPUI, University of North Carolina at Greensboro).

We trust that these new publication outlets, along with conferences, symposium, and institutes, will continue to advance research and ultimately advance good practice, for this in the end should be the goal of scholarship ... to improve lives and strengthen communities, locally and around the world.

REFERENCES

Annette, J. (2005). Community, service learning and higher education in the UK. In J. Arthur & K. E. Bohlin (Eds.), *Citizenship and higher education: The role of universities in communities and society* (pp. 39-48). New York, NY: Routledge-Falmer.

Badat, S. (2003). *Transforming South African higher education, 1990-2003: Goals, policy initiatives, and critical challenges and issues* (Unpublished paper). Retrieved from http://www.che.org.za/che_secretariat/ceo_papers/2003/SA-Transform_Dec2003.pdf

Bawden, R. (2000). *CHESP and the scholarship of engagement: Strategies towards a universe of human discourse. A report on the visit of Professor Richard Bawden to the eight CHESP pilot projects.* Johannesburg, South Africa: Joint Educational Trust.

Bringle, R. G., Clayton, P. H., & Price, M. F. (2009). Partnerships in service learning and civic engagement. *Partnerships: A Journal of Service Learning & Civic Engagement, 1*(1), 1-20.

Bringle, R. G., Hatcher, J. A., McIlrath, L., Eshimi, A. (2010). *How service learning relates to the third sector: Multi-national practice and research*. Panel presented at the Ninth International Society for Third Sector Research Conference, Istanbul, Turkey.

Bringle, R. G. & Tonkin, H. (2004). International service learning. A research agenda. In H. Tonkin (Ed.), *Service learning across cultures: Promise and achievements* (pp. 365-374). New York, NY: International Partnership for Service Learning and Leadership.

Campus Compact. (2010). *Annual report*. Retrieved from www.indianacampuscompact.org/images/stories/pdf_uploads/ICC%200910%20Annual%20Rpt%20web%20version.pdf

Corporation for National and Community Service (2008). *Community service and service learning in America's schools, 2008*. Washington, DC: Corporation for National and Community Service.

Furco, A., & Holland, B. (in press). Research on institutionalization of service learning. In P. H. Clayton, R. G. Bringle, & J. A. Hatcher (Eds.), *Research on service learning: Conceptual frameworks and assessment*. Sterling, VA: Stylus.

Giles, D. E. (2010). Journey to service learning research: Agendas, accomplishments, and aspirations. In J. Keshen, B. Holland, & B. Moely (Eds.), *Research for what?: Making engaged scholarship matter* (pp. 203-221). Charlotte, NC: Information Age Publishing.

Hatcher, J. A., & Erasmus, M. (2008).Service learning in the United States and South Africa: A comparative analysis informed by John Dewey and Julius Nyerere. *Michigan Journal of Community Service Learning, 15*(1), 49-61.

Hodgkinson, V. A. (2004). Developing a research agenda on civic service. *Nonprofit and Voluntary Sector Quarterly, 33*, 184S-197S.

Johns Hopkins Institute for Policy Studies. (2011) *Comparative nonprofit sector project*. Retrieved from http://ccss.jhu.edu/printView.php?view=9&sub=3&print=true

McBride, A. M., & Sherraden, M. (Eds.) (2007). *Civic service worldwide: Impacts and inquiry*. Armonk, NY: M. E. Sharpe

McIlrath, L., Farrel, A., Hughes, J., Lillis, S., & Lyons, A. (Eds.) (2007). *Mapping civic engagement within higher education in Ireland*. Retrieved from http://www.compact.org/wp-content/uploads/2011/03/Mapping_Civic_Engagement_final.pdf

Salamon, L. M., Wojciech Sokolowski, S., & Associates (2004).*Global civil society: Dimensions of the nonprofit sector* (Vol. 2.) Bloomfield, CT: Kumarian Press.

Saltmarsh, J., & Hartley, M. (Eds.). (2011). *To serve a larger purpose: Engagement for democracy and the transformation of higher education*. Philadelphia, PA: Temple University Press.

Thomson, A. M., Smith-Tolken, A., Naidoo, T., & Bringle, R. G. (2008). *Service learning and community engagement: A cross cultural perspective*. Presentation at the Eighth International Conference for Third Sector Research, University of Barcelona, Spain.

Thomson, A. M., Smith-Tolken, A., Naidoo, A. V., & Bringle, R. G. (2011). Service learning and civic engagement: A comparison of three national contexts. *Voluntas, 22*, 214-237.

Tonkin, H. (2011). A research agenda for international service learning. In R.G. Bringle, J.A. Hatcher, & S.G. Jones (2011). *International service learning: Conceptual frameworks and research* (pp. 191-224). Sterling, VA: Stylus.

United Nations (2010). *Millennium development goals.* Retrieved from http://www.un.org/millenniumgoals/

Watson, D. (2007). *Managing civic and community engagement.* Berkshire, England: Open University Press.

PART I

KEYNOTE ADDRESSES

CHAPTER 1

IMPROVING RIGOR IN SERVICE-LEARNING RESEARCH

Michael Q. Patton

ABSTRACT

Traditionally, rigor in research has focused on the high quality execution of a specific method, like a randomized controlled trial or an in-depth case study. This chapter offers a framework for rigor that builds on traditional attention to rigorous procedures while emphasizing greater attention to *rigorous thinking* and elevates the unit of analysis from the individual study to considering the cumulative and integrated rigor of research in the entire field of service-learning. That framework focuses on how to generate high quality, credible, and useful knowledge to test theory and inform action through systematic triangulation across realms of inquiry and knowledge generation.

Service-learning is inherently integrative. Therein resides both the challenge and opportunity for rigorous research. What I mean by being *inherently integrative* is that it begins with two distinct experiences and concepts: service and learning. Combining service and learning connects and

Understanding Service-Learning and Community Engagement:
Crossing Boundaries Through Research, pp. 3–9

integrates these operationally separate notions into a distinct arena of research on the combination: service-learning. This, I shall argue, offers unique opportunities for rigor. Traditionally, rigor in research has focused on the high quality execution of a specific method, like a randomized controlled trial or an in-depth case study. In contrast, I shall offer a framework for rigor that builds on traditional attention to rigorous procedures, emphasizes greater attention to rigorous thinking, and elevates the unit of analysis from the individual study to consider the cumulative and integrated rigor of research in the entire field of service-learning. That framework will examine how to generate high quality, credible, and useful knowledge to test theory and inform action through systematic triangulation across realms of inquiry and knowledge generation.

LEARNING FROM RIGOROUS RAILROAD ANALYSIS

For this conference, we are assembled in the Grand Hall of the Indianapolis Union Station, the first union station in the world, which opened on September 20, 1853. Let me use this setting to describe one of the most rigorous research processes I have had the privilege to be part of: *Switching Operations Fatality Analysis* (SOFA). Fifty-five railroad employees have died in switching yard accidents in the last 5 years. The first SOFA Working Group report was released in 1999 based on careful analysis of 76 railroad fatal accident case files. The 2004 report examined the 48 switching fatalities that had occurred since the first report. These analyses identified the *5 LIFESAVERS* and 10 Special Switching Hazards that contribute to fatal accidents. The 2010 report presents the latest findings on the causes of deadly accidents. The SOFA Working Group is made up of representatives from the railroad industry, labor unions, locomotive engineers, and federal regulators. These stakeholder groups are traditionally suspicious of each other and often in conflict over regulations and procedures. But they put aside those conflicts to rigorously investigate the causes of switching operations fatalities. They carefully review every case, coding a variety of variables related to conditions, contributing factors, and kinds of operations involved. They look for patterns in qualitative case data and correlations in the quantitative data across cases. They spend 3 to 4 hours coding each case and hours analyzing patterns across cases. They have found that fatalities happen for a reason. Accidents are not random occurrences, unfortunate events, or just plain bad luck. The risks to employees engaged in switching operations are real, ever present, and preventable. The data demonstrate patterns in why switching fatalities occur. Knowledge about the causes of railroad accidents has accumulated through rigorous analysis over time and across cases.

On February 25, 2010, over 50 senior industry executives, labor leaders, and Federal Railroad Administration staff were convened to discuss draft findings and their implications. The meeting opened with a moment of silence in memory of the 179 lives lost in switching operations. The group then reviewed how the SOFA Working Group arrived at its findings and determined that the results were credible, accurate, and important. The group discussed patterns in the findings and identified potential preventive initiatives. The SOFA report incorporated what was learned at this summit meeting and invited those in the railroad industry at all levels to engage with the findings and take actions to prevent fatalities. The goal is zero deaths.

The SOFA Working Group analysis process was evaluated by a team of external, independent evaluation professionals. The evaluation included examining the quality of the analysis process, the validity of findings, what lessons had been learned, and what had changed in the industry over the last decade that affected interpretation and use of the new findings. The independent evaluation concluded that the SOFA analysis process was systematic, rigorous, comprehensive, and objective. The findings were deemed valid and significant. What can be learned from this railroad example of rigorous research?

RIGOROUS THINKING SUPERSEDES RIGOROUS METHODS

The SOFA working group used multiple methods, drew on diverse sources and types of data, carefully examined and questioned assumptions, and thoughtfully triangulated findings. Rigorous thinking was more important than reliance on methodological rigor. This is a critical distinction. With concern about research rigor, adherence to method is emphasized over rigorous inquiry and critical thinking. A good example of the difference comes from a review of what constitutes rigor in information analysis done by intelligence analysts. As a result of the fiasco of faulty military intelligence leading up to and used to justify the invasion of Iraq, leaders in the intelligence community undertook a comprehensive review to reconsider what rigorous analysis means. Their findings are relevant to service-learning research.

They began by asking: "Given the many contexts in which *information analysis* occurs, what does it mean to be rigorous? Moreover, how do analysts go about achieving acceptable levels of rigor in their analysis processes? What might help them to be more rigorous?" Their work led to a model of analytical rigor that frames the concept *rigor* as an emergent multiattribute measure of sufficiency (e.g., Has the analyst done enough?) rather than as it is commonly framed, as a measure of process adherence (e.g., How rigidly has the analyst followed a particular method?). They identified eight attributes of rigorous analysis that contribute to the assessment of the quality and the sufficiency of an analysis (Woods, 2007).

Attributes of the Rigor Metric

1. *Hypothesis exploration* describes the extent to which multiple hypotheses were considered in explaining data. In a low-rigor process there is minimal weighing of alternatives. A high-rigor process, in contrast, involves broadening of the hypothesis set beyond an initial framing and incorporating multiple perspectives to identify the best, most probable explanations.

2. *Information search* relates to the depth and breadth of the search process used in collecting data. A low-rigor analysis process does not go beyond routine and readily available data sources, whereas a high-rigor process attempts to explore exhaustively all data potentially available in the relevant sample space.

3. *Information validation* details the level at which information sources are corroborated and cross-validated. In a low-rigor process little effort is made to use converging evidence to verify source accuracy, while a high-rigor process includes a systematic approach for verifying information and, when possible, ensures the use of sources closest to the areas of interest.

4. *Stance analysis* is the evaluation of data with the goal of identifying the stance or perspective of the source and placing it into a broader context of understanding. At the low-rigor level an analyst may notice a clear bias in a source, while a high-rigor process involves research into source backgrounds with the intent of gaining a more subtle understanding of how their perspective might influence their stance toward analysis-relevant issues.

5. *Sensitivity analysis* considers the extent to which analysts consider and understand the assumptions and limitations of their analysis. In a low-rigor process, explanations seem appropriate and valid on a surface level. In a high-rigor process the analyst employs a strategy to consider the strength of explanations if individual supporting sources were to prove invalid.

6. *Specialist collaboration* describes the degree to which analysts incorporate the perspectives of domain experts into their assessments. In a low-rigor process, little effort is made to seek out such expertise, whereas in a high-rigor process the analyst has talked to, or may be, a leading expert in the key content areas of the analysis.

7. *Information synthesis* refers to how far beyond simply collecting and listing data an analysts went in their process. In the low rigor process an analyst simply complies the relevant information in a unified form, whereas a high-rigor process has extracted and integrated information with a thorough consideration of diverse interpretations of relevant data.

8. *Explanation critique* is a different form of collaboration that captures how many different perspectives were incorporated in examining the primary hypotheses. In a low-rigor process, there is little use of other analysts to give input on explanation quality. In a high-rigor process, peers and experts have examined the chain of reasoning and explicitly identified which inferences stronger and which are weaker (Zelik, Patterson, & Woods, 2007).

What stands out to me about these criteria for rigor is the emphasis on engaging multiple perspectives, deep questioning, and critical thinking. With these criteria of rigor as context, let me turn to triangulation as a source of rigor in service-learning. Attention to triangulation directs attention away from the rigor of any particular study to the cumulative evidence across studies and kinds of findings. Cumulative, triangulated synthesis of research findings is how knowledge is built in a field.

Rigor Through Cumulative, Triangulated Synthesis of Research Findings

Any single method and any single study will inevitably be limited, even flawed. A field builds knowledge cumulatively through triangulated synthesis of research findings from diverse studies and using diverse sources of data. The idea is that the greater the number of supporting sources for a hypothesized proposition about service-learning, the more rigorous the supporting evidence, and the greater the *triangulation of supporting sources*, the more confidence one has in the significance and meaningfulness of that assertion of knowledge. Propositions based on only one type of supporting evidence, derived from one kind of method, is weaker than propositions supported by multiple and diverse sources of evidence. Consider these eight diverse sources of knowledge:

1. Basic and applied research on service-learning
2. Evaluation findings on service-learning programs, especially patterns across programs

3. Wisdom and reflective practice of service-learning practitioners
4. Experiences reported by service-learning program participants, clients, or intended beneficiaries
5. Expert knowledge and opinion of service-learning
6. Propositions about service-learning with strong theoretical support
7. Cross-disciplinary patterns of knowledge from other fields
8. Theory as an explanation of the lesson and its mechanism of impact

Imagine that something like a Michelin 5 star restaurant or hotel rating system is created for service-learning knowledge where each knowledge source constitutes one star. A five-star, highly rated knowledge proposition, then, would be one that was supported, over time, by cumulative evidence from multiple, triangulated sources (Patton, 2008, p. 136).

Rigorous synthesis of findings across sources and types of data is how one builds a solid foundation of knowledge in a field. Lessons learned with only one type of supporting evidence would be considered a *lessons learned hypothesis*. Nested within and cross-referenced to lessons learned should be the actual cases from which practice wisdom and evaluation findings have been drawn. A critical principle here is to maintain the contextual frame for lessons learned, that is, to keep lessons learned grounded in their context. For ongoing learning, the trick is to follow future supposed applications of lessons learned to test their wisdom and relevance over time in action in new settings.

One of the challenges facing the profession of evaluation going forward will be to bring some degree of rigor to such popular notions as *lessons learned* and *best practices*. Such rigor takes on added importance as, increasingly, the substantive contribution of research on service-learning includes not only how to conduct high quality research and evaluations but also generating knowledge based on having learned how to synthesize findings about patterns of effective interventions; that is, better practices in program design and lessons learned about effective programming generally. The future status and utility of service-learning scholarship may depend on the rigor and integrity brought to these challenges.

REFERENCES

Patton, M. Q. (2008). *Utilization-focused evaluation* (4th ed). Thousand Oaks, CA: SAGE.

Woods, D. D. (2007*). Revealing analytical rigor: A strategy for creating insight into the information analysis process.* Retrieved from http://academic.research.microsoft .com/Paper/13513837.aspx

Zelik, D., Patterson, E. S., & Woods, D. D. (2007). *Understanding rigor in information analysis.* Retrieved from http://csel.eng.ohiostate.edu/zelik/research/Rigor_files/ZelikPattersonWoods_UnderstandingRigor_1.pdf

CHAPTER 2

INTERNATIONAL SERVICE-LEARNING AS A PATH TO GLOBAL CITIZENSHIP

Barbara Lethem Ibrahim

ABSTRACT

In the past decade, globalization has had a tremendous impact on higher education as an increasing number of students worldwide now study for significant periods of time beyond their own national borders. This chapter explores the potential implications of international service-learning in higher education to enhance global citizenship. Three dimensions of global citizenship are identified (i.e., identity, allegiance, receding boundaries) and each of these is amenable to empirical study as sociological or social-psychological constructs. This conceptual framework is proposed to define some of the topics for further exploration and research.

Globalization has had a tremendous impact on higher education as an increasing number of students worldwide now study for significant periods of time beyond their own national borders. This trend has popularized the notion of educating for "global citizenship" (Lewin, 2009b; Nussbaum, 1996), one of those ideas like *diversity* which is widely perceived to be a public good but rarely subjected to critical assessment.

Understanding Service-Learning and Community Engagement:
Crossing Boundaries Through Research, pp. 11–21
Copyright © 2012 by Information Age Publishing

What does it mean to be educating citizens of the world? It becomes an important question once the cosmopolitan veneer around the phrase is removed to expose vast disparities of wealth, influence and cultural understanding that still divide our globe.

This chapter explores the potential of education to enhance global citizenship. We do so through the lens of international service-learning, a rapidly growing and popular study abroad option on many college campuses in the United States (Bringle, Hatcher & Jones, 2011; Parker & Dautoff, 2007) and across the globe (Tonkin, 2004). International service-learning is an educational endeavor that integrates community-based experiential learning, international education and study abroad and is defined as:

> A structured academic experience in another country in which students (a) participate in an organized service activity that addresses identified community needs; (b) learn from direct interaction and cross-cultural dialogue with others; and (c) reflect on the experience in such a way as to gain further understanding of course content, a deeper understanding of global and intercultural issues, a broader appreciation of the host country and the discipline, and an enhanced sense of their own responsibilities as citizens, locally and globally. (Bringle & Hatcher, 2011, p. 19)

Examples from the small but growing body of research designed to understand the impact of international service-learning experiences on student attitudes, alerts us to several complexities. One of the puzzles is that some studies of undergraduate service-learning programs abroad have uncovered a decrease, small but nonetheless real, in global civic-mindedness as one of the initial student outcomes. The area of international service-learning for global citizenship is ripe for critical research (Bringle & Tonkin, 2004; Tonkin, 2011). A simple conceptual framework is proposed to define some of the fertile topics for further exploration.

BACKGROUND AND FRAMING

At the American University in Cairo, Egypt, I recently asked a group of fairly cosmopolitan students and faculty whom they supposed was the first person to say, "I am a citizen of the world". The answers ranged from Mahatma Gandhi to Eleanor Roosevelt to John Lennon, but none of these were even close. In fact that statement "I am a citizen of the world" was first made in the year A.D. 220 by the Greek philosopher Diogenes Laertius, who saw his allegiances extending beyond Athens to other city-states and unimagined hinterlands.

The idea of global citizenship thus has a very long pedigree passing from the Greeks to Roman Stoic writers like Seneca and Cicero, through a line of pacifist global thinkers in the Enlightenment such as Immanuel Kant, on through the founding fathers in the United States. In 1791, Thomas Paine said "The world is my country; all mankind are my brethren, and to do good is my religion." This intellectual legacy has a long history as well in liberal higher education. No nineteenth century European felt himself, *rarely, herself*, to be truly well-educated until having made a requisite study trip to absorb the classical sites of Greece and the Roman Empire. Global citizenship for them meant not only relating to those in other geographies but also to people from the distant past. Likewise, contemporary analyses of the liberal education stress the increasing relevance of global citizenship (Hovland, McTighe Musil, Skilton-Sylvester, & Jamison, 2009; McTighe Musil, 2003).

The idea or ideal of global citizenship faces a backlash from time to time, and currently in the United States there are a number of high-profile detractors, ironically, just as inexpensive air travel and electronic communication finally put global connections within reach of nearly everyone. Newt Gingrich emphatically disagreed with Thomas Paine, saying in 2003 "I am *not* a citizen of the world. I think the entire concept is intellectual nonsense and stunningly dangerous" (Gerzon, 2010, p. xi). His disdain for an expansive sense of citizenship is echoed in many parts of the world today, where identity politics valorizes a local identity and spreads xenophobic fear or contempt for *the other*.

In academia, the interest in world studies, study abroad opportunities, and, more recently, developing intercultural competencies among college graduates (Deardorff, 2008; Hovland et al., 2009) can be traced to a number of historical factors (Lewin, 2009a). Certainly, among these are nation building strategies, most prevalent in the postwar and cold-war era in the United States and the United Kingdom (Kiely, 2011; Tonkin, 2011) which promoted these educational ideals in the context of postwar reintegration. A major aspect of building pan-European identities across the European Union involves educational exchange at the undergraduate level, while volunteering forms an important aspect of study abroad in countries such as Israel, Japan, Philippines, and Mexico (Tonkin, 2011).

Combining a community-based opportunity to give service as part of the international educational experience was pioneered by programs like *Teach for Africa* at Harvard and Princeton in the 1960s and the International Partnership for Service-Learning and Leadership in 1980s. The United Nations Educational, Scientific and Cultural Organization supported such early efforts in a wide range of service and service-learning activities across the globe (Berry & Chisholm, 1999).

DEFINITIONS AND INDICATORS

Bringle et al. (2011) analyze how the strengths of study abroad, international education, and service-learning converge to produce a powerful pedagogy for international civic learning and, by extension, global citizenship. As one deconstructs the phrase global citizenship into constituent parts, contradictions become readily apparent. Formal citizenship is granted by a state, or in some cases, a union of states. Citizenship almost always implies elements of legacy, birthright, geographic location, and allegiance to a sovereign, who in turn provides protection. None of that is of course possible in claiming citizenship to the entire globe (Nussbaum, 1996; Plater, 2011). So what is most likely implied in using the term global citizenship are more nebulous ideas such as affiliation, identity, empathy, and social solidarity. McTighe Musil (2003) describes six graduated levels of possible engagement that are applicable to degrees of global citizenship: (a) exclusionary, (b) oblivious, (c) naïve, (d) charitable, (e) reciprocal, and (f) generative.

The conceptual clarity of the term may be helped by putting forward some dimensions of global citizenship that are amenable to empirical study as sociological or social-psychological constructs. The following dimensions are a starting point in forming a conceptual framework to guide future research:

- Identity: In embracing global citizenship, one acknowledges a liminal threshold or porous understanding of what is embraced as *my* language, culture or heritage and that of others in distant places. Identities become intermingled and capable of expansion rather than boundary maintenance. Identity development takes on dimensions "as both a citizen of one's own community and nation as well as the world" (Plater, 2011, p. 49).

- Allegiance: The welfare and rights of distant people become relevant and motivate concern or action, regardless of residence or birthright. As fewer kinds of borders limit interaction, and modern life is characterized by technology, mobility and diversity, commitments and allegiances are formed to others beyond one's country of origin.

- Receding boundaries: As identities and allegiances expand they influence life choices. Those who embrace global citizenship are increasingly likely to be geographically mobile, to interact with people beyond their home base, and to seek jobs or interests that involve *border crossings*.

Each of these dimensions reflects a behavioral component as well as dispositions and values that can be translated into measurable indicators. Just as with more standard aspects of citizenship, then, the dimensions of global citizenship are amenable to pedagogy and can be taught inside and beyond the classroom. First, however, we expand upon the three interrelated aspects of global citizenship.

Identities That Embrace Difference

The historical figure of Richard Burton embodies what it could mean to live a life dedicated to learning about and embracing *the other*. A Victorian-era explorer remembered for his East African search for the source of the Nile and for making a disguised pilgrimage to Mecca, he reveled in and embraced human cultural diversity. Throughout an adventurous life he actively sought to understand other religions as they were experienced by believers. Burton cultivated within himself the best he discovered in other cultures (Troyanov, 2006). His appreciation for places and ideas considered alien in Victorian England, however, made him a pariah at home.

An examination of the lives of people like Burton, Mother Theresa, and others suggests that the concept of *tolerance*, which has characterized the multicultural discourse until now on many university campuses, may benefit from critical examination. Tolerance implies a distanced acceptance of *the other* but stops short of the potential for growth and understanding that comes with more active engagement *with others*. A step beyond tolerance is appreciation or integration, in which one has a positive affect for ideas and practices different from ones own.

In the few historical periods in which entire cultures embraced appreciation of difference, there was a proliferation of social, artistic and scientific advancement. This was the case during the flowering of civilization in fifteenth century Andalusia when the Moorish cities of Granada and Cordoba flourished. It was a rare moment of cultural integration in which Jewish poetry was not just tolerated, it was embraced as the court poetry of the Muslim rulers; Christian arts and commerce were emulated and all faiths worshiped as they saw fit. Appreciation of and engagement with differences is both rare and powerful, thus it can be seen as a dimensions of global citizenship which universities are challenged to promote.

Allegiances Expand

The past few years have seen a significant increase in the numbers of ordinary people, as opposed to celebrities, contributing funds for cross-border causes. It is estimated that charitable giving in the United States to international organization comprises 5% of total annual giving and over the past 2 years, international giving has increased by 18%, the largest percentage increase in any subsector (Giving USA Foundation, 2011). This kind of cross-border giving is facilitated by web-based modalities and motivated by increasing awareness and interest in global matters and new levels of empathy with the humanitarian needs of those far away. That expansion of concern and social responsibility beyond the community one is born or lives in is another dimension of global citizenship. The welfare of a child in Africa, or the suppression of women's rights far from home becomes a compelling responsibility and causes us to "contribute micro-loans in Bangladesh online as easily as we can give to the local United Way" (Plater, 2011, p. 30). However, in the postcolonial world, it is no longer acceptable to assume that we know the solutions to others problems, nor that they will welcome outside intervention (Illich, 1968; Sutton, 2011). It therefore requires a base of complex knowledge and sensitivity to be an effective support for human causes at a distance.

A very interesting literature is emerging that studies the phenomenon which signals some of these broader global allegiances, and that is dual or multiple citizenship. With increasing immigration and the fact that those movements are often quite fluid arrangements where close contact with the home country is maintained, acquiring a second citizenship and feeling allegiance to both is increasingly common. My son living in London told us in an off-hand way recently that he had three passports now, one more than his Egyptian father or American mother had any role in providing him. As people move from one national identity to two or even more, the meaning of citizenship necessarily shifts. For those individuals their loyalties, sense of rights and duties, and even emotional attachments are not singular but rather multiple. Cross-cultural and cross-religious marriages are another growing example in this category. These groups may shed light on the dispositions and behaviors that comprise indicators of global citizenship.

Boundaries Recede

In a staff of nine professionals at our civic engagement center at the American University in Cairo, over half are now living in a place different from where they were born or went to school. One 24-year-old has lived in 10 countries over his relatively short lifetime. This trend toward cross-border mobility appears to be increasing, both as the costs of travel decrease and work opportunities in multinational corporations and organizations encourage geographic movement.

However, there also appears to be an aspirational aspect to this trend; young people in particular express a *wanderlust* and desire to experience the wider world which would have been restricted in past eras to a privileged few. Those who form a part of this new migratory *tribe* have in some cases more in common with each other, whether from India or Indiana, than their counterparts who remain closer to home. These are aspects of global citizenship with both disposition and behavior dimensions that provide rich, untapped potential for further research.

EDUCATING FOR GLOBAL CITIZENSHIP

How do service-learning experiences contribute to forming citizens of the world with expanded identities, allegiances, and comfort with fluid boundaries? Plater (2011, p. 37) has noted that our desires and those of students to become global citizens are often not matched by the relevant skill set for achieving it successfully. Immersion in service projects in communities abroad, if framed with enough reflection and processing of the encounters (Whitney & Clayton, 2011) will undoubtedly have more transformational potential than classroom or library assignments. Bringle and Hatcher (2011) have challenged researchers to demonstrate the power of international service-learning on various types of outcomes by positing an *intensification effect:* that international service-learning has

> the capacity to intensify any previously documented outcome from study abroad, service-learning, or international education in isolation. That is, we expect that even short-term ISL [international service-learning] results in greater improvement in intercultural skills, more rapid language acquisition, better demonstration of democratic skills, deeper understanding of global issues, greater transformation of students' lives and careers, more sensitivity to ethical issues, and more life-long interest in global issues (to identify only a few possible outcomes) than either domestic service-learning, international education without study aboard or service-learning, and traditional study abroad. We further predict that this *intensification effect* will exceed an additive effect of combining the simple effects of the components (study abroad, service-learning, international education) taken two at a time. Finally, we expect that ISL will produce results that are more extensive, more robust, more transformational, and distinctive than any one of the components. (p. 22)

International service-learning is one avenue for gaining not simply the requisite knowledge, but also new tools and skill-sets; empathy, testing of one's perceptions against those of others, learning to navigate in situations of uncertainty, as well as effective communication across boundaries.

Without the requisite guided reflection on international service experiences, there are real risks of less fortuitous outcomes. Students who experience superficial exposure to a different cultural setting run the risk of having their prior stereotypes reinforced or misinterpreting encounters because they lacked the appropriate cognitive tools to process what they have experienced. Therefore, the responsibility of faculty, staff supervisors, and mentors in this cross-cultural learning process is crucial.

Duke University has instituted a full semester course for reflection following undergraduate international service-learning experiences (Colby, Ehrlich, Beaumont, & Stephens, 2003). The sometimes mixed outcomes for those students led to focused ways of fostering efficacy, hope, and resilience in the face of powerfully affecting experiences of human suffering or injustice. No amount of cheerful rhetoric about cosmopolitanism or global integration can mask the grave disparities that separate most of our students from the poor and disadvantaged in the countries they will visit. This can dissuade them from future engagement, or if properly incorporated into learning outcomes, could spur them on to further study or careers that address global human justices.

RESEARCH AGENDA

Another important way to support positive student learning and outcomes will be to encourage research in this emerging field. Of particular importance are program evaluations that identify effective strategies as well as those to be avoided. Impact evaluation studies of international service-learning may help to advance some of the current debates in cultural studies as well. What is the proper balance between appreciation of cultural difference (relativity) and acknowledging universal standards for the rights of all human beings? These are not questions with right and wrong answers, but the field needs to accumulate knowledge on approaches that lead to desired student outcomes. What are the lessons we wish students to take away from exposure to gender violence, state-sanctioned corruption or patriarchal social settings?

A related question concerns the limits of intervention or service projects when root causes of the problem students are engaging with (e.g., hunger, illiteracy, poverty) can only be addressed at a higher structural or governance level. These are issues that service-learning students and teachers grapple with in all community-based settings, but they take on added complexity in cross-national contexts. What are the most effective pedagogical tools and how can they be deployed given constraints of time and resources in many programs?

Another set of research questions concerns the civic education and history curricula currently in use in local settings. To what extent do they incorporate global themes and competencies? Instead, is a more parochial nationalism taught or valorized? Sometimes the sins are of omission: too many history texts taught in the United States have had a gaping lacuna in the centuries between the Roman Empire and the European Renaissance. The exclusion of Islamic civilization, for example, is unhealthy for both Muslim students and others who imbibe a slanted view of their world heritage.

I faced a personal dilemma each fall while my children were enrolled in Egyptian primary schools that began the fall term by glorifying *victory* in the 1973 October War with Israel. Facts were missing or wrong and the triumphal tone of the lessons offered no room for alternative interpretations. A more recently-issued curriculum has removed much of that material. Currently, the K-12 Egyptian curriculum in civics emphasizes hospitality to visitors, which is traced to the generosity and social support central to Arab and Bedouin culture. Cynics claim that the driving force behind these curricular reforms is the economics of tourism. Regardless, the learning outcomes aim to instill local pride alongside openness to *the other*.

A final important area for research concerns what we may call *New Generation Questions*. Are globalization and the information revolution that supports it creating substantially new human beings? Less expansively: is the current youth generation different in any significant measurable way from their parents or grandparents? The data appear to be contradictory. Political knowledge in the west is in decline, linked to a plummeting consumption of news from traditional sources like newspapers and television. However, levels of community service, international travel, and concern for global causes such as the environment or free expression are on the rise.

This is a rich field for in-depth research into the psyche of youth to understand how they integrate disparate attitudes and orientations. University of Minnesota is conducting a long-range panel study of 6000 study abroad students before and after their travel which should provide insight on a number of the issues raised above. Polling data from the 1960's and 1980's could provide cross-generational comparisons on some key issues (Fry, Paige, & Stallman, 2009).

CONCLUSION

The world is rapidly globalizing, with impact on the way students want to receive information and learn. Their orientations toward mobility, blended identities and desire to serve have all given credence to the emergence of *global citizenship* as a meaningful way to conceptualize cross-border identities and behaviors. It has also created increased demand for international service-learning opportunities. At the moment these tend largely to move in one direction, from the more developed nations toward those less developed. The same could be said for the scholarship in this relatively new field. Organizations such as the International Association for Research on Service-Learning and Community Engagement are important venues for creating a community of practice and scholarship going forward.

Areas ripe for further research should not been seen as limited to standard program evaluations or learning outcome studies. Well-designed evaluation studies will also advance scholarship on the formation of global citizenship more generally. They help to move a field that has relied on value propositions toward being more evidence-based. Other overlapping fields of inquiry include youth and generational change, and the vexing problems around cultural relativity versus the universality of human rights. This places research on global citizenship at the convergence of some of the most critical, and interesting, issues of our times.

REFERENCES

Berry, H. A., & Chisholm, L. A. (1999). *Service learning in higher education around the world: An initial look*. New York, NY: The International Partnership for Service Learning and Leadership.

Bringle, R. G., & Hatcher, J. A. (2011). International service learning. In R. G. Bringle, J. A. Hatcher, & S. G. Jones (Eds.), *International service learning: Conceptual frameworks and research* (pp. 3-28). Sterling, VA: Stylus.

Bringle, R.G., Hatcher, J.A. & Jones, S. G. (2011). *International service learning: Conceptual frameworks and research*. Sterling, VA: STYLUS.

Bringle, R. G., & Tonkin, H. (2004). International service learning. A research agenda. In H. Tonkin (Ed.), *Service learning across cultures: Promise and achievements* (pp. 365-374). New York, NY: International Partnership for Service learning and Leadership.

Colby, A., Ehrlich, T., Beaumont, E., & Stephens, J. (2003). *Educating citizens: Preparing America's undergraduates for lives of moral and civic responsibility*. San Francisco, CA: Jossey-Bass.

Deardorff, D. K. (2008). Intercultural competence: A definition, model, and implication for study abroad. In V. Savicki (Ed.), *Developing intercultural competence and transformation: Theory, research, and application in international education* (pp. 297-321). Sterling, VA: Stylus Publishing.

Fry, G. W., Paige, R. M., & Stallman, E. M. (2009, August). *Beyond immediate impact: Study abroad for global engagement*. Presentation at the International Academy for Intercultural Research, Honolulu, Hawaii.

Gerzon, M. (2010). *Global citizens*. London, England: Rider Books.

Giving USA Foundation (2011). *Giving USA 2011: The annual report on philanthropy for 2010*. Retrieved from www.givingusareports.org

Hovland, K., McTighe Musil, C., Skilton-Sylvester, E., & Jamison, A. (2009). It takes a curriculum: Bringing global mindedness home. In R. Lewin (Ed.), *The handbook of practice and research in study abroad: Higher education and the quest for global citizenship* (pp. 466-484). New York, NY: Routledge.

Illich, I. (1968, April). *To hell with good intentions*. Presented at the Conference on InterAmerican Student Projects (CIASP), Cuernavaca, Mexico.

Kiely, R. (2011). What international service learning research can learn from research on international learning. In R. G. Bringle, J. A. Hatcher, & S. G. Jones (Eds.), *International service learning: Conceptual frameworks and research* (pp. 243-274). Sterling, VA: Stylus.

Lewin, R. (2009a). Introduction: The quest for global citizenship through study abroad. In R. Lewin (Ed.), *The handbook of practice and research in study abroad: Higher education and the quest for global citizenship*. New York, NY: Routledge.

Lewin, R. (2009b). *The handbook of practice and research in study abroad: Higher education and the quest for global citizenship*. New York, NY: Routledge.

McTighe Musil, C. M. (2003). Educating for citizenship. *Peer Review, 5*(3), 4-8.

Nussbaum, M. C. (1996). Patriotism and cosmopolitanism. In J. Cohen (Ed.), *For love of country? Debating the limits of patriotism* (pp. 3-17). Boston, MA: Beacon Press.

Parker, B., & Dautoff, D. A. (2007). Service learning and study abroad: Synergistic learning opportunities. *Michigan Journal of Community Service learning, 13*(2), 40-53.

Plater, W. M. (2011). The context for international service learning: An invisible revolution is underway. In R. G. Bringle, J. A. Hatcher, & S. G. Jones (Eds.), *International service learning: Conceptual frameworks and research* (pp. 29-56). Sterling, VA: Stylus.

Sutton, S. B. (2011). Service learning as local learning: The importance of context. In R. G. Bringle, J. A. Hatcher, & S. G. Jones (Eds.), *International service learning: Conceptual frameworks and research* (pp. 125-144). Sterling, VA: Stylus.

Tonkin, H. (2004). *Service learning across cultures: Promise and achievement*. New York, NY: International Partnership for Service Learning and Leadership.

Tonkin, H. (2011). A research agenda for international service learning. In Bringle, R. G., Hatcher, J. A. & Jones, S. G. (2011). *International service learning: Conceptual frameworks and research* (pp. 191-224). Sterling, VA: Stylus.

Troyanov, I. (2006). *Collector of worlds: A novel of Sir Richard Francis Burton*. New York, NY: Harper Collins.

Whitney, B. C., & Clayton, P. H. (2011). Research on and through reflection in international service learning. In R. G. Bringle, J. A. Hatcher, & S. G. Jones (Eds.), *International service learning: Conceptual frameworks and research* (pp. 145-187). Sterling, VA: Stylus.

PART II

CULTURAL CONTEXTS FOR RESEARCH AND PRACTICE

CHAPTER 3

CENTER AND PERIPHERY IN SERVICE-LEARNING AND COMMUNITY ENGAGEMENT

A Postcolonial Approach

Lorilee R. Sandmann, Tami L. Moore, and Jocey Quinn

ABSTRACT

Power dynamics are intimately connected to the success of any relationship and are especially critical in developing and sustaining reciprocal engaged partnerships, the foundation for service learning and community engagement. This work explores the theoretical and applied understandings of postcolonial theory and the related constructs of center and periphery as they provide insight into the study of power dynamics in community engagement settings and recognizes the implications of this perspective. Suggestions are offered for improving reciprocity in university-community engagement by viewing research design through a postcolonial lens.

Understanding Service-Learning and Community Engagement:
Crossing Boundaries Through Research, pp. 25–46

Service-learning and community engagement play an important role in higher education throughout the world. Many governments and universities have endeavored to link student learning and research-based scholarship to local issues, and have called for more intentional partnerships (Serpell, 2007). Two important trends have emerged as a result of such rhetoric and initiatives. First, critical perspectives on engagement recognize that interactions between universities and the communities they serve are highly complex, shaped by relations of power and by discourse that privileges university-based knowledge above that of communities (Butler, 2001; Cruz, 2007; Quinn, 2007; Saltmarsh, Hartley, & Clayton, 2009; Sandmann, Kliewer, Kim, & Omerikwa, 2010; Smith, 1999). Second, in designing new initiatives to meet community and civic engagement goals, researchers in many settings reference western scholars as the experts in community engagement (e.g., Oldfield, 2008). The scholarly community has at the same time been slow to recognize the value of local knowledge or to identify indigenous experts, particularly in non-Western settings.

Fundamental to community engagement are active partnerships between higher education institutions and communities, defined either geographically or as virtual communities of shared common interests. Saltmarsh et al. (2009) propose a shift of focus from the place and activities of engagement to the processes and purpose of engagement. They define the processes of engagement as "the way in which those on campus, (administrators, academics, staff, and students) relate to those outside the campus" and purpose as "enhancing a public culture of democracy on and off campus and alleviating public problems through democratic means" (p. 6). Scholarship thus needs to shift from what is done, and progress to a focus on how, why, and with whom. Striving toward a democratically-centered framework of engagement (e.g., Benson, Harkavy, & Hartley, 2005) partners collaborate as coeducators, co-learners, and cogenerators of knowledge in public problem solving (Jameson, Clayton, & Jaeger, 2010; Kirby, 2010; Saltmarsh et al., 2009).

As the theory and scholarship in this area develop, partners are learning more about the critical need to address power issues in developing and sustaining reciprocally engaged partnerships. Most literature that investigates and theorizes power dynamics of community-university partnerships adopts the perspective of the university. However, there has recently been an effort to add a community voice in community engagement research (e.g., Community Partner Summit Group, 2010; Sandy & Holland, 2006; Mondloch, 2009). In this undertheorized arena, Sandmann et al. (2010) provide a conceptual, theoretical, and philosophical analysis of power as it relates to reciprocity in community-university partnerships. These discussions call into question the nature of such partnerships, specifically, claims of mutual benefit and reciprocity, with reciprocity meaning work done *with* rather than *in* or *for* one of the partners. Scholars are drawing on cultural and social theories to develop new tools for understanding these relationships and this chapter supports these efforts.

Building on these earlier perspectives, this chapter brings together the Sandmann et al. (2010) discussion of power theories with the Saltmarsh et al. (2009) discussion of democratic engagement. Postcolonial theory is proposed as one example of social and cultural theories that can be brought to bear in this scholarship to support the shift to process-oriented engagement. First, this chapter describes the origins as well as the theoretical and applied understandings of postcolonial theory. In this context, it analyzes the underlying concepts of center and periphery as they provide insight into power dynamics in community engagement. It begins to deconstruct dominant modes of binary thinking that position universities as central producers of knowledge and communities as peripheral to that production. Spivak's (1985, 1988a, 1988b) concept of *the other* is introduced and suggested as a tool for further analyzing community and civic engagement. Second, this work suggests employing a postcolonial theory lens as part of an a priori theoretical framework to shape methodological decisions in general (LeCompte & Priessle, 2003). This lens can guide an emerging research agenda that examines the purposes, processes, and power relationships in engagement activities. Finally, recommendations are offered for future practice and research using postcolonial theory.

CENTER AND PERIPHERY IN POSTCOLONIAL THEORY

Postcolonial theory deals with the relationship between dominant groups that have the power to shape the norms and values of a community, and those on the margins of that culture who do not have access to those power structures. Using the notions of *colonizer* (center) and *colonized* (periphery), postcolonial scholarship explores the experience of people in colonized societies who have been positioned by the colonizer as beyond the center.

Origins of Postcolonial Theory

Postcolonial theory offers the social and cultural complement to theories of political economy and economic development. Historians began using the term *postcolonial* as a chronological marker of events occurring after independence in formerly colonized countries in Southeast Asia and Africa in the 1970s. Literary scholars took up the term in the 1980s in their discussions of works from those countries. The term was not used by people now considered the early contributors to postcolonial theory such as Frantz Fanon (1952/1968), Homi Bhabha (1994), Edward Said (1977/1991, 1993), and Gayatri Spivak (1985) until the 1990s. Ashcroft, Griffiths, and Tiffin (1989) brought these various traditions together in *The Empire Writes Back*, their volume of literary criticism, which has served as a touchstone compilation of key theoretical concepts. Postcolonial theory is now fairly universally understood to address and ultimately support the resistance to social and cultural impacts of nineteenth century European colonization. Its central concepts have been used primarily by people from formerly colonized cultures to deconstruct history, culture, and personal experiences.

Spivak's (1985, 1988a, 1988b, 1988c) early work in this field asked significant questions about the ability of colonized or marginalized people to speak and, more importantly to be heard by those in power. Her questions go directly to the workings of power in a particular setting. Similarly, the postcolonial theorists' questions and theoretical constructs may be useful tools (Nealon & Giroux, 2003) for scholar-practitioners wishing to examine and conduct research on the workings of power in partnerships between communities and universities. Spivak's work aligns with the goal of postcolonial theory, which, according to Dirlik's (1994) critique, is straightforward: "to abolish all distinctions between center and periphery as well as other 'binarisms' that are allegedly a legacy of colonial(ist) ways of thinking" (p. 329).

Othering

Spivak grounds her work in the experience of formerly colonized peoples ,especially in India; in particular, she has written extensively about indigenous identities being reclaimed in a postcolonial world. To do so, she extends the discussion of the *other*, or *othering* (e.g., Spivak, 1985, 1988a, 1988b). Scholars explain othering as a process occurring "through discourses ... establishing the binary separation of the colonizer [center] and the colonized [periphery] and asserting the naturalness and primacy of the colonizing [center's] culture and world view" (Ashcroft et al., 1989, p. 169). Primacy, as it is used here by Ashcroft et al. (1989), is synonymous with power. It thus forges the link between Sandmann et al.'s (2010) analysis of power in service-learning and community engagement and the conceptual tools potentially found in postcolonial theory.

For Spivak (1985), the experience of othering connects specifically to "the necessary yet contradictory assumption of an uninscribed new earth," or the premise that nothing was there before the arrival of the colonizer. This absence is itself "a condition of possibility of the worlding of a world" (p. 133). In her reading of *The Rani of Sirmur*, the story of an Indian raja's *monarch's* wife, Spivak introduces Captain Geoffrey Birch of Her Majesty's Royal Army, whose career personified this concept of "worlding" an uninscribed world. Birch wrote in his correspondence to superiors about traveling through rural India on horseback "to acquaint the people who [*sic*] they are subject to" (p. 133). Spivak interprets this travel as an act of othering: the explicit image of Birch, "the European on the hills," being implicitly "reinscribed from stranger to Master ... as the native shrinks into the consolidating subjected subject" (p. 133).

A similar example of the concept of othering in university-community relations is seen in the needs-based development assumption (Kretzman & McKnight, 1993). This approach holds that the community's problems need to or can best be solved by *experts* employed by the university. Othering (Said, 1978), in this sense, is synonymous with marginalization in that it is grounded in "the necessary yet contradictory assumption of an uninscribed earth which ... generates the force to make the 'native' [someone on the periphery] see himself as 'Other' [than those at the center of the dominant/colonizer's culture]" (Spivak, 1985, p. 133). In order to think of a particular geographic place as suddenly part of an empire, the region must be understood as having been dark, silent, and ignorant prior to the arrival of civilization. Where the knowledge and experience of communities are devalued in favor of research or knowledge generated through the academy, a community can also appear as uninscribed earth, dark and silent prior to introduction of the expert knowledge valued in the new culture.

Community Engagement Binaries

Talking of the center and periphery recalls several common phrases in the engagement lexicon, including *university and community, researcher and community partner,* and *town and gown.* Through such terminology, academics position communities and community leaders as peripheral in a geographic sense, and potentially marginal in the activity of community-university engagement. These phrases can also reflect a sense of privileged students or academics working with disadvantaged communities, particularly where engagement is responding to the needs of people in socially or economically marginalized areas. Clyburn, Saltmarsh, and Driscoll (2011) refer to this approach as "a 'charity model' with the one-way application of resources, expertise, student, and faculty support to community without acknowledging community assets, expertise, knowledge, and resources" (para. 8).

Some practitioners of engagement, particularly those attuned to building reciprocal relationships with communities, express concern about the impact of this binary language. Their specific concern focuses on the resulting dialectic that can never be quite equal and perpetuates the status of the university as superior to the community in its knowledge and problem-solving capacity. This issue arose in South Africa around the implementation of the Community Higher Education Service Partnership academic coursework/modules implemented between 1999 and 2002 at six South African universities (Mitchell & Rautenbach, 2005). Working with these modules, university faculty and administrators established links between university faculty, community organizations, and local communities through service-learning. David Maughan Brown, deputy vice-chancellor of the University of KwaZulu-Natal, cautioned his audience at the 1998 International Partnership Conference about the possible impact of this initiative:

> On the one hand I fully endorse the idea of service-learning. On the other hand, it would seem to me to be a betrayal of the mutuality of the partnership relationship [for the university] to assume a dominant role in the partnership and promote an educational intervention to be espoused by the partnership as a programme which is manifestly to the advantage of the university and fixes the university squarely back in the centre of a wheel of relationships which may turn out to be little better than the extension relationships of the past. (Mitchell & Rautenbach, 2005, p. 102)

Discussing the University of KwaZulu-Natal's implementation of a Community Higher Education Service Partnership module in South Africa's Inadi community, Mitchell and Rautenbach (2005) call Maughan Brown's comments "prophetic" (p. 102) in that in practice the university remained the dominant partner. They describe the Community Higher Education Service Partnership documentation as implying the descriptor "previously disadvantaged" (p. 107) in conceptualizing communities. These terms can be read as connoting a community in need of external assistance to address its local issues, as in the needs-based community development model critiqued by Kretzman and McKnight (1993).

Holland and Gelmon (1998) describe similar instances in the early examples of U.S. community-university engagement, when institutions saw community partnerships as an opportunity to use members of the community as research subjects in their research projects. They attribute this approach to the way academic researchers are socialized to the role of experts in their work with communities, which put the researchers in a position of identifying community problems and needs as well as offering an expert solution *for* their subjects. Gillespie (2002) describes partnerships like these located in Canada as overemphasizing the university's interests, while deemphasizing the causes of the problem, thereby doing what Mitchell and Rautenbach (2005) describe as "perpetuating oppression and marginalization in communities" (p. 109).

The binary constructs underlying such experiences surfaced by looking through a postcolonial lens reflect a fundamental understanding of the nature of power in community-university relationships (Sandmann et al., 2010). These examples point to the increasing salience of cultural and social theory to this field of study, complementing the wealth of knowledge gathered from organizational development literature (Eckel, Hill, & Green, 1998; Kezar, 2011; Schein, 1985; Tierney, 2008). Community-university engagement scholarship from multiple countries points to underlying binaries, such as community-university, researcher and community partner, or academic research and indigenous ways of knowing. The existence of these binaries in turn suggests the utility of postcolonial theory in shaping the future development of a research agenda for scholarship related to service-learning and community engagement.

A Postcolonial Reading of Engagement

In 1984, the University of Essex invited scholars to a conference titled *Europe and Its Others*, focused on a single topic: "how Europe [in the imperial era] consolidated itself as a sovereign subject by defining its colonies as 'Others'" (Spivak, 1985, p. 128). Conference organizers invited participants to consider further the way imperialists and colonial officials also simultaneously "constituted [the colonies], for the purposes of administration and the expansion of markets, into programmed near-images of [the] sovereign self" (Barker, Hulme, Iversen, & Loxley, 1985, p. 128). These "programmed near-images" (p. 128) emerge through an intellectual process similar to Said's (1978) *orientalism*, or the construction by westerners of an image of *oriental* people and customs that reflects more of the west's fantasies than of the lived realities of Asian peoples. In her paper delivered at this conference, Spivak argued that the near-image of "*third world* countries" has become "a discursive field ... a pain-stakingly constructed ... cultural commodity with a dubious function" (1985, p. 128, emphasis in the original). Such depictions of *British India* ultimately reinforce an image of Britain as a colonial power rather than reflecting the lived realities of Indian people in the colonial era. This meshing of image and reality has made it difficult, Spivak argued, to consolidate a figure from British nineteenth century India as a knowable subject, understood in terms that would be recognizable by Indians either then or now without a colonial lens.

Spivak (1988a) also addresses the experience of the other in one of her most important pieces, "Can the Subaltern Speak?" In effect, she argues, the subaltern, those on the periphery in a colonial society, cannot speak. Instead, the stories that marginalized people might tell to portray their reality will forever be covered up by dominant groups that have tried to speak for them, first British colonial officials, then Indian bureaucrats supporting the empire, and now academics writing about them. One popular press writer has summarized Spivak's point this way: "The experiences of such [peripheral] groups are inevitably distorted by the perspectives of the elite who are describing them" (Smith, 2002, p. B-7).

The pressing issue is not a person on the periphery's ability to speak, but the willingness of those at the center to listen and to hear what is being said. Spivak (1984-1985/1990) explained,

> For me, the question "Who should speak?" is less crucial than "Who will listen?" ... [T]oday ... the real demand is that, when I speak from [the] position [of a Third World person], I should be listened to seriously, not with ... benevolent imperialism ... because I happen to be an Indian or whatever.... A hundred years ago it was impossible for me to speak, for the precise reason that makes it only too possible for me to speak in certain circles now. (pp. 59-60)

In the context of community-university partnerships, a particular marginalized group who, for example, is offered financial support might have the same reaction. Suddenly the researchers are listening and engaging because funding is available to help *study* impoverished communities, or to address a global health crisis.

Reading Spivak's analysis of the construction of a formerly colonized nation as a discursive field and cultural commodity, framed by a colonial lens, raises a question: Is anything similar happening to the *community* in community-university partnerships? Scholars in different national contexts have suggested that universities may indeed be constructing community as a cultural commodity, in the same way the British colonial forces constructed an imaginary India, by imposing their agendas on communities (see Holland & Gelmon, 1998; Gillespie, 2002, and more recently in a South African context, Mitchell & Rautenbach, 2005). This colonizing approach has limited higher education institutions' capacity to realize the goals of the community engagement activities as they were initially articulated by leaders such as Boyer (1996). Participants at the 2008 Kettering Foundation discussion concluded that "while the [civic engagement in higher education] movement has created some change, it has also plateaued and requires a more comprehensive effort to ensure lasting commitment and institutional capacity" (Saltmarsh et al., 2009, p. 1).

Objections to This Postcolonial Reading of Engagement

Some might object to the use of postcolonial theory as a tool for exploring power imbalances in the relationships between universities and the communities they serve. The authors of this chapter are from countries that actively colonized other nations in the nineteenth century. Further, they are well-educated White women who appear to stand firmly in the center of dominant society on many levels. Should privileged people such as these authors be the ones speaking about the experience of those on the periphery of the university-community relationship? Perhaps not. As Smith (2002, p. B-7) cautions, being firmly situated in *elite* roles as university researchers brings a risk of distorting the perspective of community members. The authors of this chapter are very likely unaware of what they do not know that they do not know about communities both internationally and in their own countries.

However, if, as Spivak (1985, 1984-1985/1990) argues, the issue is the center's willingness to listen and to hear what is being said, anti-oppression or radical organizing models (Tinkler, 2010) suggest that because of their privileges, the authors may in fact represent precisely the people to speak out for change in the academy. Adopting Johnson's (2005) definition of privilege as an "unearned advantage" (p. 24) leads to the conclusion that those in such roles are not to speak for communities but to be reflexive and critical about their own position, power, and privilege. Further, Johnson and McIntosh (2000) advance an argument that after first recognizing the privilege one has within a particular social system or cultural matrix, one is then to actively mobilize that privilege to make a difference in the lived experience of those lacking it. For example, the Center for Urban Research and Learning at Loyola University in Chicago employs a team model (Nyden, 2009) in its work, effectively "recognizing the privilege" (Johnson, 2005, p. 24) conveyed through researchers' access to capital valued by the university administration. Center for Urban Research and Learning uses the team model to add seats to the research design table, thereby engaging community members and university researchers as active participants in the process. This model echoes Fear, Rosaen, Bawden, and Foster-Fishman's (2006) call for "coming to critical engagement," creating "opportunities to share ... knowledge and learn with [all] those who struggle for social justice; and to collaborate ... respectfully and responsibly for the purpose of improving life" (p. xiii). Fear et al. (2006) differentiate critical engagement from the instrumental engagement models common in community-university engagement literature, models that focus on completing tasks and projects. Critical engagement is, above all else, a transformative experience for all involved: "The primary value is the effect it has on participants, helping them think intentionally and deeply about themselves, their work, and how they approach their practice" (Fear et al., 2006, p. 257). Although their work focuses on community-engaged scholars, Fear et al. understand that their discussion of critical engagement applies to all participants in the engagement initiatives, meaning those representing the larger community as well as the university (F. Fear, personal communication, March 15, 2006).

The Utility of the Theoretical Framework

Theory-informed data analysis calls for deep reading of the body of work of the theoretical tradition. This is necessary to avoid what Scheurich and McKenzie (2005) refer to as *cherry picking*, one particularly useful concept which, upon deeper reading, "does not really integrate with the rest of the [theorist's] assumptions" (p. 859). This section foregrounds the experimental nature of the reading of engagement vis-à-vis postcolonial theorists. It asks what postcolonial theory reveals, what issues it obscures, what pointers for practice and further research it gives, and how might scholars and practitioners utilize it to achieve more equitable university-community engagement?

The prevalence of implicit binaries in the structure and functioning of service-learning, community-university partnerships, and other informal interactions, as seen through a postcolonial lens, is deeply implicated in the possible failure of those in the university to realize the values, processes, and goals of democratic engagement (Saltmarsh et al., 2009). These include the promise of engagement to empower communities, to advance civic participation, and to realize achievements in both democratic citizenship and community economic development. Serpell (2007) asks a pertinent question here: How can universities make the knowledge they produce simultaneously relevant to the needs of the modern nation and to its people? (p. 25). The answer lies in the challenges highlighted by the previous postcolonial reading of engagement. Production of knowledge relevant to the needs of communities requires engaging with communities to realize concepts such as *relevant* and *reciprocal*. These concepts are critical to definitions of engagement (e.g., American Association of State Colleges and Universities, 2002; Driscoll, 2008). This also moves community development from a needs-based deficit model, further toward what Kretzmann and McKnight (1993) refer to as asset-based development which recognizes and builds upon community strengths rather than drawing in outside experts to solve problems.

The history and continued success of projects such as the placement by Colombian universities of medical and law students on short-term externships (Moore, Quinn, & Sandmann, 2009; Moore, Sandmann, & Quinn, 2008) demonstrates that not all community-university partnerships are othering projects. Mitchell and Rautenbach (2005), Holland and Gelmon (1998), and Gillespie (2002) suggest that some projects do, however, unintentionally reinforce a center-periphery binary relationship. In doing so, the scholars reveal misalignments between the rhetoric of reciprocity and the actual practice of community-university engagement.

If, as Spivak (1984-1985/1990) argues, "practice is an irreducible theoretical moment [and] no practice takes place without presupposing itself as an example of some more or less powerful theory," (p. 2) the community-university partnership itself represents a "situatable moment" (p. 2) of practice that may be understood differently by individual participants. Boyer (1996), introducing the scholarship of engagement, asks a pertinent question: "[W]hat would happen if the [U.S.] university would extend itself more productively into the marketplace of ideas?" (p. 15). He suggested drawing on the many different perspectives of a university faculty by raising two significant questions: "How many different weeks were there that week? And who is interpreting them?" (p. 15). Boyer seems to contend that universities and faculty researchers in particular should be the interpreters. However, the questions he posed converge with Spivak's description of practice as an "irreducible theoretical moment" that is interpreted differently by different people as a reflection of the individual's positionality.

The scholarship of or about engagement itself, that is, the peer-reviewed literature, also has the potential to obfuscate further the experience of community partners. This body of literature contains what the academy considers the official record of engagement activities that have been written up, using Wolcott's (2005) notion for the requisite final stage of ethnographic fieldwork. However, Spivak (1984-1985/1990) cautions against taking any one case or narrative as representative of all narratives. Following this logic, any effort by an academic researcher to offer a narrative of a partnership, or as representative of everyone's experience of that partnership, is inherently problematic. Indeed, as Spivak argues in her early writings, the subordinates' voices are in danger of forever being covered up by those who are describing them.

Postcolonial theory provides a specific perspective for the (re-)reading of community-university partnership narratives. By surfacing underlying power structures and suggesting opportunities to reinterpret this data, considering the relationships between center and periphery offers an interesting new understanding of what it means, and what is possible, when researchers work with local communities. Cox (2000) argues that an organization's decision to participate in a community-university partnership activity is directly connected to serving its fundamental interests in a given situation. The success of the partnership depends upon these diverse interests: "Only sufficient types and levels of specific individual interests can create and sustain the partnership" (Cox, 2000, pp. 9-10). The nuanced view of community-university partnerships emerging through a postcolonial reading, suggests some utility of the center/periphery binary in theorizing and doing engagement. It also highlights some challenges that scholars must acknowledge and address in designing new research projects.

IMPLICATIONS

Postcolonial concepts draw the scholar's attention to ways in which both knowledge and physical resources are valued differently according to their relative proximity to the center of a particular cultural or community system. Postcolonial theorists explore power dynamics as manifest in the standards by which a culture values human and intellectual resources, with special attention to how those standards are set and by whom. In this way, scholars and practitioners of what is often, and somewhat problematically, referred to as *university-community engagement* can draw on a new set of theoretical constructs to examine in a new light the partnerships between various participants in community-building activities. The use of postcolonial theory tools by engagement participants will have implications for the theory itself; it will also generate recommendations related to community-university engagement practice and research.

The common binary of community and university, or *town and gown*, evokes an almost fatuous distinction, reinforcing a false dichotomy. University employees (gownies) are simultaneously residents of the community, making them members of the university and also of the municipal community; many people not employed by the college or university (townies) access campus facilities and programs on a regular basis, rendering them members of the geographical community represented by the city and also members of an amorphous university community. Such blurry distinctions between town and gown make it difficult to maintain firm definitional boundaries between the two. Further, the constructs of postcolonial theory suggest that such boundaries are themselves problematic in the context of practices intended to reduce or eliminate the distance between center and periphery.

Scholars typically pick up postcolonial concepts as tools to understand elements of *anthropological* culture, or texts that are representative of a particular culture or set of cultural dynamics. However, these constructs developed for use in an anthropological setting will likely need to be redefined or reimagined to serve in the analysis of formal and informal efforts involving the multiple segments of a community. Kezar's (2011) findings emphasize the heterogeneity of cultures among universities and the non-profit/community agency sector; this suggests that postcolonial theory may not be appropriate for macro-level discussions of partnerships or informal collaborations in general. Kezar work also reinforces the importance of locale, emphasizing that place matters in the study of community-university engagement. Accordingly, postcolonial theory may be most effective as a piece of an a priori theoretical frame in which a variety of theoretical constructs guide research design (LeCompte & Preissle, 2003). For instance, by drawing on critical geography (Cresswell, 2004; Harvey, 1993, 1996) researchers could focus more closely on power as it shapes the social construction of a particular geographic place (Moore, 2008). Or, from a different perspective, the deliberative relationships and informational restraints of the Rawlsian *original position*, could be used to highlight and eliminate inherent bias, based on a position of power, constructed into many social, political, economic institutions (Rawls, 1971, 1999).

RECOMMENDATIONS FOR PRACTICE AND RESEARCH

Miller and Hafner's (2008) recommendations for building what they call "dialogic" (Freire, 1970) collaborations point to what might be the key contribution of postcolonial theory to the practice of community-university engagement. These writers place with the partnership's leaders the responsibility to "create environments where mutuality of participation is maximized" (Miller & Hafner, 2008, p. 105). It is, they argue, the "responsibility of leaders to create collaborative conditions" (p. 101), paying specific attention to who is at the table, when those people are speaking, and who is listening. One strategy to this end: educate university representatives about collaborative community-based work. Referring to something or someone as "community-*based*" (emphasis added), as Miller and Hafner do here, consciously marks that individual/partner as socially located (Keith & Pile, 1993) in a particular place, rather than geographically located within or outside particular physical parameters. Focusing on the university as separate from the community reinforces the possibility that university employees will continue to be seen and to see themselves as the *experts* or in some other way distanced from other partners.

However, the social location of *community agency* carries with it the connotation of expertise. Kretzmann and McKnight (1993) emphasize the mobilization of community assets, often embodied in individuals' and agencies' knowledge and experiences to strengthen communities. Cruz (2007) discusses the necessity of many different kinds of knowledge to solve problems or grow communities. What she is describing is, at its heart, the dialectic proposed by postcolonial thinkers as a way out of binary thinking. By emphasizing the dialectical nature of the binary relationships, theorists, and thus scholar-practitioners, recognize and draw upon on the interdependence of the two halves of the dichotomy, rather than reinforcing the distance between center and periphery (Ashcroft, Griffiths, & Tiffin, 2000).

Recommendations for Practice

Postcolonial theoretical constructs also challenge or provide tools for scholar-practitioners. Hoyt (2010) presents a four-stage model of the practice of engagement which is not informed by postcolonial theory, but offers an excellent example of the kind of reciprocity and shared social location discussed previously. The final stage of her model, "authentic engagement," is characterized by "lasting relationships" and the partners' commitment to "building knowledge together over time" (p. 81). This stage embodies characteristics closely related to the postcolonial idea of dialectical.

> Practice and ideas flowered, were fed, back and improved within a complex and dynamic system of relationships. Here, a city was no longer simply a lab under a microscope … but a living partnership between a university and a city for the purpose of reciprocal knowledge. (p. 81)

Although preserving the dichotomy, between university and community, Hoyt's description of the working relations of the partners reflects the kind of cultural formation that might prove an "increasingly important factor in the imperial society's constitution and understanding of itself" (Ashcroft et al., 2000, p. 27). When scholars use postcolonial theoretical constructs for the purposes of social critique, they often develop strategies intended to reframe the relationship between two ideas or entities as dialectical rather than dichotomous. The interaction between center and periphery is "in fact transcultural, with a significant circulation of effects back and forth between the two cultures" (Ashcroft et al., 2000, p. 27).

Looking at formal and informal relationships among community-based and university-based entities through this frame reveals specific points to be emphasized for shaping the practice of collaboration:

1. *The success and sustainability of collaborative partnerships involving community- and university-based actors relies on the relationships among the partners at least as much as on funding.* Following Miller and Hafner (2008), establishing and maintaining these relationships is crucial. Participants need to pay attention to who is involved, who is not being invited, and who is allowed to speak and to be heard in the collaborative space. A corollary to this point reflects the concerns of tenure track faculty, who need institutional support to balance this work with expectations for promotion and tenure (Moore & Ward, 2008, 2010).

2. *University administrators and faculty must recognize that they are an integral part of the community, not separate from it.* By taking up the stance of *neighbor,* equally invested in the outcome of an initiative that will impact all members of the community, partners begin to dismantle the hierarchies that otherwise maintain distance and build trans-cultural (dialectical) partnerships more firmly grounded in mutuality and reciprocity.

Recommendations for Research

First, further work can be done to draw on a wider range of postcolonial writing, such as that of Bagile Chilisa (2005), who challenges Euro-centric conceptions of both knowledge and research methodologies. In discussing the failure of western orientated health promotion work on HIV/AIDS in Africa, she suggests that in many cultures knowledge is not text based but is transmitted in visual and spoken forms, such as rituals, songs, myths and legends. If researchers take this seriously then both the research data they gather in collaboration with communities and the methodologies they employ need to change. At present, researchers in many countries ground their research in U.S.-based scholarship related to community- university engagement, in effect situating U.S. scholars at the center of the knowledge related to engagement. Scholars and practitioners everywhere can benefit from more models and deeper cross-cultural reflection on issues related to this work. Decentering the U.S. experience will move scholarship away from what Gillespie (2002) criticizes as over-emphasizing the interests of the center and deemphasizing the periphery.

The strength of postcolonial theory is in its application for utilizing relevant constructs first to highlight oppressive power structures, and then to ameliorate them to some degree. Foucault (1977) has theorized power as an essentially neutral force. The problem, he argues, is how people exert this power to shape cultural norms and individual access to economic and social resources. Postcolonial theorists for the most part understand power as an oppressive force, eliminating Foucault's distinction between power and how people use it. The power of the center is the tool by which those on the periphery are marginalized. This power of the center cannot simply be wished away and therefore research requires a sustained reflexivity that recognizes and accounts for power inequalities when interpreting research data and understanding what it means. Nevertheless, in Foucault's (1977) terms, power is exercised in diverse ways in all situations, it is not a thing but a process, and subversion and resistance can exist on all levels. Thus the community is not merely the passive object of the university's power. This is also an important factor to recognize and account for in researching university/community partnerships

Looking through the postcolonial lens, all engagement is cast as transcultural in the sense that the various entities represented in the formal and informal partnerships have their own, usually very distinct, cultures (Kezar, 2011; Tierney, 2008). These partnerships have also become very important in the university's understanding and portrayal of itself as serving the community (Morphew & Hartley, 2006), a characteristic which has become increasing crucial to shore up state funding (Weerts & Ronca, 2006), to meet accreditation criteria (Higher Learning Commission, 2003), and to appeal to donors' desire to support service to the community (Weerts, 2007). By reframing the relationships among community and university as dialectical in nature, postcolonial theory also has the potential to contribute to community-university engagement scholarship in several interesting ways. Such research would focus on power and how it works among partners in the collaboration, introducing perspectives that offer the potential to more fully realize the goals of reciprocity (Driscoll, 2008).

To that end, concepts from postcolonial theory could also be useful in rethinking each element of research design (LeCompte & Preissle, 2003), beginning with the research team. This implies that there must be a process of research capacity building and that this process is two way: a research team should include community representatives but not as tokens. The university researchers should work with them to share research skills, but in turn the community researchers need to share their knowledge with the other members of the team: for example about ways in which certain issues are conceptualized, about local traditions and legends and who holds valuable local historical information, This should not be a cursory process, but substantial preparation time should be given to this as part of the research design. As noted earlier, Nyden (2009) describes "add[ing] chairs to the research table" (p. 2), a process he commonly facilitates through the Center for Urban Research and Learning at Loyola University in Chicago. This team model represents a different approach to identifying and defining problems for study. Fear et al. (2006) encourage "coming to critical engagement," (p. xiii) bringing together partners from across collaborations, and highlighting opportunities to develop professional communities of practice (Wenger, 1998) focused on colearning strategies for building community asserts.

New research questions become visible through the postcolonial lens. A pressing issue presents itself : Is the distinction between community and university (still) relevant in these relationships? If so, what can deeper understanding of the distinction contribute to research, theory, and practice? If not, what are the overlaps? What are the ways in which many people and organizations are both of the community and of the university? How do they fuse the knowledge gained from each sphere and how can this act as a catalyst for positive change? Also, again in keeping with postcolonial theory's focus on people on the margins of a society, researchers might overtly examine power, asking questions about who is not involved in the partnership, who is or is not speaking, any discourse that might be rewriting the contributions of marginalized groups, and the process of setting the agenda for a partnership.

Holland and Gelmon (1998), Gillespie (2002), and Saltmarsh et al. (2009) have discussed the *potentially* negative impact of the expert model of university outreach. Academic discussion has suggested exploring an alternative framework for understanding the dynamics of doing research *with*, rather than research *on,* the community. However, talking of either research *with* or *on* or even *for* communities keeps the conversation stuck in distinction. Some differentiation remains appropriate, given the cultural differences between university and community that Kezar (2011) has discussed. Nonetheless, distinguishing university and community limits the degree to which new paradigms can be applied in operationalizing and understanding the role of universities in the communities they serve. Research needs to shift the focus from what communities or universities *do* to what the desired vision of the future is among a particular group of people, particularly those currently positioned on the periphery or margin. That future will be fluid and might involve multiple agencies collaborating together: the reification of either university or community thus becomes less likely and their part in a bigger whole can be better understood.

In the discussion in this chapter, university has been set as analogous to center, and community to periphery. However, situations can be explored where community might be conceived as the core and the university the periphery. Can elements of the community be seen as colonizing the university, for example in corporate research centers that shape organizational and research structures of universities or in student unions and activities with corporate sponsors and private firms providing goods and services to students on a university campus? The ways in which these corporate forms of partnership influence and shape what counts for relevant knowledge within the university need to be researched and explored. So, finally, further study can be posited not as dialectic between community and the university but rather the concepts of core and periphery can be richly researched as fluid and based on context when dealing with university-community partnerships.

TO A POSTCOLONIAL FUTURE

The theory extended through this chapter provides new insight into the power dynamics of community-university engagement; supports cross-cultural, comparative study of various types of engagement; and offers an alternative framework for understanding the dynamics of doing research *with*, rather than research *on*, the community. By doing so it represents an important turn in the scholarship related to community-university engagement, bringing a critical eye to discussions about the purposes, processes, and power relationships necessarily involved in efforts to foster authentic democratic engagement.

REFERENCES

American Association of State Colleges and Universities. (2002). *Stepping forward as stewards of place*. Washington, DC: Author.

Ashcroft, B., Griffiths, G., & Tiffin, H. (1989). *The empire writes back: Theory and practice in post-colonial literatures*. London, England: Routledge.

Ashcroft, B., Griffiths, G., & Tiffin, H. (2000). *Post-colonial studies: The key concepts* (2nd ed). New York, NY: Routledge.

Barker, F., Hulme, P., Iversen, M., & Loxley, D. (Eds.). (1985). *Europe and its others*. Colchester, England: University of Essex Press.

Benson, L., Harkavy, I., & Hartley, M. (2005). Integrating a commitment to the public good into the institutional fabric. In A. J. Kezar, A. C. Chambers, & J. C. Burkardt (Eds.), *Higher education for the public good: Emerging voices from a national movement* (pp. 185-216). San Francisco, CA: Jossey-Bass.

Bhabha, H. (1994). *The location of culture*. London, England: Routledge.

Boyer, E. (1996). The scholarship of engagement. *Journal of Public Service and Outreach, 1*(1), 11-20.

Butler, J. (Ed.). (2001). Ethnic studies as a matrix for the humanities, the social sciences, and the common good. In *Color-lines to borderlands: The matrix of*

American ethnic studies (pp. 18-41). Seattle, WA: University of Washington Press.

Chilisa, B. (2005). Educational research within postcolonial Africa: A critique of HIV/AIDS research in Botswana. *International Journal of Qualitative Studies, 18*(6), 659-684.

Clyburn, G., Saltmarsh, J., & Driscoll, A. (2011, January). Carnegie selects colleges and universities for 2010 community engagement classification [Web post]. Retrieved from http://www.carnegiefoundation.org/newsroom /press-releases/carnegie-selects-colleges-and-universities-2010-community-engagement-classification

Community Partner Summit Group. (2010). Achieving the promise of community-higher education partnerships: Community partners get organized. In H. Fitzgerald, C. Burack, & S. Seifer (Eds.), *Handbook of engaged scholarship: The contemporary landscape: Community-campus partnerships* (Vol. 2, pp. 201-221). East Lansing, MI: Michigan State University Press.

Cox, D. (2000). Developing a framework for understanding university-community partnerships. *Cityscape, 5*(1), 9-25.

Cresswell, T. (2004). *Place: A short introduction.* Malden, MA: Blackwell.

Cruz, N. (2007, March). *Reflection and response to Katrina: Engaged educators on fire with urgency, clarity and hope.* Keynote address presented at the Gulf South Summit on Civic Engagement, New Orleans, LA.

Dirlik, A. (1994, Winter). The postcolonial aura: Third world criticism in the age of global capitalism. *Critical Inquiry, 20*, 328-356.

Driscoll, A. (2008, January/February). Carnegie's community engagement classification: Intents and insights. *Change,* 38-41.

Eckel, P., Hill, B., & Green, M. (1998). *On change: En route to transformation.* Occasional paper no. 1. Washington, D.C.: American Council on Education.

Fanon, F. (1968). *Black skin: White masks* (C. L. Markmann, Trans.). London, England: MacGibbon and Kee. (Original work published 1952)

Fear, F. A., Rosaen, C. L., Bawden, R. J., & Foster-Fishman, P. G. (2006). *Coming to critical engagement: An autoethnographic exploration.* Lanham, MD: University Press of America.

Foucault, M. (1977). *Discipline and punish: The birth of the prison.* New York, NY: Random House.

Freire, P. (1970). *Pedagogy of the oppressed.* New York, NY: Continuum.

Gillespie, J. (2002). *University community collaboration: Understanding incentives, challenges, and approaches.* Vancouver, Canada: University of British Columbia Centre for Human Settlements.

Harvey, D. (1993). From space to place and back again: Reflections on the condition of postmodernity. In J. Bird, B. Curtis, T. Putnam, G. Robertson, & L. Tickner (Eds.), *Mapping the futures: Local cultures, global change* (pp. 3-29). London, England: Routledge.

Harvey, D. (1996). *Justice, nature and the geography of difference.* Malden, MA: Blackwell.

Higher Learning Commission. (2003). *Handbook of accreditation* (3rd ed). Retrieved from http://www.ncahlc.org/download/Handbook03.pdf

Holland, B., & Gelmon, S. (1998). The state of the "engaged campus." *AAHE Bulletin, 51*(2), 3-6.

Hoyt, L. (2010). A city-campus engagement theory from, and for, practice. *Michigan Journal of Community Service Learning, 17*, 75-88.

Jameson, J., Clayton, P., & Jaeger, A. (2010). Community engaged scholarship as mutually transformative partnerships. In L. Hater, J. Hamel-Lamber, & J. Millesen (Eds.), *Participatory partnerships for social action and research* (pp. 259-277). Dubuque, IA: Kendall Hunt.

Johnson, A. G. (2005). *Privilege, power and difference* (2nd ed.). New York, NY: McGraw-Hill.

Keith, M., & Pile, S. (Eds.). (1993). Introduction Part 1: The politics of place. In *Place and the politics of identity* (pp. 1-21). London, England: Routledge.

Kezar, A. J. (2011). Organizational culture and its impact on partnering between community agencies and postsecondary institutions to help low-income students attend college. *Education and Urban Society, 43*(2), 205-243.

Kirby, E. L. (2010). The philosophy of "co-": Acting with to maximize potential in participatory partnerships. In L. Harter, J. Hamel-Lambert, & J. Millesen (Eds.), *Participatory partnerships for social action and research* (pp. 377-384). Dubuque, IA: Kendall Hunt.

Kretzman, J., & McKnight, J. (1993). *Building communities from the inside out: A path toward finding and mobilizing a community's assets.* Chicago, IL: ACTA.

LeCompte, M., & Preissle, J. (2003). *Ethnography and qualitative design in educational research* (2nd ed). San Diego, CA: Academic Press.

McIntosh, P. (2000). White privilege and male privilege: A personal account of coming to see correspondences through work in women's studies. In A. Minas (Ed.), *Gender basics: Feminist perspective on women and men* (2nd ed., pp. 30-38). Belmont, CA: Wadsworth.

Miller, M. M., & Hafner, P. M. (2008). Moving toward dialogic collaboration: A critical examination of a university-school-community partnership. *Educational Administration Quarterly, 44*(1), 66-110.

Mitchell, C., & Rautenbach, S. (2005). Question service-learning in South Africa: Problematising partnerships in the South African context. A case study from the University of KwaZulu-Natal. *South African Journal of Higher Education, 19*(1), 101-112.

Mondloch, A. S. (2009). One director's voice. In R. Stoecker & E. A. Tryon (Eds.), *The unheard voices: Community organizations and service learning* (pp. 136-146). Philadelphia, PA: Temple University Press.

Moore, T. L. (2008). *Placing engagement: Critical readings of interaction between regional communities and comprehensive universities* (Unpublished dissertation). Washington State University, Pullman, WA.

Moore, T.L., & Ward, K.A. (2010). Institutionalizing faculty engagement through research, teaching, and service at research universities. *Michigan Journal of Community Service Learning, 17*(1), 44-58.

Moore, T. L., & Ward, K. A. (2008). Documenting engagement: Faculty perspectives on self representation for promotion and tenure. *Journal of Higher Education Outreach and Engagement, 12*(4), 5-28.

Moore, T., Quinn, J., & Sandmann, L. (2009, June). *A comparative analysis of knowledge construction in community engagement.* Paper presented at the 5th International Conference on Lifelong Learning, Centre for Research on Lifelong Learning, University of Stirling, Scotland.

Moore, T., Sandmann, L., & Quinn, J. (2008, November). *International engagement: A critical discussion.* Paper presented at the annual meeting of the Association for the Study of Higher Education, Jacksonville, FL.

Morphew, C. C., & Hartley, M. (2006). Mission statements: A thematic analysis of rhetoric across institutional type. *The Journal of Higher Education, 77*(3), 456-471.

Nealon, J., & Giroux, S. (Eds.). (2003). Why theory? In J. *The theory toolbox: Critical concepts for humanities, arts, and social sciences* (pp. 1-8). Oxford, England: Rowan & Littlefield.

Nyden, P. (2009). Collaborative community-university research team. Retrieved from http://www.compact.org/wp-content/uploads/2009/04/nyden-final.pdf

Oldfield, S. (2008). Who's serving whom? Partners, process, and products in service-learning projects in South African urban geography. *Journal of Geography in Higher Education, 32*(2), 269-285.

Quinn, J. (2007, April). *Mutual learning between universities and communities.* Paper presented at the annual meeting of the American Educational Research Association, Chicago, IL.

Rawls, J. (1971). *A theory of justice.* Cambridge, MA: The Belknap Press of Harvard University Press.

Rawls, J. (1999). *The law of people.* Cambridge, MA: Harvard University Press.

Said, E. (1978). *Orientalism: Western conceptions of the Orient.* New York, NY: Pantheon.

Said, E. (1991). *Orientalism: Western conceptions of the Orient.* London, England: Penguin. (Original work published 1977)

Said, E. (1993). *Culture and imperialism.* London, England: Chatto and Windus.

Saltmarsh, J., Hartley, M., & Clayton, P. H. (2009). *Democratic engagement white paper.* Retrieved from http://futureofengagement.files.wordpress.com/2009/02/democratic-engagement-white-paper-2_13_09.pdf

Sandmann, L. R., Kliewer, B. W., Kim, J., & Omerikwa, A. (2010). Toward understanding reciprocity in community-university partnerships: An analysis of select theories of power. In S. H. Billig (Series Ed.) & J. Keshen, S. H. Billig, & B. A. Holland (Vol. Eds.), *Advances in service learning: Vol. 10. Research for what? Making engaged scholarship matter* (pp. 3-23). Charlotte, NC: Information Age.

Sandy, M., & Holland, B. (2006). Different worlds and common ground: Community partner perspectives on campus-community partnerships. *Michigan Journal of Community Service Learning, 13*, 30-43.

Scheurich, J. J., & McKenzie, K. B. (2005). Foucault's methodologies: Archaeology and genealogy. In N. Denzin & Y. Lincoln (Eds.), *Handbook of qualitative research* (3rd ed., pp. 841-868). Thousand Oaks, CA: SAGE.

Serpell, R. (2007). Bridging between orthodox western higher educational practice and an African sociocultural context. *Comparative Education, 43*(1), 23-51.

Schein, E. H. (1985). *Organizational culture and leadership.* San Francisco, CA: Jossey-Bass.

Smith, D. (2002, February 9). Creating a stir wherever she goes. *New York Times,* p. B-7.

Smith, L. (1999). *Decolonizing methodologies: Research and indigenous peoples.* London, England: Zed Books.

Spivak, G. (1985). The Rani of Sirmur. In F. Barker, P. Hulme, M. Iversen, & D. Loxley (Eds.), *Europe and its others* (pp. 128-151). Colchester, UK: University of Essex.

Spivak, G. (1988a). Can the subaltern speak? In C. Nelson & L. Grossberg (Eds.), *Marxism and the interpretation of culture* (pp. 271-316). Chicago, IL: University of Illinois Press.

Spivak, G. (1988b). *In other worlds: Essays in cultural politics.* New York, NY: Routledge.

Spivak, G. (1988c). Subaltern studies: Deconstructing historiography. In R. Guha & G. Spivak (Eds.), *Selected subaltern studies* (pp. 3-34). New York, NY: Oxford University Press.

Spivak, G. (1990). Criticism, feminism, and the institution. In S. Harasym (Ed.), *The post-colonial critic: Interviews, strategies, dialogues.* New York, NY: Routledge, Chapman, and Hall. (Reprinted from *Thesis Eleven, 10/11,* 175-187, 1984-1985, November/March)

Tierney, W. G. (2008). *The impact of organizational culture on organizational decision-making.* Sterling, VA: Stylus.

Tinkler, B. (2010). Reaching for a radical community-based research model. *Journal of Community Engagement and Scholarship, 3*(2), 5-19.

Wenger, E. (1998). *Communities of practice: Learning, meaning, and identity.* Cambridge, England: Cambridge University Press.

Weerts, D. J. (2007). Toward an engagement model of institutional advancement at public colleges and universities. *International Journal of Educational Advancement, 7*(2), 79-103.

Weerts, D. J., & Ronca, J. M. (2006). Examining differences in state support for higher education: A comparative study of state appropriations for research universities. *Journal of Higher Education, 77*(6), 935-965.

Wolcott, H. F. (2005). *The art of fieldwork* (2nd ed.). Walnut Creek, CA: AltaMira Press.

CHAPTER 4

ANOTHER LOOK AT THE DISSEMINATION OF THE RACIAL IDENTITY INTERACTION MODEL IN A CULTURAL-BASED SERVICE-LEARNING COURSE

Lori Simons, Nancy Blank, Lawrence Fehr, Kevin Barnes, Denise Georganas, and George Manapuram

ABSTRACT

The findings of this research highlight the importance of the diffusion of the racial identity interaction model in a cultural-based service-learning (CBSL) course. Students increased their awareness of racial privilege, institutional discrimination, and racism, as well as they improved their racial and ethnic identity attitudes, social justice attitudes, and problem-solving and multicultural skills by the end of the term. Students also demonstrated multicultural awareness and knowledge in their papers and they exhibited multicultural skills in their reflections. Students developed a deeper understanding of privilege and oppression through their critical reflections of the course content and service context. The incorporation of a racial identity interaction development paradigm in a CBSL course resulted in students

Understanding Service-Learning and Community Engagement:
Crossing Boundaries Through Research, pp. 47–71
Copyright © 2012 by Information Age Publishing

engaging in a meaningful dialogue about racial differences with both peers and recipients and it assisted with the transformation of their world views.

Investigations on academic-based service-learning (ABSL) have noted both improvements and changes in students' diversity attitudes that resulted from service experiences with recipients who differed from them in race and class at placement sites located in culturally-diverse communities (Hess, Lanig, & Vaughan, 2007). Baldwin, Buchanan, and Rudisill (2007) found that some students changed while others maintained their preconceived notions about those with whom they were paired in the service activity. Brody and Wright (2004) and Quaye and Harper (2007) propose that service-learning provides students an opportunity for informal interracial contact and these interactions allow them to rethink their assumptions about others who are racially and ethnically different. In contrast, Dunlap, Scoggin, Green, and Davi (2007) suggest that students retain their stereotypical attitudes and beliefs after engaging in interracial interactions with recipients who reinforce their prejudicial attitudes, or participating in service experiences that do not negate their cognitive biases. Students may change their racial precognitions, but they do so only after they were required to connect directly service experiences to the course content (Bell, Horn, & Roxas, 2007; Hill-Jackson, Sewell, & Waters, 2007). Failure to find ABSL effects on students' diversity attitudes may reflect a program limitation (Moely, McFarland, Miron, Mercer, & Illustre, 2002a). ABSL may not sufficiently encourage students to think about how race and class influence their interactions with recipients; therefore, service experiences reinforce the "power dynamic" between White students and service recipients (Moely et al., 2002, p. 24).

Cultural-based service-learning (CBSL) is an extension of the ABSL pedagogy that requires students to connect the race, class, and culture content to the service context, examine personal dispositions toward diverse racial and ethnic recipients, and think critically about the relationships among power, privilege, and oppression (Baldwin et al., 2007; Sperling, 2007). The purpose of this study was to determine if students improved their multicultural attitudes and skills after participation in CBSL and to explain any change of cognitions and behaviors through the racial identity interaction paradigm.

RACIAL IDENTITY INTERACTION MODEL

Racial identity models (as similarly described in Simons, Blank, Russell, Williams, & Willis, 2009) were developed to explain the psychological process of minority identity transformation for Blacks (Cross, 1995) and other People of Color (Sue & Sue, 2003). Cross's model of psychological nigrescence (the process of becoming Black) described a five-stage process in which Blacks developed a racial identity during the Civil Rights movement (Cross, 1991). Helms (1995) reformulated racial identity models to suggest interpersonal interactions between Whites and individuals belonging to different racial groups serve as a catalyst for White identity development. Helms (1990, 1995) postulates that each stage be considered a cognitive schema or status individuals use to organize racial information and to structure their reactions to each other. White racial identity development occurs through six statuses in which they transform their views of themselves as privileged and colorblind to perceptions of themselves as racialized (i.e., having a racial identity) and less racist.

The six statuses of White racial identity development are contact, disintegration, reintegration, pseudo-independence, immersion-emersion, and autonomy (Helms, 1990, 1995). In the contact stage, the person is oblivious to racial issues and adopts a colorblind view. Service-learning students have a naïve view of race and are resistant to think of themselves in racial terms (i.e., "I treat everyone the same, I don't see race."). In the disintegration stage, the person becomes aware of the social implications of race on a personal level. Service-learning students begin to think of themselves in racial terms and recognize White privilege (i.e., "I do not think Whites are taught to see themselves as racial beings or how White privilege contributes to racism."). In the reintegration stage, the person understands, but is resistant to accept that Whites are responsible for racism. Service-learners are resistant to acknowledge and accept that White privilege contributes to racism (i.e., "I understand the benefits of being White, but why should I feel guilty for something I am not responsible?"). In the pseudo-independence stage, the person understands the unfair advantages of growing up White and the disadvantages of growing up Black in the United States. Service-learning students adopt liberal views in which they perceive affirmative action and other types of social programs as way to improve racial, economic, and educational disparities (i.e., "I plan on participating in the Teach for America program at this school after I graduate because I am inspired to make a difference."). In the immersion-emersion stage, the person searches for a personal meaning of racism and the ways in which one benefits. In this phase, service-learning students acquire a deeper understanding of racism (i.e., "My mother noticed my interview questions and informed me that it was inappropriate for me to ask the questions I wrote. I informed her that if I didn't ask these questions or engage in this type of dialogue then I was perpetuating the cycle of oppression by maintaining a colorblind view."). In the autonomy stage, the person develops a positive, less-racist self-concept. Service-learning students develop a positive racial identity in which they embrace their Whiteness, recognize the connection between privilege and oppression, and engage in activities to combat racism (i.e., "I realize that I have been a passive racist because I did not correct my boss when she was being an active racist. It's hard for me to admit that I have partaken in racism, but I need to understand my behavior in order to change it.").

The racial identity interaction model (as similarly described in Simons et al., in press) was developed to explain how Whites develop a positive, less-racist identity by engaging in four-types of interpersonal interactions with others who differ racially from them. Helms (1995) suggested that Whites modify their racial schema with each new interpersonal experience. The context of interpersonal interactions allows Whites to express cognitive, affective, and behavioral components of more than one status and the quality of these interactions may decrease their prejudice. The first type of interpersonal interaction is the parallel interaction in which service-learning students are agreeable to avoid racial tension (i.e., "Although I was offended I did not respond when the children asked me if I am White."). The second type is the regressive interaction in which both service-learning students and recipients experience tension about racial differences, but one of them relinquishes an opinion to preserve the harmonious relationship (i.e., "My preceptor teacher could not believe that my parents could afford to send me to college, I felt uncomfortable by her reaction so I stopped talking to her about my personal life."). The third type is the progressive interaction in which service-learners acquire new racial information, experience dissonance, and modify their racial statuses (i.e., "A Black female with whom I lost touch requested to be my friend on Facebook. When I did not accept her request, she sent me a message that said I was a racist. This experience made me rethink the way I interact with the children at the school."). The fourth and final type is the crossed interaction in which service-learning students perceive and react to racial material directly opposite of each other (i.e., "There was a great deal of discussion in my dorm about the Democratic Presidential candidate, Barack Obama's visit to campus. Many students stated that having a Black President would end racism. I tried to reason with them, but after they refused to hear my perspective, I retreated to my room."). The racial identity interaction model may be useful in describing students' cognitive, affective, and behavioral changes over the semester.

The three questions guiding this study were:

1.   Do students reformulate their racial attitudes and acquire multicultural skills through participation in CBSL by the end of the term as indicated by increases in their awareness of racial privilege; institutional discrimination and racism; civic, social justice, diversity, eth-

nic identity and pro-Black attitudes; and multicultural awareness, knowledge, and skills?

2. What and how do students learn through participation in CBSL?

3. How consistent are the qualitative and quantitative findings? Do these findings enhance understand of the impact of CBSL on students' attitude-formation and skill-development from a racial identity interaction paradigm?

COURSE DESCRIPTION

The multicultural psychology course is a 200-level undergraduate class that requires 15-hours of service-learning at an elementary or secondary public school and serves as a social science distribution requirement in the general education curriculum of the college of arts and sciences. The course objectives were to foster students' cultural competence (i.e., multicultural awareness, knowledge, attitudes, and skills). In-class time (50 minutes, three times per week, 15 weeks) began with a discussion on students' concerns about taking this class, guidelines for this course, and a lecture on multiculturalism. The next two classes consisted of an orientation on cultural-based service-learning activities by guest speakers representing the three placement sites. The first two placements required students to assist the teacher in the classroom and to tutor or mentor children who differed from them in race, ethnicity, and socioeconomic status at one of two elementary public schools in a district that consistently ranks low on state performance indicators (Pennsylvania Department of Education [PDE], 2009). State assessment indicators reveal that in the fourth-grade, 31% score at the proficient level in reading, 34% score at the proficient level in math, and 42% score at the proficient level in science (PDE, 2009). The third placement required students to work with high school students who differed from them in race, ethnicity, socioeconomic status, and exceptionalities on their senior projects. The senior project required high school students to write a research paper, participate in field work connected to their topic of study, deliver an oral presentation, and compile a portfolio of their work. Service-learning students helped seniors with their research papers and presentations at a high school located in a district that has a 47% drop-out rate and a combine average scholastic aptitude test (SAT) score of 788 (RMC Research Corporation, 2008). Eighteen percent of 11th-graders enrolled at this high school score at the proficient level in math and 12.6% score at the proficient level in reading (School District of Philadelphia [SDP] Report, 2009).

The rest of the course was devoted to lecture, reflective and experiential activities, and discussion. Topics covered in this course included multicultural psychology, stereotypes, ageism, sexism, classism, and racism, as well as racial identity development, oppression and privilege, prejudice reduction, and cultural competence. Topics were based on lectures and discussions that corresponded to assigned readings. Students were required to read *The Psychology of Prejudice* by Nelson (2006), *White Privilege* by Rothenberg (2008), and *Why Are All the Black Kids Sitting Together In The Cafeteria?* by Tatum (1997). They also read supplemental articles on racial-ethnic identity development (Cross, 1991; Helms, 1990). Experiential activities (i.e., crossing-the-line) (Goldstein, 2008; Kivel, 2002; Pedersen, 2004; Singelis, 1998), talking circles (Wolf & Rickard, 2003), and videoclips (i.e., "People Like Us, Blue Eyed") were used to stimulate reflection and discussion.

Students were required to complete a multicultural observation paper, a movie critique of a diversity film, an intercultural interview paper, and reflections about their course and service experiences (Simons, 2008). The multicultural observation is an immersion experience. Students attended an activity associated with a culture or ethnic group that is distinctively different from them. For example, some students attended a church service other than their own, dined at a restaurant that serves ethnic food, or went to a part of the community or city to which they have never been. Then they wrote a short description about what they did, how it felt while they were doing it, and what they learned. Students were also required to watch a diversity film (i.e., *Crash, Mississippi Burning*), apply diversity theories to explain the main theme of the movie, and describe what they did or did not learn in terms of racial identity development and multicultural competence (i.e., awareness, knowledge, & skills). In addition, students were required to complete an intercultural interview paper. This assignment requires students to develop an interview on any topic related to multicultural psychology (i.e., classism, ageism, racism), interview two individuals who differ in one cultural characteristic (i.e., age, race, religion, sexuality, nationality, education, gender, or socioeconomic status), and compare and contrast their responses. Students integrated theory and research to explain the main findings from the interviews. Students were also required to complete structured reflection questions after each class and service experience so they could critically analyze their thoughts and feelings about race and class concepts within the course and service context over the semester. The course ended with a social network activity (Trimble, Stevenson, & Worth, 2004) and a reflective discussion about how student concerns about taking this class have changed throughout the semester.

METHOD

College students from a private teaching university in a northern metropolitan area completed a pretest and a posttest survey. Data were gathered from 54 students at the beginning and at the end of the semester during three academic years (2007-2008, 2008-2009, 2009-2010). All of the students completed the pretests and posttests. Cultural-based service-learning students in Sample 1 (2007-2008) did not differ from those in Sample 2 (2008-2009) and Sample 3 (2009-2010). One-way analysis of variance with post-hoc Tukey and chi-square tests were used to measure possible differences in gender, race, and age among the three groups. Most students identified themselves as White (70%) and female (76%) as shown in Table 4.1.

Measures (as Similarly Described in Simons et al., 2009)

A demographic questionnaire, developed by the researchers, was used to gather information on gender, race, age, GPA, area of study, and year in school.

The Civic Attitudes and Skills Questionnaire (CASQ), developed by Moely, Mercer, Ilustre, Miron, and McFarland (2002b), assessed civic attitudes and skills. The CASQ, an 84-item self-report questionnaire, yields scores on six scales: (a) *Civic Action* respondents evaluate their intentions to become involved in the future in some community service; (b) *Interpersonal and Problem-Solving Skills* respondents evaluate their ability to listen, work cooperatively, communicate, make friends, take the role of the other, think logically and analytically, and solve problems; (c) *Political Awareness* respondents evaluate their awareness of local and national events and political issues; (d) *Leadership Skills* respondents evaluate their ability to lead; (e) *Social Justice Attitudes* respondents rate their agreement with items expressing attitudes concerning the causes of poverty and misfortune and how social problems can be solved; and (f) *Diversity Attitudes* respondents describe their attitudes toward diversity and their interest in relating to culturally different people. Internal consistencies for each scale reported by Moely et al. (2002b) ranged from .69 to .88, and time test-retest reliabilities for each scale ranged from .56 to .81

The Color-Blind Racial Attitude Scale (CoBRAS), developed by Neville, Lilly, Duran, Lee, and Browne (2000), assessed contemporary racial issues. The CoBRAS, a 20-item self-report measure, yields scores on three scales: (a) *Unawareness of Racial Privilege* respondents evaluate their lack of awareness of White racial privilege; (b) *Unawareness of Institutional Discrimination* respondents evaluate their lack of awareness of racial issues associ-

**Table 4.1.   Demographic Characteristics
of Cultural-Based Service-Learners**

Variables	Students (n = 54) %
Age (M, SD)	20.01 (1.17)
Gender	
Male	24
Female	76
Ethnicity	
African American	23
White	73
Latino	2
Asian American	2
GPA (M, SD)	3.06 (1.84)
Year in school	
Freshman	2
Sophomore	43
Junior	35
Senior	20
Major	
Psychology	72
Social science	5
Nursing	15
Social work	4
Business	2
English/secondary education	2
Service placement	
Elementary public school	83
Public high school	17
Service hours (M, SD)	15.39 (28.00)
Continued to participate in service hours	48
Kept in touch with the placement	40
Previous service-learning course	77
One prior service-learning course	53
Two prior service-learning courses	20
Previous volunteer work	23
Volunteer hours	2.16 (3.80)
Future service-learning course	69

ated with social policies, affirmative action, and discrimination against White people; and (c) *Unawareness of Blatant Racial Issues* respondents evaluate their lack of awareness of blatant racial problems in the United States. Item scores are added together to produce three subscale scores. Cronbach's coefficient alpha for each scale ranged from .86 to .88 (Neville et al., 2000).

The Multicultural Awareness-Knowledge-Skills Survey (MAKSS), developed by D'Andrea, Daniels, and Heck (1991) assesses multicultural competence. The MAKSS, a 60-item self-report measure, yields scores on three scales: (a) *Awareness* respondents examine their multicultural awareness; (b) *Knowledge* respondents assess their multicultural knowledge; and (c) *Skills* respondents evaluate their multicultural counseling skills. Item scores are added together to produce three subscales. Cronbach's coefficient alpha for each scale ranged from .75 to .96.

The Multicultural Counseling Inventory-for Educators (MCI), developed by Sodowsky, Taffe, Gutkin, and Wise (1994) measures cultural competence on four scales: (a) *Awareness* respondents assess the degree of their cultural awareness; (b) *Knowledge* respondents assess the degree of their cultural knowledge; (c) *Skills* respondents assess the degree of their cultural skills; and (d) *Relationships* respondents assess their interactional process and relationships with others who differ from them. Cronbach's coefficient alpha for each scale ranged from .68 to .80. The MCI served as a reliability check for the MAKSS because the MAKSS was designed to be used with graduate students.

The Multigroup Ethnic Identity Measure (MEIM), developed by Phinney (1992), measures two aspects of students' ethnic identity: (a) Ethnic identity achievement based on exploration and commitment; and (b) Sense of belonging to and attitudes toward, one's ethnic group. Mean scores are calculated to produce two subscale scores. Reliability for this scale is strong ($\alpha = .80$).

The Pro-Black Scale and Anti-Black Scale, developed by Katz and Hass (1988), measures positive and negative components of people's contemporary racial attitudes. The Pro-/Anti-Black scale, a 20-item self-report measure, yields scores on two subscales: (a) *The Anti-Black Scale* respondents indicate higher prejudicial attitudes towards Blacks; and (b) *The Pro-Black Scale* respondents indicate less prejudicial attitudes toward Blacks. Items are added together to produce two separate subscale scores. Intercorrelations ranged from .16 to .52 (Katz & Hass, 1988) and Cronbach's coefficient alpha ranged from .75 to .84 (Plant & Devine, 1998).

Design and Procedure

A triangulation mixed-methods design was used to measure differences and similarities in students' attitudes and skills. Quantitative and qualitative data were collected at the same time and the quantitative and qualitative results were considered together to understand the transformation of student attitudes and skills. The qualitative data were used to refine, explain, and extend the quantitative findings (Creswell, 2005).

All of the students completed an informed consent form and a pretest survey measuring attitudes and skills at the beginning of the semester. Students completed the survey, placed it in a coded, confidential envelope, and gave it directly to the researcher. Surveys took about 45 minutes to complete. Students answered structured reflection questions about the course content and service context for each class and day of service so that their notations occurred throughout the semester (Simons, 2008). Reflection responses ranged from 40 to 60 pages in length. Students also completed three additional assignments for this course—a multicultural observation paper, a movie critique of a diversity film, and an intercultural interview paper. In addition, students completed a racial identity attitude scale (i.e., White Racial Identity Attitude Scale (WRIAS), Black Racial Identity Attitude Scale (BRIAS), People of Color Racial Identity Attitude Scale (PRIAS) (Helms & Carter, 1991) at their own pace during a class discussion in the middle of the semester. The racial identity attitude scales measure race-related developmental schemas and each scale took approximately 10 minutes to complete. Students were also required to complete a seven-item course evaluation and a posttest survey at the end of the course. The seven-item course evaluation was based on the Multicultural Environmental Inventory (MEI) (Pope-Davis, Liu, William, Nevitt, & Toporek, 2000). The MEI measures the degree to which multiculturalism is integrated in a graduate counseling program, and the course evaluation took about 5 minutes to complete.

RESULTS

A repeated measure analysis of variance (ANOVA) was conducted on the Anti-/Pro-Black, CASQ, CoBRAS, MAKSS, MCI, and MEIM scores to detect differences in pretest and posttest attitudes and skills for three student groups (i.e., 2007-2008, 2008-2009, 2009-2010). There were no significant differences in attitudes and skills between student groups during the three academic years; however, students made increases in their attitudes and skills over time. A paired t test was conducted on the Anti-/Pro-Black, CASQ, CoBRAS, MAKSS, MCI, and MEIM scores to further assess differences in student attitudes and skills. Students increased their awareness of racial privilege, institutional discrimination, and racism by the end of the term as shown in Table 4.2.

The constant comparative method was used to construct a common framework about what students learned through participation in CBSL (Creswell, 2005). Open coding consisted of categorizing and naming the data from the multicultural movie, intercultural interview, and structured reflection assignments according to service-learning (Eyler & Giles, 1999)

**Table 4.2.   Pretest and Posttest Mean Scores
and Standard Deviations on CASQ and
Culture Competence Measures for Cultural-Based Service-Learners**

| | Time Points | | | | | |
| | Pretest | | Posttest | | | |
Measure	M	SD	M	SD	df	t
CASQ						
Civic action	44.77	5.53	32.60	4.68	47	16.03***
Problem solving	41.56	4.30	42.63	4.54	45	-2.14*
Political awareness	17.83	3.44	18.08	3.77	47	-.65
Leadership skills	15.08	2.57	15.35	2.38	47	-.89
Social justice attitudes	29.60	4.33	30.76	3.56	45	-2.40*
Diversity attitudes	18.65	3.13	19.73	3.61	48	-1.78
Cultural Competence						
MEIM						
Ethnic identity achieve-ment	15.87	4.50	22.33	2.35	32	-8.94***
Sense of belonging	25.78	6.80	26.15	2.88	32	-.33
CoBRAS						
Racial privilege	32.18	8.73	20.31	5.49	43	11.02***
Institutional discrimina-tion	23.59	5.34	21.95	5.79	43	2.20*
Racism	14.86	4.54	12.63	4.56	45	3.02**
Pro-/Anti-Black Scale						
Anti-Black	-.62	7.87	-2.92	7.94	42	1.96
Pro-Black	7.55	8.06	11.16	6.86	42	-3.64***
MAKSS						
Awareness	28.82	2.48	29.92	3.64	27	-1.89
Knowledge	34.67	5.62	41.48	4.98	30	-4.87***
Skills	30.22	5.07	31.12	4.84	30	-.94
MCI						
Awareness	23.90	3.34	25.25	4.60	31	-1.88
Knowledge	22.75	3.01	26.67	6.40	27	-3.26**
Skills	18.38	2.18	19.38	2.26	30	-1.96
Relationship	19.75	2.02	19.48	2.06	28	.63

Note: *p < .05. **p < .01. ***p < .001.

and multicultural models (Howard-Hamilton, 2000). Two coders counted the number of responses for each category and divided the responses by the number of students ($n = 54$) to obtain the percentages. Table 4.3 shows the percentages of the different categories for the multicultural movie, intercultural interview, and structured reflection assignments. Students demonstrated multicultural awareness and knowledge in their multicultural movie and intercultural interview assignments, as well as a deeper understanding of the diversity content, privilege and oppression, and multicultural skills in their reflections. The seven-item course evaluation served as a reliability check for the course content and the percentages for evaluation items are shown in Table 4.4.

In addition, student reflections were used to describe how students learned through participation in CBSL. Structured questions were used to guide student reflections and required them to make entries after each class and service experience over the semester so that data could be analyzed according to early-, mid-, and late-entries. Selective coding consisted of systematically analyzing data from student reflections using topical codes based on the racial identity interaction model (Helms, 1995). Coders counted the responses for each racial identity development (RID) category—contact, disintegration, reintegration, psuedo-independence, immersion-emersion, and autonomy and divided the number of responses for each category by the total number of student reflections to obtain the percentage. Topical codes based on RID categories were further compared using the constant comparative method. Coders compared RID categories with service-learning and multicultural themes that emerged across time over the semester. Coders counted the number of responses for each thematic characteristic that emerged for each category within each time period and divided the number of student reflections to obtain the percentage. Table 4.5 illustrates student reflections of racial identity development grouped into early-, middle-, and late-entry themes. The majority of this sample was White; therefore, student reflections illustrated White racial identity development. The White racial identity attitude scale (WRIAS) served as a reliability check for student reflections and the WRIAS profiles are shown in Table 4.6.

DISCUSSION

This study illuminates the value of the racial identity interaction model in a CBSL course. The first objective of this study was to measure changes in students' attitudes and skills. Students increased their awareness of racial privilege, institutional discrimination and racism, made improvements in ethnic identity and reductions in prejudice attitudes, and acquired multicultural knowledge by the end of the semester. These findings are consistent with previous studies that found students increased their awareness of racism and White privilege after participation in a diversity course (Case, 2007; Kernahan & Davis, 2007). In addition, students increased their understanding of social injustices and ability to work cooperatively with service recipients in the community, but they decreased their intentions to

Table 4.3.   Major Categories From Student Assignments

Topics	Movie Paper %	Intercultural Interview %	Journal Reflections %
Culture	29	61	100
Prejudice	29	46	100
Racism	94	72	100
White privilege	47	25	96
Socioeconomic privilege	0	25	89
Resistant to discussing racial issues in class	0	0	96
Learned communication skills	02	0	91
Racial identity development	68	18	91
Knowledge or skills gained through social interactions	0	64	100
Value of the course	0	0	98
Multicultural awareness	68	68	98
Multicultural knowledge	50	43	100
Multicultural skills	35	50	96
Self-knowledge	20	61	93
Development of new or less-racist attitudes	0	0	89
Prejudice reduction	0	0	82
Deeper understanding of content knowledge/ Application skills	35	39	89
Impact of race	0	0	93
Adopting a perspective of a Person of Color	0	0	89
Stereotyping	16	53	93
Tolerance	0	0	86
Awareness of racial differences between self and recipients	0	0	86
Community or social responsibility	0	0	77
Culture shock/Eye-opening experience	0	0	31
Value of service	0	0	85
Ageism	02	1	87
Sexism	08	46	75
The intersection between privilege and oppression	31	11	79
Steps to confront racism and privilege	0	0	86
Awareness of racial similarities between self and recipients	0	0	64
Preconceived notions about recipients	0	0	88
Classism	11	43	68
Whiteness	02	0	82
Discrimination	26	46	39
Steps to become an ally	0	0	79
Colorblind attitudes	02	03	71
Resistance in adopting a perspective of a Person of Color			11
Resistance in steps to confront racism and privilege			14
Resistance in Steps to become an Ally			11

**Table 4.4. Percentages of Course Evaluation Items
for Cultural-Based Service-Learners**

	%				
Items	Strongly Disagree	Disagree	Neither Agree/ Disagree	Agree	Strongly Agree
1. This course helped me examine my own cultural biases.	0	0	3	23	74
2. This course helped me learn about multicultural competencies.	0	0	3	17	80
3. The service-learning experiences in this class have increased my knowledge about multiculturalism.	0	0	9	40	51
4. The assignments in this class has increased my knowledge about multiculturalism.	0	2	6	29	63
5. The experiential activities in this class have increased my knowledge about multiculturalism.	0	0	3	43	54
6. I will take another course that utilizes service-learning.	0	9	34	20	37
7. I will take another course that focuses on diversity or multiculturalism.	0	3	11	37	49

continue in ongoing service beyond the course. These findings are partially congruent with Moely et al. (2002a), who found that service-learning students increased their social justice attitudes, problem-solving skills, and interest in service participation over time. The service context provided students an opportunity to observe the limited resources in both districts. For example, the high school did not have a library and both elementary schools had outdated computers. Students may have attributed these educational inequities to racial privilege, institutional discrimination, and racism, thus contributing to their greater awareness and knowledge of privilege and oppression, understanding of educational inequities in public schools located in inner-city communities, and resourcefulness for working with scarce resources (i.e., students brought their laptop computers to the high school).

A second objective was to describe what and how students learn through participation in CBSL. Students demonstrated multicultural

Table 4.5. White Racial Identity Development Interaction Model

	Status	%	Characteristic	%	Examples
Initial or early	Contact	93	Resistance and fear	95	I'm a little worried about the discussions we will be having in class especially those involving race and racism. I do not want to offend anyone with my questions or opinions.
			Preconceptions	88	I'm not sure what I am getting into with this class; it could be either fun or a nightmare. I have never worked with diverse children and I am afraid they will reject me.
Early	Disintegration	71	Racial awareness	100	When I look in the mirror, I don't see the color of my skin. I see me as a person. The service experience was an eye-opener; because it forced me to think about what it means to be White.
			Impact of race	93	I have grown up with privileges because I am White. I never saw my race because I was not denied privileges because of it. In fact, most White people are unaware of the privileges they have. However, we need to understand these privileges and make them visible before we can change them. This is the first step in understanding and changing how White privilege contributes to inequalities.
			Racial differences	86	I was colorblind and never thought any different. This is because I never had to think about my race until now. After reading Tatum's book, I understand that I never thought about my race because I am White. The color of your skin dictates opportunities. For instance, the Black children I work with attend a school that does not have up-to-date technology. This would never be tolerated in a White school.
Middle	Reintegration	92	White privilege	96	As a White student, I can add to McIntosh's list of privileges that I can walk into the school to tutor the children and will not get questioned by the security guard or administrative staff.
			Socioeconomic privilege	87	My parents forbid me to go into the City because of what they heard about the community surrounding campus, but after venturing into this community for this course, I realize I have been living in fantasyland because of the advantages I have been given as an upper-class male.
	Pseudo-independence	84	Prejudice reduction	82	I have tried to unlearn the racism that I was taught but I still do not feel guilty for being White; I have stood up for People of Color to Whites who have made derogatory remarks.

(Table continues on next page).

Table 4.5. (Continued)

Status	%	Characteristic	%	Examples
		Tolerance	86	I have learned to identify my own "isms" and put myself in other people's shoes before I think and speak through activities and readings in class.
		Racial Attitudes	88	I am ashamed to admit how ignorant I was at the beginning of this course. My preconceptions changed once I became aware of them and I learned not to stereotype.
Middle	82	Deeper understanding of the course content	89	After we watched the Blue-Eyed film, I wrote down questions for my interview assignment. My mother noticed and told me that it was inappropriate to ask such questions. I informed her that if I did not ask these questions then I was perpetuating the cycle of racism by maintaining a colorblind view.
Late		Adopting a perspective of a Person of Color	79	I would feel that all eyes are on me when discussing race and privilege in a mostly all-White class. I would feel like an outcast or that I did not belong. I would think that White people can't understand what racism is until they spend a day in my shoes. I would not want White people to relate to my experiences, but I would need them to be aware of racism and contribute to reducing it.
		The link between privilege and oppression	79	After participating in the backward/forward activity, I felt guilty because I had so many privileges. I realized that my socioeconomic privileges are a result from my race and racism. The opportunities for White, middle and upper class individuals exceed those available for People of Color regardless of their social class.
		Steps to confront racism on campus	86	As students, we can write letters to the President of the college requesting a more diverse student body and faculty, and request better tuition plans for underprivileged and that this class is mandatory.
		Acting as an ally	79	I have acted as an ally by educating my family on racism and the things I have learned in class. I have spoken my mind and challenged others when they have said racist things. I think about how I say things and try not to get defensive, but that part is hard.
Late or final	95	Communication skills	100	The fear I had about discussing race in class has vanished. The course empowered me to have a voice. I learned how to express my thoughts without feeling any discomfort, because there wasn't any judgment in the course.

Stage	Category		Theme	Score	Quote
			Course value	98	The course forced me to step out of my box and open up to people who are different from me. The discussions were deep, sometimes awkward, but healthy at the same time. The journals were tedious, but forced me to think, really think about where I came from, what I was doing, and who I want to become as a White male.
			Self-knowledge	97	I realize that I have been a passive racist. It's hard for me to admit that I have partaken in racism in the past, but I need to understand what I have done in the past in order to move forward with being an ally in the future.
			Multicultural awareness	98	I learned that I do not know as much about race, class, culture, and diversity as I thought I knew. This class made me aware how different each person is by the discussions between classmates. It opened my eyes to both White and socioeconomic privileges I have.
			New less-racist attitudes	89	Through this course, I became aware of my stereotypes and have learned to change them; The knowledge I acquired from my mentee contradicted my stereotypes. I have changed my thoughts and attitudes about recipients. I am more aware how White and socioeconomic privilege contributes to the social disparities in the community and the inequities in the school system.
			Multicultural knowledge	100	The course provided information I can carry with me the rest of my life. It really helped me understand who I was and the privileges I have because of my skin color, as well as understanding what those privileges mean for People of Color.
			Service value	82	A little girl asked me to read her a story that was about Ruby Bridges, the first African-American to go to an integrated school. I started to read the story and then realized what I was reading and got embarrassed. This situation demonstrated exactly what we learning in class. White people get embarrassed when they talk about race and there I was embarrassed, but I grew from this experience.
Late or final	Autonomy	95	Skills	96	As I reflected on the yarn activity, I realized how important it is to establish relationships with others who differ from me and to engage in a dialogue with them about race; The test we took in class showed me how much I have grown and what areas I need to keep working on to be more culturally competent.
			Whiteness	82	Tatum's book made me feel the dry concepts you were teaching us in class. I learned that I am White and with being White there are privileges which afford me the opportunity to fight against racism and make a difference. I learned just because I am White, it doesn't mean I am a bad person.

**Table 4.6.   Means and Standard Deviations
for White Racial Identity Attitudes**

Variable	M	SD	Schema Profile
White Racial Identity Attitudes (WRIAS)			
Contact	30.25	4.48	High
Disintegration	24.88	4.35	Low
Reintegration	21.14	5.27	Low
Pseudo-independence	32.80	4.64	High
Immersion	31.14	5.25	High
Autonomy	34.31	3.80	High

Notes: Higher scores indicate stronger levels of racial identity. The subscales measure different race-related schemas including: (1) Contact refers to respondents' lack of awareness of their own racial-group membership; (2) Disintegration refers respondents' ambivalent awareness of the implication of race for members of other racial groups; (3) Reintegration refers to respondents' passive endorsement of White superiority and Black inferiority; (4) Pseudo-independence refers to respondents acceptance of one's Whiteness and quasi-recognition of the sociopolitical implications of racial differences; (5) Immersion-Emersion refers to respondents' self-initiated development of their positive White identity; and (6) Autonomy refers to respondents' appraisal of their positive White identity orientation.

awareness and knowledge in the multicultural movie and intercultural interview assignments, and they demonstrated a deeper understanding of the diversity content, privilege and oppression, and multicultural skills in their reflections. Students acquired multicultural awareness, knowledge, and skills through their own learning process of racial identity development, congruent with previous research (Dunlap et al., 2007; Helms, 1995; Tatum, 1992).

Helms (1995) proposes that interracial interactions between Whites and Blacks contribute to a positive racial identity. She contends that initial interracial contact in which Whites avoid racial tension with Blacks is the hallmark of the parallel relationship, and the avoidance of racial conflict allows Whites to preserve their naive or colorblind view of race in the contact stage. Almost all students were resistant to engage in class discussions about race and racism at the beginning of the semester. Most students also described having preconceived notions about working with diverse recipients at a public elementary or high school in an inner-city neighborhood in their early reflections. Their resistance to discuss racial issues represents the parallel relationship, and their preconceived notions represent the contact status of the racial identity interaction model.

Helms (1995) suggests that the regressive interaction is the experience of racial tension between Whites and Blacks. The context for this tension forces Whites to think about themselves in racial terms and to recognize the social implications of their race in the disintegration stage. The service context appears to have served as a catalyst for triggering students' racial cognitive, affective, and behavioral responses. All students described their initial visits at the school as an eye-opening experience that led to their racial awareness in their early reflections. White students reported that they never consciously thought about being White or the implications of their race until they engaged in interpersonal interactions with recipients at the school. For instance, White students made notations about the differences in available resources in White, middle-class suburban school districts compared to Black, lower-income, urban school districts. Student reflections about racial differences represent the regressive relationship, and their racial awareness represents the disintegration status of the racial identity interaction model.

Helms (1995) refers to the progressive interaction as continual interracial contact between White and Blacks in which Whites acquire information that contradicts their assumptions and contributes to cognitive dissonance as manifested in their ambivalent attitudes toward racial privilege as perpetuating the cycle of racism in the reintegration stage. Students' relationships with recipients in the service context appear to have contributed to their comprehension of racial or socioeconomic privilege beyond racial privilege awareness. Most students expressed a wide range of emotions ranging from shame and guilt to sadness and anger in their examples illustrating White privilege in the middle of their reflections. Students' affective responses or cognitive dissonance represent the progressive relationship, and their recognition of racial privilege represents the reintegration status of the racial identity interaction model.

Helms (1995) suggests that the quality of interpersonal interactions between Whites and Blacks provides Whites with opportunities to adopt liberal attitudes about social programs to improve racial and educational disparities as a way to resolve cognitive dissonance felt by their recognition of racial privilege in the reintegration stage. The course content and the service context appear to have assisted students with their resolution of cognitive dissonance and development of new racial attitudes. Most students provided examples of racial tolerance and prejudice reduction to illustrate how the course and service experiences contributed to the development of their new attitudes toward others who are racially different from them in the middle of their reflections. Students' racial attitudes represent the progressive relationship, and their racial tolerance and prejudice reduction represent the pseudo-independence status of the racial identity interaction model.

Helms (1995) proposes that the context and quality of continual interpersonal interactions between Whites and Blacks allows Whites to develop a deeper understanding of racism and ways in which they benefit in the immersion-emersion stage. Few students described discomfort or resistance in their reflections of adopting a perspective of a Person of Color (Rothenberg, 2008), steps to confront racism on campus (Kivel, 2002; Rothenberg, 2008), or ways to serve as an ally (Kivel, 2002; Rothenberg, 2008). Most students described acquiring a deeper understanding of racism and the ways in which privilege contributes to oppression. It appears as if the course assignments contribute to students' conceptions of and dispositions toward privilege and oppression beyond tolerance. Students' resistance represents the parallel relationship, while their thoughts and feelings about racism represent the progressive relationship, and their comprehension of the connection between privilege and oppression represents the immersion/emersion status of the racial identity interaction model.

Helms (1995) refers to the crossed interaction as situations in which Blacks and Whites engage in meaningful dialogue about racial differences. The context and quality of crossed interactions contribute to the development of a positive, less-racist identity in the autonomy stage. All students described how they learned to engage in a dialogue about race without feeling uncomfortable, and almost all students described the value of CBSL in assisting the development of their multicultural awareness, attitudes, knowledge, and skills in their final reflections. Many students also provided examples of how the course taught them about themselves. White students learned to view themselves as racial beings and to understand their Whiteness and the privileges it affords them. Students' ability to engage in a racial dialogue represents the crossed relationship, and their acquisition of multicultural awareness, attitudes, knowledge, and skills represent the autonomy status of the racial identity interaction model.

A final objective was to compare the quantitative and qualitative findings to determine the impact of CBSL on students' attitude formation and skill development from a racial identity interaction paradigm. The consistency among student reflections, surveys, and course evaluations indicated that most students thought the course content, experiential activities, class assignments, and service experiences assisted their attitude formation and skill development, congruent with previous studies (Dunlap et al., 2007; Tatum, 1992). Students made improvements in their awareness of racial privilege, institutional discrimination, and racism. Students reformulated their racial and social justice attitudes and gained knowledge of multicultural competence (i.e., awareness, attitudes, knowledge, and skills) through their participation in CBSL. White students further developed positive, less-racist identity through their interpersonal experiences in both course and service contexts. Similarities were observed in racial identity development between student profiles and reflections. High scores on the contact, immersion/emersion, pseudo-independence, and autonomy subscales suggest that White students transformed their colorblind views of race and privilege. White students embraced their Whiteness, understood the implications of being White and privileged, and made an effort to engage in activities that promoted justice and fairness. Low scores on the disintegration and reintegration subscales indicate that students exhibited a mild level of racial ambivalence or intolerance toward other racial groups, which is consistent with their reflections of racial awareness and recognition of White privilege. The combination of the quantitative and qualitative data indicates that the interpersonal experiences in the course and service context influenced student development of their ethnic identity and cultural competence.

LIMITATIONS

There were limitations associated with this study that prevents generalizing results beyond our student sample of White females. The undergraduate student population is also demographically homogenous. Most participants came from middle-class backgrounds and were the first-generation to attend a 4-year college. Further, participants worked in public schools in inner-city communities where the majority of children and adolescents were African-American and came from lower-income backgrounds. The various developmental levels of recipients and the educational disparities associated with both public school districts make these service experiences unique and unlikely to be replicated elsewhere. Moreover, history effects were most likely associated with student responses. President Obama's visit to the campus and his election as the first African-American President of the United States may have enhanced students' multicultural knowledge. The observed racial tension between Black and Asian students and the assault of Asian students that resulted in a student boycott at the high school allowed participants to experience racial privilege and racism first-hand, which may have further contributed to the improvement of their racial and social justice attitudes. These events would probably not be observed by other participants at this or another school at any other time. Further, the use of student assignments, reflections, and surveys does not prevent participant bias in written materials. There is the potential for testing and social desirability effects to be associated with participant responses that were collected with multiple methods at different points in time. Finally, the lack of randomization methods precludes disentangling the effects from the course content and the service context on participants' attitudes and skills.

CONCLUSION

CBSL is an extension of social justice pedagogy (Cipolle, 2010). It can be a transformative process in which students shift from passive to active learners. Students achieved an awareness of racial and economic conditions that influenced the policies and practices of the public school system. They became agents of social change by thinking critically about the impact of oppression and privilege on education and challenging the practices that perpetuate inequality and injustice through their course and service work.

This study indicates that the incorporation of a racial identity interaction development paradigm in a CBSL course taught students how to engage in a meaningful dialogue about racial differences with both peers and recipients in the course and the service context and it assists them with the transformation of their world views.

ACKNOWLEDGMENTS

This study was supported through a grant from Project Pericles and the Philadelphia Higher Education Network Development.

REFERENCES

Baldwin, S. C., Buchanan, A. M., & Rudisill, M. E. (2007). What teacher candidates learned about diversity, social justice, and themselves from service-learning experiences. *Journal of Teacher Education, 58*, 315-327.

Bell, C. A., Horn, B. R., & Roxas, K. C. (2007). We know its service, but what are they learning? Preservice teachers' understanding of diversity. *Equity & Excellence in Education, 40*, 123-133.

Brody, S. M., & Wright, S. C. (2004). Expanding the self through service-learning. *Michigan Journal of Community Service, 11*(1), 14-24.

Case, K. A. (2007). Raising White privilege awareness and reducing racial prejudice: Assessing diversity course effectiveness. *Teaching of Psychology, 34*, 231-235.

Cipolle, S. B. (2010). *Service learning and social justice: Engaging students in social change*. Lanham, MD: Rowman and Littlefield.

Creswell, J. W. (2005). *Educational research* (2nd ed). Upper Saddle River, NJ: Pearson Prentice Hall.

Cross, W. E. (1991). *Shades of Black: Diversity in African-American identity.* Philadelphia, PA: Temple University Press.

Cross, W. E. (1995). The psychology of Nirgrescence: Revising the Cross model. In J. G. Ponterotto, J. M. Casas, L. A., Suzuki, & C. M. Alexander (Eds.), *Handbook of multicultural counseling* (pp. 93-122). Thousand Oaks, CA: SAGE.

D'Andrea, M., Daniels, J., & Heck, R. (1991). Evaluating the impact of multicultural counseling training. *Journal of Counseling Development, 70,* 143-150.

Dunlap, M., Scoggin, J., Green, P., & Davi, A. (2007). White students' experience of privilege and socioeconomic disparities: Toward a theoretical model. *Michigan Journal of Community Service, 13*(2), 19-30.

Eyler, J. S., & Giles, D. E., Jr. (1999). *Where's the learning in service learning?* San Francisco, CA: Jossey-Bass.

Goldstein, S. (2008). *Cross-cultural explorations: Activities in culture and psychology.* Boston, MA: Allyn & Bacon.

Helms, J. E. (1990). *Black and white racial identity: Theory, research, and practice.* Westport, CT: Greenwood Press.

Helms, J. E. (1995). An update of Helms's White and People of Color racial identity models. In J. G. Ponterotto, J. M. Casas, L. A., Suzuki, & C. M. Alexander (Eds.), *Handbook of multicultural counseling* (pp. 181-198). Thousand Oaks, CA: Sage.

Helms, J. E., & Carter, R. T. (1991). Relationships of white and black racial identity attitudes and demographic similarity to counselor preferences. *Journal of Counseling Psychology, 38,* 446-457.

Hess, D. J., Lanig, H., & Vaughan, W. (2007). Educating for equity and social justice: A conceptual model for cultural engagement. *Multicultural Perspectives, 9*(1), 32-39.

Hill-Jackson, V., Sewell, K. L., & Waters, C. (2007). Having our say about multicultural education. *Kappa Delta Pi Record, 43* (4)174-181.

Howard-Hamilton, M. (2000). Programming for multicultural competencies. *New Directions for Student Services, 90,* 67-78.

Katz, I., & Hass, R. G. (1988). Racial ambivalence and American value conflict: Correlational and priming studies of dual cognitive structures. *Journal of Personality & Social Psychology, 55,* 893-905.

Kernahan, C., & Davis, T. (2007). Changing perspectives: How learning about racism influences student awareness and emotion. *Teaching of Psychology, 34,* 49-52.

Kivel, P. (2002). *Uprooting racism: How White people can work for racial justice.* Gabriola Island, Canada: New Society.

Moely, B. E., McFarland, M. Miron, D., Mercer, S., & Ilustre, V. (2002a). Changes in college students' attitudes and intentions for civic involvement as a function of service learning experiences. *Michigan Journal of Community Service Learning, 9*(1), 18-26

Moely, B. E., Mercer, S. H., Ilustre, V., Miron, D., & McFarland, M. (2002b). Psychometric Properties and correlates of the civic attitudes and skills questionnaire (CASQ): A measure of student's attitudes related to service learning. *Michigan Journal of Community Service Learning, 8*(2), 15-26.

Nelson, T. D. (2006). *The psychology of prejudice.* Boston, MA: Allyn & Bacon.

Neville, H. A., Lilly, R. L., Duran, G., Lee, R. M., & Browne, L. (2000). Construction and initial validation of the Color-Blind Racial Attitude Scale (CoBRAS). *Journal of Counseling Psychology, 47*, 59-70.

Pederson, P. B. (2004). *One-hundred and ten experiences for multicultural learning.* Washington, DC: American Psychological Association.

Pennsylvania Department of Education (2009). *Pennsylvania System of School Assessment (PSSA).* Retrieved August 10, 2010. http://www.pde.state.pa.usa.

Phinney, J. (1992). The Multigroup Ethnic Identity Measure: A new scale for use with adolescents and young adults from diverse groups. *Journal of Adolescent Research, 7*, 156-176.

Plant, E. A., & Devine, P. G. (1998). Internal and external motivation to respond without prejudice. *Journal of Personality and Social Psychology, 75*, 811-832.

Pope-Davis, D. B., Liu, William, M., Nevitt, J., & Toporek, R. L. (2000). The development and initial validation of the multicultural environmental inventory: A preliminary investigation. *Cultural Diversity and Ethnic Minority Psychology, 6*(1), 57-64.

Quaye, S. J., & Harper, S. R. (2007). Faculty accountability for culturally inclusive pedagogy and curricula. *Liberal Education, 93* (3), 32-39.

RMC Research Corporation (2008). *Partnerships in Character Education: Senior Project Evaluation.* Philadelphia, PA: Author

Rothenberg, P. (2008). *White privilege.* New York, NY: Worth.

School District of Philadelphia. (n.d.). *School profile, South Philadelphia High School, high school region.* Retrieved from https://sdp-webprod.phila.k12.pa.us/school_profiles/servlet/

Singelis, T. M. (Ed). (1998). *Teaching about culture, ethnicity, and diversity: Exercises and planned activities.* Thousand Oaks, CA: SAGE.

Simons, L. (2008). *Multicultural psychology.* American Psychological Association, Office of Teaching Resources in Psychology (OTRP) Project Syllabus website. Retrieved November 4, 2008, from http//:www.teachpsych.org/otrp/syllabi/syllabi.php?category=special topics cross listed with diversity

Simons, L., Blank, N., Russell, B., Williams, E., & Willis, K. (2009). An exploration of the value of cultural-based service learning for student and community partners. In B. E. Moely, S. H. Billig, & B. A. Holland (Eds), *Creating our identities in service learning and community engagement* (pp. 189-216). Charlotte, NC: Information Age.

Simons, L., Fehr, L., Blank, N., Russell, B., Goodman, A., DeSimone, R., Manampuram, G., & Georganas, D. (in press). Let's talk about pedagogy, research, and practices centered on racial identity development theory in cultural-based service-learning. In M. W. Ledoux, S. C. Wilhite, & P. Silver (Eds). *Civic engagement and service learning in a metropolitan university: Multiple approaches and perspectives.* Hauppauge, NY: Nova Science.

Sodowsky, G. R., Taffe, R. C., Gutkin, T. B., & Wise, S. L. (1994). Development of the multicultural counseling inventory: A self-report measure of multicultural competencies. *Journal of Counseling Psychology, 41*, 137-148.

Sterling, R. (2007). Service learning as a method of teaching multiculturalism to white college students. *Journal of Latinos and Education, 6*, 309-322.

Sue, D. W., & Sue, D. (2003). *Counseling the culturally diverse: Theory and practice* (4th ed.). New York, NY: Wiley.

Tatum, B. D. (1992). Talking about race, learning about racism: The application of racial identity development theory in the classroom. *Harvard Educational Review, 62*(1), 1-24.

Tatum, B. D. (1997). *Why are all the black kids sitting together in the cafeteria?* New York, NY: Basic Books.

Trimble, J. E., Stevenson, M. R., & Worell, J. P. (2004). *Toward an inclusive psychology: Infusing the introductory psychology textbook with diversity content.* Washington, DC: American Psychological Association.

Wolf, P. R., & Rickard, J. A. (2003). Talking circles: A Native American approach to experiential learning. *Journal of Multicultural Counseling and Development, 31*, 39-43.

CHAPTER 5

CIVIC ENGAGEMENT IN/ACTION

A Cross-Cultural Comparison of Youth Involvement

Elizabeth M. Goering and Crystal Henderson

ABSTRACT

This study uses thematic content analysis to examine focus group conversations about civic-mindedness and civic engagement conducted with approximately 50 youth (ages 11-19) in the United States and Germany. At the heart of the research is a keen interest in how young people define, understand, and participate in acts of civic engagement. The research is rooted in standpoint theory, a framework that assumes life experiences shape a person's worldview. The results offer empirical evidence of differences in the construction of civic-mindedness among youth from the diverse cultural standpoints represented in the sample. In addition, the findings have practical implications for educators seeking to design global service-learning programs or civic engagement opportunities that are appropriate for culturally diverse populations.

Understanding Service-Learning and Community Engagement:
Crossing Boundaries Through Research, pp. 73–99
Copyright © 2012 by Information Age Publishing
All rights of reproduction in any form reserved.

An engaged citizenry is a cornerstone of democracy. Carol Geary Schneider, the president of the Association of American Colleges and Universities (AACU), reminds us in her foreword to *Civic Responsibility*, that "the sustainability of a democracy depends on its citizens' possession of knowledge, judgment, skill, and willingness to engage with other citizens" (Dey, Barnhardt, Antonaros, Ott, & Holsapple, 2009, para. 11). Indeed, research has established the benefits of an engaged citizenry to the individual (e.g., Astin, Vogelgesang, Ikeda, & Yee, 2000) as well as to the community at large (e.g., Zeldin, McDaniel, Topitzes, & Calvert, 2000).

Not surprisingly, educational institutions have been earmarked as a primary site at which "education for citizenship" (Platt, 1998, p. 18) should take place. Schools, colleges, and universities have responded to this call by integrating service-learning and other civic engagement activities into the curriculum. In fact, according to the results of an AACU poll, 68% of its member institutions identify civic engagement as an expected learning outcome for their graduates (Dey et al., 2009). Generally the results of these efforts to promote civic-mindedness through service-learning and other civic engagement programs have been positive (Bringle & Hatcher, 2000; Bringle & Kremer, 1993; Duffy, Franco, Gelmon, Jones, Meeropol, & Zlotkowski, 2004; Jarjoura, 1999). Conville and Weintraub (2002) summarize the positive impacts of service-learning, noting that it "evokes a high level of student engagement," affirms the "personal responsibility for civic participation and institutional responsibility to participate with the community to improve society," and it "enhances deeper student learning" (p. 5-6).

In recent years, civic engagement has been "crossing boundaries," with a rapid upsurge in service-learning initiatives designed to provide students opportunities for exposure to and dialogue with diverse cultural groups (e.g., Hunt & Swiggum, 2007). In some instances, these initiatives are domestic programs, crossing boundaries between the various cocultures that make up a country. The impact of these domestic cross-cultural civic engagement experiences appears to be positive. One of the major findings reported in Keen and Hall's (2009) study of college student participants in cocurricular service-programs in 23 U.S. colleges hosting the Bonner Scholars program is that "dialogue across difference" is of significant developmental importance during all 4 years of the undergraduate experience. Increasingly, civic engagement programs have been building bridges across national borders as well. Sherraden, Lough, and McBride (2008) note the "unprecedented recent expansion of international volunteering and service" (p. 396).

In addition to the rapid growth in intercultural civic engagement initiatives, both domestic and international, other countries have also acknowledged the value of civic engagement and are developing domestic engagement strategies of their own. Germany, for example, in October 2010, adopted its first *National Engagement Strategy*, designed to foster civic involvement in Germany. In introducing the new program, Kristina Schröder, the Federal Minister of Family Affairs, Senior Citizens, Women and Youth, explained: "We need the civic participation of our citizens because those who do volunteer work make a contribution to progress and cohesion in our society through their work, their creativity and personal initiative" (Federal Ministry of Labour and Social Affairs, 2010, para. 4). This upsurge in the emphasis placed on civic engagement is, in fact, rooted in a remarkable world-wide increase in volunteerism, philanthropic giving, and the activities of nongovernmental organizations (Salamon, 2010; Toepler & Salamon, 2003).

The growing trend towards the internationalizing of service-learning and civic engagement highlights the need to recognize that these constructs vary considerably from one culture to the next. As multicultural models of civic engagement are developed, the importance of adapting those models to diverse cultural standpoints becomes salient. Tonkin (2004) warns of the dangers inherent in failing to recognize cultural differences that may influence the cultural transferability of civic engagement. Indeed, an experience of one of the authors of this paper illustrates the potential for substantial cultural difference in perceptions of civic engagement. While on sabbatical leave, a German colleague was visiting the U.S. and accompanied a class on a service-learning trip to a local food bank. As part of their service-learning activity, the students filled weekend *sack packs* for needy youth. When asked for her impressions about the experience, the German visitor commented positively on her interaction with the American students. However, after a brief silence, she added, "But isn't it hegemonic to marshal all these students to take care of a problem that your government really should be taking care of?"

This anecdote illustrates that there are cultural differences in how people conceptualize civic-mindedness and as models of civic engagement cross national and cultural boundaries, paying attention to these differences is important. This study seeks to understand the diverse ways in which German and American youth experience and describe concepts such as civic engagement and civic-mindedness. Specifically, it identifies cultural differences in understandings of what it means to be an engaged citizen and in the assumptions that are made about how citizens should relate to one another, the responsibilities they have to one another, and the responsibilities their government has to them.

REVIEW OF LITERATURE AND DEVELOPMENT
OF RESEARCH QUESTIONS

Scholars have explored several aspects of the relationship between civic engagement and culture. Some researchers (i.e., Almond & Verba, 1963; Bennett, 2008; Janmaat, 2006) have examined the concept of *civic culture*, seeking to describe and categorize the various ways in which citizenship is defined across cultures. Bennett (2008), for example, identifies two broad patterns of citizenship among younger people who have grown up in the age of globalization: the *actualizing citizen* and the *dutiful citizen*. The actualizing citizen has a diminished sense of obligation to the government, views voting as less meaningful than other acts such as consumerism or volunteering, mistrusts politicians and media sources, and acts politically through loose networks of community action rather than through civic organizations. On the other hand, the dutiful citizen feels a greater sense of obligation to participate in government, views voting as a core democratic act, joins civic organizations and political parties, and uses mass media to stay informed about key issues.

A second aspect of the relationship between civic engagement and culture that has received considerable attention is the underlying *cultural frames* or *worldviews* that account for differences in civic culture. Kecskes (2006), building on the work of Thompson, Ellis and Wildavsky (1990) and Douglas's (1970) group and grid cultural theory, proposes four cultural frames that inform human behavior: hierarchical, individualistic, fatalistic, and egalitarian. Kecskes notes that although service-learning has traditionally been rooted in egalitarianism, not all culture's frames are egalitarian. He calls for the examination of what service-learning might look like within the other cultural frames.

Yet another body of literature has explored the impact these culturally-variable frames have on conceptualizations of civic engagement or particular civic engagement initiatives. Thornton and Jaeger (2007), for instance, explore this relationship quite locally, offering a case study analysis of how the organizational culture of one particular university shaped their civic engagement programs. Kecskes and Elshimi (2010), on the other hand, take a much broader view, analyzing the perceptions of civic engagement within Arab cultures. Their preliminary findings suggest that the political, religious, social, and historical context of cultures within the Arab world likely contribute to culturally unique understandings of civic engagement.

Finally, some research (e.g., Carr, 2002; Tonkin, 2004) has explored strategies for designing and implementing successful international service-learning and civic engagement in light of underlying cultural differences. In his edited volume, Tonkin (2004) makes a compelling case for starting to plan international service-learning programs by conducting a preliminary analysis of shared values, identifying what the cultures have in common and the ways in which they differ.

As this review of literature indicates, the relationship between culture and civic engagement has received scholarly attention; however, little of this research examines the perspectives of young people. That is unfortunate, because the need to engage young people is well established. According to Sanchez-Jankowski (2002), "If a country is to maintain its democratic appeal it must teach young people what it means to be both civic minded and engaged" (p. 239). If young people are to be engaged, then they must be given an opportunity to talk and be listened to. As Carlson (2006) explains, "We have learned that we do not want them 'at the table' because they are our future leaders.... We need them 'at the table' because they contribute a unique perspective today, and they alone have the experience of living as young people in this time and place" (p. 91). Golombek (2006) concurs, advocating for "looking at the world through children's eyes" and the "recognition and inclusion of children's opinions, worldviews, and experiences" (p. 14).

A theoretical framework that seems particularly well-suited for this research is standpoint theory, because it recognizes that the "unique perspective" or "standpoint" from which an individual views the world influences how individuals socially construct their world. Specifically, standpoint theory acknowledges that "individuals have similar and different vantage points from which they see the world, and the vantage points are the result of the person's field of experience as defined by social group membership" (Kinefuchi & Orbe, 2008, p. 73). Furthermore, one's cultural standpoint significantly shapes ones' worldview and, thus, the way in which one interprets and participates in life events. This perspective provides a framework for exploring the ways in which concepts such as civic-mindedness come to have meaning within particular social and cultural groups and how those meanings may vary across diverse standpoints.

The specific research questions of this study were:

- Research Question 1: According to youth, what constitutes civic engagement? Are there cultural differences in how youth define civic engagement?

- Research Question 2: In what acts of civic engagement do youth report participating? Are there cultural differences in reported acts of civic engagement?

- Research Question 3: What communication factors promote or dissuade civic engagement among youth? Are there cultural differences in these factors?

METHODS

Data Collection

Arguably one of the best ways to study civic engagement among youth is to talk with young people about their own experiences. Consequently, the method selected for this study was thematic content analysis of focus group interviews with youth between the ages of 11 and 19 (average age = 16.2) in the United States and in Germany. Germany was selected as the country to contrast with the United States because of the extensive literature on civic-mindedness within that culture (e.g., Janmaat, 2006; Silbereisen, Tomasik, & Grümer, 2008) and because of access of one of the authors.

Twenty-five youth in a major metropolitan area in the Midwest of the U.S. participated in four focus groups. The participants were recruited through community programs for at-risk youth. In Germany, 21 youth participated in three focus group interviews. The German participants were recruited from upper-level English classes in a Gesamtschule in a mid-sized city in central Germany. At the request of school officials, the German focus groups were conducted in English. Each focus group lasted between 75 and 120 minutes, and the following questions were used to guide the focus group discussions: What does it mean to be civic-minded? How do you define civic engagement? Tell me of a time when you had to decided to either participate or not participate in a civic engagement activity. What decision did you make and what factors influenced your decision? What institutions (i.e., schools, religious institutions) influence and/or cultivate civic-mindedness and civic engagement among youth? What degree of influence do your peers have on whether or not you become civically engaged? What messages do you receive that dissuade you from becoming civically engaged? What obstacles do you encounter as it relates to you participating in a civic event? What would you suggest as a way to promote the value of civic-mindedness and civic engagement among youth? Institutional Review Board (IRB) approval was requested and received for the project from the IRB at the authors' home university.

Data Analysis

The focus group transcripts were analyzed using thematic content analytical methods, as described by Bereleson (1971). Through this method, the primary issues and concerns related to each of the topic areas included in the focus group guide (e.g., definitions of civic engagement, acts of civic engagement, factors promoting civic engagement, obstacles to engagement) were identified and categorized into relevant themes. This process involved the following steps: First, the focus group transcripts were unitized by demarcating segments of conversation related to each topic area. For example, talk related to definitions of civic-mindedness was separated from talk related to specific acts of engagement. Then, the content related to each topic area was analyzed using a *constant comparison technique* (Glaser & Strauss 1967) to index common and divergent themes related to the topic. The constant comparative technique is an inductive analytical approach, in which themes emerge from the data rather than being superimposed on the data. The themes emerging in the first focus group provided the framework for the analysis of subsequent focus groups. As additional focus group data were analyzed, findings were constantly compared to the previously identified themes, and the thematic categories related to each topic area were fine-tuned and refined.

RESULTS

Definitions of Civic Engagement

American youth. The primary goal of this research was to give voice to young people from two diverse cultures, to find out from them how they, from their unique standpoints, view and live civic engagement. However, in analyzing the focus group data, it became clear that the data from the American youth could not be combined into a single cultural profile. In fact, two unique perspectives, representing two diverse standpoints, were evident in the responses from the American youth. The first standpoint, labeled Standpoint A, is represented by youth with a relatively strong collectivist orientation (Hofstede, 1980) and strong institutional affiliations. The second standpoint, labeled Standpoint B, is represented by youth with a relatively strong individualist orientation (Hofstede, 1980) and relatively limited institutional affiliation. These results suggest that these two standpoints provide quite different vantage points from which young people view civic engagement.

The first question asked in the focus groups, and the first research question this study sought to answer, was "What is civic engagement?" The initial response given to this question by the American interviewees in all four focus groups was "I don't know." This response was often followed by puzzled looks and what appeared to be genuine confusion. However, as the participants talked with one another, they were able to come to a consensus about what civic engagement is. The definitions of civic engagement constructed by the four American focus groups included: "It's doing things to help others, coming together with a group of people and 'doing good' in the community," "civic engagement is community service, giving back by helping others," it is "coming together to do something good in your community" and it is "helping others by doing good things, but it doesn't benefit you."

A more in-depth analysis of the focus group talk related to defining civic engagement reveals several noteworthy themes. First, although the definitions given by the four American groups varied in construction, all of them included some or all of the following components: *community service, coming together, and helping others*. Second, two of the four groups (interestingly, those labeled Standpoint A) defined civic engagement as something their parents did and not something they did themselves. Finally, in some instances, the initial definitions provided by the groups were congruent with the acts of engagement reported by group members, but in other instances, this was not the case, and there was inconsistency between how the youth defined civic engagement as an abstract construct and their actual behavior. The two groups that conceived of civic engagement as something their parents did and not something they did, for instance, proceeded to provide many examples of acts of engagement in which they participated on a regular basis. This finding suggests that behavioral acts of civic engagement are not always perceived by youth as civic engagement.

German youth. As with the American focus group participants, the German youth responded to the question "What is civic engagement?" with confusion. In part, their confusion was related to semantics, because although the students knew the meanings of the two words "civic" and "engagement" separately, they were less familiar with the phrase "civic engagement." They, however, were able to offer definitions of what it means to be an "engaged citizen."

There are some subtle but intriguing differences in the themes emerging in the German youths' conversation in response to this question as compared to the definitions generated by the American youth. According to the German respondents, one component of being an engaged citizen is "living peacefully in community," which entails getting along with people and nature, avoiding violence, and "not to have an argument with other people." A second component of the German conceptualization of civic engagement is being politically active. As one respondent explains, "You have to have an interest in what is happening politically. You would not just walk away from the politics." A third theme emerging in the German's definition of civic engagement is the importance of being well-educated, watching the news, and staying informed. Finally, the German respondents included taking care of one's self in their definition of what it means to be an engaged citizen. One respondent explained, "Taking care of myself is part of being a good citizen," and another chimed in, "Yeah, being responsible, because the way I live affects other people."

Acts of Civic Engagement

American youth. Once the conceptual, definitional understandings of civic engagement had been gleaned from the focus group interviews, attention shifted, in keeping with the second research question, to analyzing how young people operationalize civic engagement. Specifically, narrative accounts of the particular acts of civic engagement in which young people actually participate were elicited. Table 5.1 provides a summary of the acts of engagement reported by all focus group participants. The majority of these activities are behaviors typically associated with civic engagement, such as volunteering in churches or within their communities. However, the youth also provided some examples of civic engagement which may be considered atypical. For example, one participant shared a story of a time when he "helped a guy whose car was on fire. I did my best to help him with what objects I had at hand. ... It's not donating money, but it's still helping. I almost caught myself on fire." Another more atypical example is the group members who defined their *court ordered community service* as *civic engagement*.

In keeping with the thematic analytical method employed in this analysis, the authors initially sought to discern patterns in the specific activities identified by the youth as acts of civic engagement. This analysis revealed that the acts of engagement discussed by the young people in the study varied along two dimensions: (a) the initiator of the act, and (b) the target, or beneficiary, of the act. The reported acts of engagement from all focus group participants are plotted along these two dimensions in Figure 5.1. The vertical axis in Figure 5.1 represents whether the act was initiated by an individual or a group, and the horizontal axis indicates how local versus global the target of the act was. These two dimensions intersect to create four types of civic engagement activity. Some actions, such as helping out on an uncle's farm or cleaning an aunt's house, are individual-initiated, local acts. Others, such as working with a school club to clean a community park, are group-initiated, local acts. Going with a church group on an international mission trip is an example of a group-initiated act with a more global target, and an individual donating to disaster relief illustrates the individual-initiated, global quadrant.

The majority of the reported acts of civic engagement target local rather than global issues. However, although the number of individually-initiated acts is nearly equal to the number of group-initiated acts, the vast majority of the civic engagement activities reported by the youth rep-

**Table 5.1.   Acts of Civic Engagement Reported
by Youth in the United States and Germany**

| | American Youth | | |
Action Initiated by	Standpoint A	Standpoint B	German Youth
Educational institutions	• 10 required hours of service-learning • Color guard • National Honor Society • ROTC • Student council • Grant writing for after-school program		
Religious institutions	• Clean up after disaster • Mission trips • Vacation Bible school		
Community organizations	• Grant writing for community center programs • Mentoring • Park clean up		• Volunteered through sports clubs to teach younger children
Family and friends	• Community and park clean up	• Julian Center • Helped on uncle's farm • Cleaned aunt's house • Cleaned church for grandmother	• Volunteered in food pantry • Volunteered at summer camp for people with disabilities • Participated in political protest (i.e., demonstrations for better education)
Self		• Helped stranger with burning car • Donated clothes to Am Vets, Salvation Army • Collected tabs for Ronald McDonald's House • Collected Yoplait lids for cancer research	• Participated in political protest (i.e., anti-Fascism rallies) • Personal protest against cruelty for animals (not eating meat)
Judicial affiliation		• Court-ordered community service	

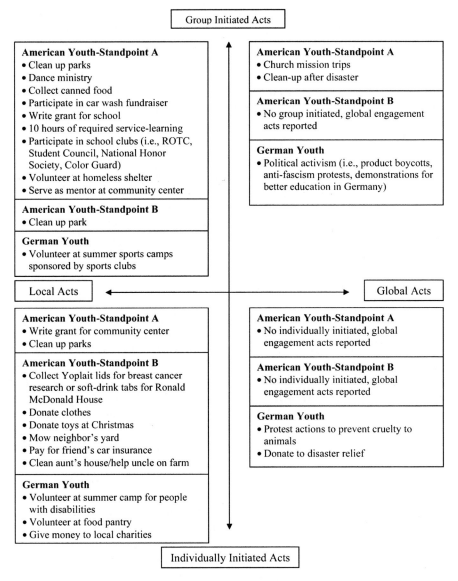

Figure 5.1.   Youth-reported acts of civic engagement plotted by act initiator and act target.

resenting Standpoint B were individual-initiated; whereas, a majority of acts reported by those representing Standpoint A were group-initiated.

An analysis of the narratives shared by the focus group participants about their specific acts of engagement revealed several noteworthy themes. Perhaps most evident is the important role institutional affiliations play in shaping civic engagement activities. For many of the youth interviewed in this study, educational institutions provided opportunities which framed and contextualized engagement as a way for them to personally excel while also contributing to the community good. For example, some youth reported that their schools required them to perform ten hours of community service, and they listed these activities as examples of *civic engagement*. In these particular situations, youth chose from a variety of available activities including cleaning up parks, planting trees, or reading books to kindergartners and first graders. The students who received school credit for some of their civic engagement activities were more likely to list additional similar acts in which they have participated without being required to do so. For example, one American respondent who was required to do community service through her school also reported writing grants on her own time as a way to ensure that after school youth programs were created and maintained within her community. She explained that she did it so that young people "don't get in trouble or go to jail, do drugs or be places they're not supposed to be, act out and do things they're not supposed to do."

Another institutional affiliation that significantly was associated with the acts of civic engagement reported by the American youth was church membership. Two of the groups interviewed identified participation in Vacation Bible School, mission trips to other countries and cleaning up disaster areas with their churches as examples of civic engagement. Without this particular institutional membership, these specific and unique opportunities identified by the youth would likely not have been present in their responses. Further, such opportunities, as referenced by the youth's own examples, fostered a collective mindset while exposing the youth to different worldviews, interpretations, and perspectives.

This, institutional affiliation played a significant role in shaping American youths' understandings of what it means to be an engaged citizen. The standpoint vis-a-vis civic engagement of the American youth seemed to be influenced primarily by institutional affiliation. The youth situated in Standpoint B did not cite educational or church affiliations at all as influencing factors in defining their acts of civic engagement. This discrepancy is particularly noteworthy when one considers the role institutions play in motivating civic involvement. In the narratives shared in these focus groups, when an institutional framework that promoted embedded opportunities for civic engagement was present, the motivations behind the individuals' giving their time and resources were very different than when an institutional structure providing these opportunities was not present. When institutional support was present, the youth conveyed a more collective cultural frame, expressing a perceived obligation to their communities. This is shown repeatedly in the responses the focus group participant's gave when asked, "What factors influence you to take on some of the projects that you do?" One student explained that she participated in a park clean-up day because "this is our environment, so I am going to pick it up." Another explained that "kids are our future so I am going to be a mentor." Yet another explained why she took the time to write a grant: "So I ask, what can I do for the programs that are not going to be funded this year because [our school] says they can't afford it. Of course I am going to write them a grant, especially if it keeps or gets kids engaged." All of these examples imply a motivation that is rooted in a strong sense of connection with and commitment to community. Interestingly, as noted above, all of these narratives were shared by individuals with strong institutional affiliations.

In contrast, the narratives shared by students who did not report having institutionally embedded support for civic engagement were characterized by much more of an individualistic mindset. The motivations for why these respondents performed the acts they defined as *civic engagement* included: "20 hours, it's court-ordered." "It's a tax write off." "We get extra credit." "I feel good about myself." "You do it or you pay a fine and do more time." Many of the acts that are labeled as civic engagement by the youth in these groups are individual acts which do not typically represent the altruism often associated with engagement. For these individuals, acts of engagement are loosely linked to the community at large, but they are motivated by an individual orientation. Collecting Yoplait lids for breast cancer research, collecting tabs from soft-drink cans for the Ronald McDonald House, and giving clothes to the American Veterans organization, for example, are all linked to a sense of community at some level, but the reasons the youth gave for performing these acts of engagement belie a much more individualist orientation.

The narratives shared by youth without institutional support of civic engagement also seem to construct community very differently from those shared by teens with strong institutional support. The groups with limited institutional affiliation targeted local recipients—friends, family, and self—as their idea of community. The acts of engagement they reported were performed locally, for this more narrow community. For example, one individual defined as civic engagement the time he spent working on his uncle's farm when his uncle was unable to lift and bale hay, plant trees or work because of shoulder surgery.

Finally, in the absence of institutional membership, the propensity for future civic engagement appears to be reduced. One individual defined mowing his neighbor's yard as civic engagement, but stated, "I will never do it again; the old man never thanked me." Yet another respondent spent some time cleaning at her aunt's house when her aunt was ill. She also stated that she would never do it again because her aunt only complained.

German youth. The acts of civic engagement reported by the German youth were less in quantity and fundamentally different from those reported by the American participants. Although volunteering was the first thing the German youth mentioned as something an engaged citizen does, they reported that they actually do very little volunteer work. In fact, their immediate response to the focus group facilitator's question, "So, do you volunteer?" was laughter. "We really think it's important, but most of us don't do it," one student summarized. Indeed, the examples of volunteering shared by the German youth were limited. One student reported that she has worked in a food pantry at her mother's urging, and two shared stories of volunteering with other members of their sports clubs to teach diving and soccer to young children.

A second act of civic engagement that was mentioned by the German youth is philanthropic giving, but, again, actual giving reported by the respondents was limited. One student explained: "Some people don't donate because they think that money won't get to the people."

For the German youth, the primary acts of civic engagement were acts of political activism, a form of civic engagement that was noticeably absent from the American students' responses. The importance of participating in political activism was explained by one student who said, "I think [protesting when you see injustice is important], because if the whole community thinks it's not okay, we need to work against it. We have to do that." Another student added, "When rights and privileges are being taken away, it's important to protest. It's important to protest to protect the things you have." The specific protest activities the German students report having participated in include anti-Nazi protests, strikes, signing online petitions, participating in boycotts, demonstrations for better education, and demonstrations against fascism. Not all of the examples of political activism were organized collective activities, though. One student talked about her own efforts to raise awareness about vegetarianism as civic engagement. She argued that in and of itself, her decision not to eat meat is an act of protest, noting: "I think it is a protest to refuse to eat meat. Animals are living creatures, so to not eat meat is a kind of protest." She explained further that she chooses not to participate in the violent protests of some animal rights groups, opting instead to "talk with people one on one."

Although the primary acts of civic engagement identified by the German respondents were acts of political activism, students were quick to point out that protesting by itself is not enough. As one respondent explained, "Very often it's very easy to say 'Oh I'm against it.' And many people do this. They complain. It's also really important to stand for something and do something. You can't just be against something, though, you have to present an alternative."

Figure 5.1 plots the acts of engagement described in the narratives shared by the German focus group participants according to the two dimensions described above. For the most part, the acts of engagement in which the German youth report participating are group-initiated activities with some global impact. Only a few of the narratives evidenced individually-initiated engagement. Even in those instances where an individual reported initiating an act alone, such as the student who shared the story of taking the train to Berlin for an anti-Nazi protest, the act of engagement is an organized, collective initiative.

Communicative Construction of Civic Engagement

The final research question guiding this research is "What communication factors promote or dissuade civic engagement among youth, and are there cultural differences in these factors?" To answer this research question, the civic engagement narratives shared by the focus group participants were analyzed to discern the specific spheres of discourse that contributed to the youths' understanding of what it means to be an engaged citizen. In addition, the students were asked directly to reflect on and talk about the impact schools, religious institutions, family, and friends have had on their understandings of civic engagement. Their conversation in response to these prompts was thematically analyzed using the constant comparative technique. The findings are summarized in Table 5.2.

American youth. As noted in the previous section, schools and religious institutions play a significant role in shaping the American youths' understandings of civic engagement. Within this data set, this appears to be more true for the youth representing Standpoint A than for those representing Standpoint B.

Family is another institution that appears to play a significant role in shaping the American youths' experiences and expectations related to civic engagement. The narratives of engagement shared by the focus group participants suggest that individuals often have key individuals who are particularly influential, and often those individuals are family members. For one young woman, that influential person was her grandmother. She explains, "Our choir goes to nursing homes, and my grandma lives there. If she tells me that there is no one to minister to them, then I think this is a priority because my grandma is telling me that there's not been anyone to minister to the nursing home." In this example, the opinions of the grandmother play an important role in communicatively constructing

Table 5.2.   The Communicative Construction of Civic Engagement by Youth in the United States and Germany

Spheres of Discourse	American Youth		German Youth
	Standpoint A	*Standpoint B*	*German Youth*
Family, friends, and peers	• It starts at home. My grandfather and my uncle are involved in stuff. • It's how you're raised. My dad's in the military; we have done community service in lots of places. • My brother and sister told me: "as long as you're doing what is right than why not clean it up?"	• Grandma and I fixed breakfast for Sunday School ... but I don't do it anymore because I got lazy and like to sleep in. • I have to do it, I still clean the church, I do it to help my grandma she gets paid for it being done. • I cleaned my aunt's house who was sick and my aunt complained.	• I volunteered because I have a friend and the mother is a member of this organization. • We don't really feel a responsibility to do this, because nobody does it. Our peers don't do it, so we don't. • My mother suggested that I do it.
School programs and teachers	• Teachers want you to do something better in life and be more active in something positive. • AmeriCorps Volunteers involve us in community projects so we meet more older people in the community and so I choose to be more like them. • Student Council, National Honor Society, Color Guard, ROTC and sports allow us to do more things and require higher grades.	• I do it to get school credit.	• I think the schools in Germany should do more to teach us what kinds of volunteer work there is in Germany. • Political parties should go to schools and make presentations—start discussions with students and young people.
Church	• Pastor, I want to be like him, I want his job. • Dance Troop Leader grabs us all the time takes us to do things in the community.	• Church is one of the major places people get involved in their communities.	• The church is not so important--not so important as in America. • That's something our grandparents do.
Judicial system	•	• You got to do it (court-ordered community service) or you have to pay a fine and do more time.	•

the value the story teller places on the particular act of engagement. If the grandmother saw the choir's visit as important, the young person did as well.

As one might expect for this age group, friends and peer group are especially influential in framing civic engagement. One student shared the following story, which effectively illustrates the power of peer influence on civic engagement:

> At my school we started a canned food drive. I don't know why I didn't do it but I think why I didn't want to do it was because at the time I wasn't educated about giving people things or if you don't receive anything back from giving people things it's ok you choose to help somebody but we were in class and my classmates helped me understand it would be helpful to give away the cans we are not using to people who need them so they talked me into it. We were in class and we were talking and they said it was a good chance to give back or whatever, give to others who need the cans. So after talking, so yeah, I decided it was a good thing.

This narrative demonstrates the role of friends and peer groups in communicatively constructing attitudes towards civic-mindedness. Although initially this student did not place the same value on the particular act (donating to the canned food drive) as her peers, through peer-to-peer discussion the individual was challenged to rethink the meaning she associated with the act, and ultimately her opinions about the act converged with those of her classmates. Through the group communication process, an act of civic engagement and the values associated with this act actually became cultivated within this individual's value system. This is just one example of how peer group interaction assists youth in defining civic engagement, their role within their communities, and their level of responsibility within their communities. In this case, the individual was influenced by the group communication process in a way that ultimately cultivated civic-mindedness. However, peer influence does not always work this way. Several of the narratives shared in these focus groups also describe instances where individuals decided to forego participating in a particular civic engagement activity because their friends were not participating.

The above narratives demonstrate that peers can influence the decision to engage in a specific act, but that is not the only way in which peers contribute to the communicative construction of civic engagement. In fact, at a more fundamental level, peers played an important role in shaping understandings of what it means to be engaged and in creating expectations of community responsibility. This is effectively illustrated in the following narrative:

I got one for you. This happened on Friday before I was heading down to Bloomington. My buddy's girlfriend, she just got her driver's permit so I let her drive my buddy's car to take her and the baby home, but she wrecked the car in the driveway and her brother called the cops on her. What brother would do something like that? But my buddy didn't have insurance so I went inside and went online and put insurance on the car before the cops got there, and it cost me $2,000 dollars.

When asked, "Why did you do that?" the storyteller stated, "I didn't want her to go to jail and they have helped me out before, I don't have no money right now [*sic*] but he can drive."

In this narrative, as in the previous one, one can trace the communicative construction of the storyteller's notions of civic-mindedness. In this story, the peer group played a significant role in shaping expectations about what a *good citizen* was expected to do. Furthermore, if other spheres of discourse, such as schools, churches, or families, do not play an active role in communicatively constructing those expectations, the peer group may play a disproportionately significant role in shaping young peoples' understandings of what it means to be an engaged citizen.

Although peers play an undeniably important role in fostering civic-mindedness among youth, several of the narratives emphasized the fact that the youth also acted as individuals. One respondent exclaimed, "If we were given the opportunity, we would go to New Orleans and help out with the recovery effort even if our friends were not going to do it because it's the right thing to do." A particularly interesting feature of this story, however, is the fact that the content of the message supports individual action "we would go ... even if our friends were not going", but the speaker chooses to use the *we* pronoun, implying a collective component even when the act is conceptualized as an individual act.

A final communication sphere of influence affecting young peoples' decision making related to civic engagement that emerged from the thematic analysis of the focus group data is emerging technologies. Table 5.3 summarizes the themes emerging related to this topic for all of the focus groups.

While the American youth report using communication technologies to gather information that helps them be more engaged, the specific technologies used and the specific uses of those technologies varied, depending on standpoint. The more collectively-oriented, institutionally-embedded youth representing Standpoint A reported watching several local and national political debates and regularly reading political blogs, print newspapers, and online newspapers. In addition, these youth reported using cell phones and pagers to disseminate information regarding community alerts and civic engagement opportunities and using the internet for informational and tangible purposes. The narra-

**Table 5.3. Technology Use and Civic Engagement
Among Youth In U.S. and Germany**

American Youth		German Youth
Standpoint A	*Standpoint B*	
Use technology to gather information:	**Use technology to gather information:**	**Use technology to gather information:**
• Local news (TV & print)	• Local news (mostly TV)	• Local news (TV & print)
• National news (TV & print)	• Only one person reported using media to keep up with politics (watching presidential debates) or for civic engagement	• National news (TV & print)
• International news (TV & print)		• International news (TV & print)
• Online TV and newspapers	• The majority reported using computers primarily for online games, music and movies	**Use technology to support political activity**
• Use Social networking sites (MySpace, Facebook, Political Blogs)		• Use internet to find out about planned political protests
• Get bus route information		• Use social networking sites to "exponentially increase" the impact of protest activity
Use of cell phones:	**Use of cell phones:**	
• To disseminate community alerts and civic opportunities across counties, peer groups & cultures	• Text message friends about social activities and relational matters (limited use for civic engagement)	**Use technology to raise awareness about social issues**
		• Rock stars promoting causes through the internet
		• Pink protest song ("Dear Mr. President") going virile on Youtube

tives they shared talk about using the internet to research particular topics, to keep up with local, national and international news, or to look up bus routes to get to a civic engagement activity. One student stated that when he missed the local news in the morning, "I take my laptop to school and watch it online."

The youth whose standpoint is less institutionally embedded, on the other hand, reported using cell phones primarily as a means to keep in touch with friends and family. This finding is consistent with the tendency reported above that these respondents conceptualized acts of civic engagement in terms of providing assistance to friends and family. In addition, the civic engagement narratives shared by these youth provided no indication of internet use for civic engagement purposes. These students admitted that they used the Internet predominantly to play online games and download music and videos.

One final noteworthy finding related to the relationship between technology use and civic engagement emerging from this data was that although a majority of the youth reported that they used technology to access information on local community events as well as the local and national news, they also reported that the messages and images they see often have a "negative impact on their desire to become civically and/or politically engaged." Although the data collected in these focus groups does not provide enough detail to explain this finding, it is worthy of further exploration.

German youth. A comparison of the responses from the German and American focus groups revealed some intriguing differences in terms of how understandings of civic engagement are communicatively constructed. Whereas religious institutions played a significant role in fostering civic-mindedness in America, they had very little influence on the German youth participating in this study. When asked, "Do churches, synagogues, and mosques provide opportunities for you to do volunteer work?" the German youth responded, saying "Not so much." One teen explained, "That's something our grandparents do." The German youth expressed the perception that this is a notable difference between their experience in Germany and what they assume the experience of their counterparts in America might be. One student noted, "The church is not so important here. Not so important as in America." Another added, "In much of the rest of the Western world, the link to the church is going down, but in America it seems to be on the rise."

One role religious institutions were seen as playing related to civic engagement in Germany was fundraising. One student explains: "There are many organizations in Germany that are covered by the church, so you can help people who don't have that much money." The students were able to brainstorm several organizations that *do good* under the auspices of religious institutions, such as "Caritas, Brot für die Welt, or Miserior." It is interesting to note that for the most part, those civic engagement initiatives are globally focused. It is also important to note that while the young people were aware of the fundraising activities of religious institutions, none of them donated money through these initiatives.

According to the German youth, the primary function of educational institutions in terms of civic engagement is as a site for educating an engaged citizenry. The students reported that they think their schools do a fairly good job of preparing them to stay informed about the world in which they live and teaching them about political processes in a general sense. They challenged schools to do more, however, to provide them with civic engagement opportunities. One student argued: "I think that the schools in Germany should do more to teach us what kinds of volunteer work there is in Germany." In addition, they suggested that schools work more closely with political parties to engage students in the political process. One respondent recommended, "Political parties should go to schools and make presentations, start discussions with students and young people." Another student expanded on the idea: "Maybe they can combine that with concerts or bands. Make it an event that young people will be drawn to." Yet another suggested, "In my opinion it's a good idea to connect politics and sports." The riff of responses from the focus group participants indicated that the German students saw a need for more experiential civic engagement in their schools to supplement the academic study of what it means to be an engaged citizen than is already there.

As in the United States, German youth report that family and friends play a particularly important role in their personal involvement in civic engagement. In most of those instances where German youth reported doing volunteer work, it was because of the influence of family or friends. For example, one student explained: "I have done something with handicapped people. It was during a holiday. For 2 weeks. The handicapped people were teenagers, my age, and we went hiking with them." When asked why she volunteered there, she said "I have a friend and the mother is a member of this organization." Another female respondent who said she volunteers at a food pantry explained that it was her mother who encouraged her to go.

As with the American youth, the impact of friends can either encourage or discourage civic engagement. According to the German respondents, however, for them the latter is more likely. One respondent clarified, "We don't really feel a responsibility to do this; because nobody does it. Our peers don't do it, so we don't."

Another factor contributing to the communicative construction of civic engagement in Germany is organizational affiliations. Clubs and organizations that are not associated with educational or religious institutions are especially important in Germany in motivating civic engagement. One student shared a story of working with his diving club to teach diving to children. He explained, "I volunteer because I want to give the club this work back." "I'm a part of an organization and I do the volunteer work to help out the organization." In this narrative, the role of the organization itself in shaping what it means to be an engaged citizen and the expectations that go along with that are clear.

As did the American youth, German youth also talked about the role of emerging technologies related to civic engagement. The uses of emerging technologies related to civic engagement reported by the German youth were similar to and different from the patterns emerging in the data from the American youth. The German youth identified one of the primary civic engagement applications of new technology as being the promotion of particular "causes." They gave the example of rock stars promoting their causes through the internet. Although the German youth reported being aware of this use of technology, they were quick to point out that they do not see themselves as being influenced by these messages. One respondent explained, "We don't respond to these messages. Not as much as young people in America do. I don't think the stars are so near to us like in America." The German youth also reported that, in fact, they are suspicious of the motives behind online efforts to engender civic engagement. One student elaborated: "I think many famous people do that because they care about their image. It's not motivated by their desire to do good—it's their desire to promote themselves."

The primary use of technology for civic engagement purposes discussed by the German youth was their use of the internet and social networking tools to spread the word about protest activities. One student explained, "If the protest is reported on the internet, it can reach a lot more people." The students admitted that they personally use the internet to learn about protest activities, and they acknowledged that the internet can be used to exponentially increase the impact of a particular protest. One student shared a story of attending an anti-fascism rally in Berlin. An important element in her narrative is reporting her experience online through a social network site, which made "a lot more people aware of the event."

Understanding how youth use technology to connect themselves to their communities is a critical component to understanding the factors that promote or hamper civic engagement among young people. Furthermore these data suggest that cultures and cocultures may be using technology differently to connect to their communities. These differences need to be recognized, understood, and taken into account in planning civic engagement initiatives that cross cultural boundaries.

DISCUSSION

This study explored cultural differences in how youth conceptualize and enact civic engagement. The results indicate that the views of civic engagement expressed by young people are shaped by their cultural standpoint and that youth in Germany and the United States have different standpoints and, thus, unique perspectives about engagement. Furthermore, the results suggest that even within larger national cultural groups, cocultures may inhabit different standpoints related to civic engagement. This was most evident in the focus groups conducted with American youth. In this section, the major findings revealed through our analysis will be discussed, with particular emphasis on their implications for internationalizing civic engagement.

Cultural standpoint is a powerful force, shaping an individual's understanding of what it means to be an engaged citizen. On the one hand, the American and German youth define civic engagement in a similar manner: a common thread in all of the definitions of civic engagement presented by the young people is that it involves working to meet community needs. However, closer analysis reveals that German and American young people approach the construct of civic engagement from very different conceptual standpoints. To the American youth, *working to meet community needs* means tangibly solving problems (i.e., working at food pantries, tutoring, helping clean up after a disaster), but to the German youth, *working to meet community needs* means taking the political actions necessary to ensure that the government meets its obligations to the people. For example, German youth are more likely to engage in protests against poverty or for policies that ensure fee-free access to education for all than they are to participate in projects that provide direct material aid to people in need. This represents a fundamental difference in the conceptualization of civic engagement, a difference that is not inconsistent with existing research on civic involvement within these two countries. A study of political activity and volunteerism conducted as part of the American Democracy Project's Political Engagement Project discovered that young people in the United States are more likely to engage in apolitical community service than in political activities (Colby, 2008). This stands in stark contrast to the emphasis placed on political activism as civic engagement reported by the German youth in the current study.

This difference has obvious implications for designing civic engagement initiatives that involve individuals from these two cultures. The success of civic engagement programs relies on convergence between young people's conceptualizations of what it means to be an engaged citizen and the engagement opportunities they are provided. Either the engagement activities must be tailored to fit within the existing conceptualizations of the student, or the student's concept of what it means to be engaged must be altered to foster such convergence. This latter alternative is evident in the Political Engagement Project's goal to promote the inclusion of explicitly political activities within the conceptualization of civic engagement at American universities (American Association of State Colleges and Universities, 2011).

A second key finding supported by our data is that the conceptualization and enactment of civic engagement within the lives of young people are strongly associated with the institutional support provided for engagement within a particular cultural context. Research has shown "a spectacular expansion of philanthropy, volunteering, and civil society organizations throughout the world" (Salamon, 2010, p. 167); however, the types of activities supported by the civil society sector varies considerably from country to country. In their analysis of NGOs around the world, Toepler and Salamon (2003) found that NGOs promoting culture and recreation are most prevalent in Central Europe, while NGOs offering welfare services are less common. Given this institutional context for engagement, it is not surprising that volunteer activities reported by the German youth in our sample were related primarily to culture and recreation, activities such as volunteering with summer camps for children with disabilities or with soccer clubs.

The engagement activities reported by the American youth also were shaped by their institutional support for engagement; however, the two standpoints represented in the American sample differed considerably on this dimension. The Standpoint A youth are firmly embedded in a variety of institutions that encourage and offer opportunities for civic engagement. The conceptualization of civic-mindedness revealed in the talk of the young people in this cultural context grows out of messages from family members about the responsibilities of good citizenship. These messages are, in turn, institutionally reinforced by schools, churches, and community organizations. The Standpoint B youth, on the other hand, appear to be much less embedded within institutions that promote civic engagement. The youth situated within these diverse standpoints view civic engagement differently, they engage in different engagement opportunities, and they use communication technologies quite differently for the purposes of civic activity.

The practical implications of this finding are clear: embedding opportunities for civic engagement within institutions appears to be of particular importance, especially for fostering a civic mindset in young people. The results of this study indicate that those young people with institutional affiliations that support civic engagement were more likely to engage in acts that supported their communities, and they were more likely to express a collective, community-oriented mindset. Perhaps most important, though, is that young people who were civically engaged through their schools and religious institutions were more likely to participate in other civic engagement activities on their own. It seems as if the institutionally mandated civic engagement does get transformed into an embraced ideology.

A third finding from this research is the importance of interaction within peer groups and with respected opinion leaders in shaping attitudes related to civic engagement. As the results of this study suggest, across cultures young people were heavily influenced by the actions and interactions of their peers. Although this finding is not surprising, it is important when it comes to designing civic engagement initiatives that will speak to young people.

A final finding emerging from this data is the incongruence observed between civic engagement as a defined concept and a lived reality. The fact that young people can tell researchers what civic engagement is, but that they do not necessarily live it, suggests that civic engagement programs do not always result in students identifying with the ideology of engagement. Promoting self-reflection and encouraging individuals to think of themselves as engaged citizens may help align the conceptual and behavioral aspects of engagement among young people. This recommendation is consistent with the Project on Civic Reflection, which encourages intentional reflection on the "values and the choices you make in serving your community" as an important element in fostering civic-mindedness (Project on Civic Reflection, 2011).

The results of the current research have practical implications for community partners and educators who seek to provide civic engagement and service-learning opportunities that are appropriate for the populations they serve. As civic engagement becomes increasingly global, cultural differences in conceptualizations of what it means to be an engaged citizen must be intentionally considered in program design. Students need to be taught to recognize the ways in which their own standpoint affects their perception of and interpretation of civic engagement activities. In addition, they need to be taught that other cultures may have quite different understandings of what it means to be an engaged citizen. Finally, as we help students reflect on international service-learning experiences, this should be done through the lens of sensitivity to those differences. The human tendency is to evaluate experiences through our own cultural lenses. Even what an individual sees as *civic responsibility* or *the obligations of an engaged citizen* will vary from culture to culture. Educators can help students learn that the lenses individuals from other cultures are wearing may be different and to prepare them to interact effectively and appropriately in diverse cultural contexts.

REFERENCES

Almond, G. A., & Verba, S. (1963). *The civic culture: Political attitudes in five democracies*. Princeton, NJ: Princeton University Press.

American Association of State Colleges and Universities. (2011). American democracy project: Political engagement project (PEP). Retrieved from http://www.aascu.org/programs/adp/engagement.htm.

Astin, A. W., Vogelgesang, L. J., Ikeda, E. K., & Yee, J. A. (2000). *How service-learning affects students*. Los Angeles, CA: University of California, Higher Education Research Institute.

Bennett, W. L. (2008). Civic learning in changing democracies: Challenges for citizenship and civic education. In P. Dahlgren (Ed.), *Young citizens and new media: Learning and democratic engagement*. New York, NY: Routledge.

Berelson, B. (1971). *Content analysis in communication research*. Glencoe, IL: Free Press.

Bringle, R. G., & Hatcher, J. A. (2000, Fall). Meaningful measurement of theory-based service-learning outcomes: Making the case with quantitative research. *Michigan Journal of Community Service-learning*, 68-75.

Bringle, R. G., & Kremer, J. F. (1993). An evaluation of an intergenerational service-learning project for undergraduates. *Educational Gerontology, 19*, 407-416.

Carlson, C. (2006). The Hampton experience as a new model for youth civic engagement. *Journal of Community Practice, 14*, 89-106.

Carr, K. (2002).Building bridges and crossing borders: Using service-learning to overcome cultural barriers to collaboration between science and education departments. *School Science and Mathematics, 102*, 285-298.

Colby, A. (2008). The place of political learning in college. *Peer Review, 10*, 4-8.

Conville, R. L., & Weintraub, S. (Eds.). (2002). *Service-learning and communication: A disciplinary toolkit*. Washington, DC: National Communication Association.

Dey, E. L., Barnhardt, C. L., Antonaros, M., Ott, M. C., & Holsapple, M. A. (2009). *Civic responsibility: What is the campus climate for learning?* Washington, DC: Association of American Colleges and Universities.

Douglas, M. (1970). *Natural symbols: Explorations in cosmology*. London, England: Barrie and Rockliff.

Duffy, D., Franco, R., Gelmon, S., Jones, S., Meeropol, J., & Zlotkowski, E. (2004). *The community's college: Indicators of engagement at two-year institutions*. Providence, RI: Campus Compact.

Federal Ministry of Labour and Social Affairs. (2010). *Strengthen civic engagement*. Retrieved from http://www.bmas.de/portal/48606/

Glaser, B. G., & Strauss, A. L. (1967). *The discovery of grounded theory: Strategies for qualitative research*. New York, NY: Aldine de Gruyter.

Golombek, S. B. (2006). Children as citizens. *Journal of Community Practice, 14*(1), 11-30.

Hofstede, G. (1980). *Culture's consequences: International differences in work-related values*. Newbury Park, CA: SAGE.

Hunt, R. J., & Swiggum, P. (2007). Being in another world: Transcultural student experiences using service-learning with families who are homeless. *Journal of Transcultural Nursing, 18*, 167-174.

Janmaat, J. G. (2006). Civic culture in Western and Eastern Europe. *AES, 47*, 363-393.

Jarjoura, G. R. (1999). Delinquent youths and their futures: Can outreach on the part of the university make a difference? In A. Driscoll & E. A. Lynton (Eds.) *Making outreach visible: A guide to documenting professional service and outreach*. Herndon, VA: Stylus.

Kecskes, K. (2006, Spring). Behind the rhetoric: Applying a cultural theory lens to community-campus partnership development. *Michigan Journal of Community Service-Learning*, 5-14.

Kecskes, K., & Elshimi, A. (2010, October). *Arab world perceptions of civic engagement*. Paper presented at the meeting of the International Association for Research on Service-Learning and Community Engagement, Indianapolis, IN.

Keen, C., & Hall, K. (2009). Engaging with difference matters. *The Journal of Higher Education, 80,* 59-79.

Kinefuchi, E., & Orbe, M. P. (2008). Situating oneself in a racialized world: Understanding student reactions to *Crash* through standpoint theory and context-positionality frames. *Journal of International and Intercultural Communication, 1,* 70-90.

Platt, C. (1998). Civic education and academic culture. *Liberal Education, 84,* 18-25.

Project on Civic Reflection. (2011). Project on civic reflection. Retrieved from http://www.civicreflection.org/

Salamon, L. M. (2010). Putting the civil society sector on the economic map of the world. *Annals of Public and Cooperative Economics, 81,* 167-210.

Sanchez-Jankowski, M. (2002). Minority youth and civic engagement: The impact of group relations. *Applied Developmental Science, 6,* 237-245.

Sherraden, M. S., Lough, B., & McBride, A. M. (2008). Effects of international volunteering and service: Individual and institutional predictors. *Voluntas, 19,* 395-421.

Silbereisen, R. K., Tomasik, M. J., & Grümer (2008). Soziodemografische und psychologische korrelate des bürgerschaftlichen engagements anfang 2000 in Deutschland [Sociodemographic and psychological correlates of civic engagement at the beginning of the new millennium in Germany]. In R. K. Silbereisen & M. Pinquart (Eds.) *Individuum und sozialer wandel* (pp. 197-227). Weinheim, Germany: Juventa.

Thompson, M., Ellis, R., & Wildavsky, A. (1990). *Cultural theory.* Boulder, CO: Westview.

Thornton, C. H., & Jaeger, A. J. (2007). A new context for understanding civic responsibility: Relating culture to action as a research university. *Research in Higher Education, 48,* 993-1020.

Toepler, S., & Salamon, L. M. (2003). NGO development in Central and Eastern Europe: An empirical overview. *East European Quarterly, 37,* 365-378.

Tonkin, H. (Ed.). (2004). *Service-learning across cultures: Promise and achievement.* New York, NY: International Partnership for Service-learning.

Zeldin, S., McDaniel, A., Topitzes, D., & Calvert, M. (2000). *Youth in decision-making: A study on the impacts of youth on adults and organizations.* Retrieved from http://www.glsen.org/binary-data/GLSEN_ATTACHMENTS/file/130-1.pdf

CHAPTER 6

DIGITAL
CLASSROOM PROJECT

Impact of Service-Learning and Information and Communication Technology on Student Learning in Hong Kong

Alfred C. M. Chan, Carol H. K Ma, Sharon S. Y. Chan, Polly Y. N. Chiu, and Sandy S. S. Yeung

ABSTRACT

This paper describes a collaborative service-learning model between Lingnan University and a primary school in Hong Kong that developed a hybrid model of university-community partnerships in service-learning and internet-based learning. Echoing the trend of advancing technology in education and the need for holistic education, the Digital Classroom Project integrated the pedagogy of service-learning and information and communication technology. With the aim of creating a learning environment unconstrained by time and location, the digital classroom project encouraged learners to develop independent learning skills and share knowledge with a diverse and global audience. Primary school students participated in guided reading and group discussions led by university students utilizing both online and face-to-face activities. A comprehensive evaluation of effective-

Understanding Service-Learning and Community Engagement:
Crossing Boundaries Through Research, pp. 101–125

ness was implemented that examines eight different areas. This paper reports on these outcomes, which found overall positive impacts on student learning.

In today's rapidly progressive environment, students need to be technologically skilled and capable of independent learning in order to keep up with the increasing pace of technological development. By incorporating service-learning, reading, and information and communication technology (ICT), the Digital Classroom Project (DCP) created a learning environment unconstrained by time and location. It enabled learners and teaching professionals in different regions and with different education levels to share, build, and transform knowledge and educational experiences.

The rising popularity of e-learning has urged government and education professionals to develop strategies for further integrating technology education (TE) and information technology (IT) in education in Hong Kong. The Curriculum Development Council of the Education Bureau of Hong Kong positions TE as an essential component in preparing students for the e-learning environment. To equip students with the ability to keep pace with advanced technological development, skills in manipulating technology and independent learning habits should be developed when children are of young ages.

Despite rapid technological development, reading is still regarded as the most effective means to develop students' independent learning ability. "Reading to Learn" is one of the four key tasks of Hong Kong's education curriculum. The Curriculum Development Council (2001) highlighted the importance of reading in enhancing students' interest, appreciation, knowledge, and experience, in addition to improving their language proficiency and adding value to their quality of life.

The DCP was designed to respond to this intersection of technological advancement and the importance of reading in education. The project begins with the pedagogy of service-learning and a guided reading approach. The participating primary school students, no matter what their educational level, were asked to read a list of books (mostly classical novels and storybooks with themes of civic and moral education), which were selected in accordance with the general reading capability of primary school students. University students acted as mentors to guide primary school students in reading the selected books. They shared their reading experience on an online discussion platform established by adopting the "Knowledge Management* System +" (KM*S+). This platform enables them to share their knowledge and come up with new ideas without geographical or time constraint.

OBJECTIVES

With the pedagogy of service-learning and the advantage of technology (especially the online platform established by KM*S+), this project aimed to (a) foster participants' reading ability and reading incentives through multiple forms of interaction; (b) cultivate a reading culture among primary school students; (c) enhance participants' learning abilities and skills; (d) facilitate technological application in education; (e) encourage participants to share knowledge and thoughts through online discussion; and (f) build intergenerational relationships among different age groups.

The project included an evaluation to analyze the effectiveness of the project and to explore the learning outcomes of the participants. The research aimed to explore the primary school students' and the university students' learning outcomes in eight different areas: (a) reading habits, (b) internet utilization habits, (c) subject-related knowledge, (d) communication skills, (e) organizational skills, (f) social competence, (g) problem solving skills, and (h) research skills.

THEORETICAL FRAMEWORK

The DCP integrates the pedagogy of service-learning and the application of ICT. According to Bringle and Hatcher (1995), service-learning is a "course-based, credit bearing educational experience that allows students (a) to participate in an organized service activity that meets identified community needs; (b) to reflect on the service activity in such a way as to gain further understanding of course content, a broader appreciation of the discipline, and an enhanced sense of civic responsibility" (p.112). Unlike community volunteer work, S-L combines theoretical and practical learning experiences. Through performing voluntary community service, students' academic study can be reinforced through the process of critical thinking and self-reflection (Chan, Ma, & Fong, 2006).

Not only university students can benefit from S-L, but also students of any educational level. The Education Bureau in Hong Kong recommends service-learning to be one of the key strategies in promoting moral and civic education in the primary school curriculum. The Curriculum Development Council recognizes that service-learning provides authentic learning experiences for students to learn through active participation in thoughtfully organized services. Service-learning should not be merely treated as community service, an educational visit or an extra-curricular activity (2001); it should be integrated into the overall academic experience.

AN INEVITABLE TECHNOLOGICAL TIDE: INFORMATION AND COMMUNICATION TECHNOLOGY

With the rapid development of advanced technology, governments around the globe have put resources into formulating strategies and exploring technological potentials in education, and Hong Kong is no exception. According to the Curriculum Development Council, the curricular aim of technology education in Hong Kong is to develop technological literacy in students through the cultivation of technological capability, understanding, and awareness. The Education Bureau in *Right Technology at the Right Time for the Right Task: Consultation Document on the Third Strategy on Information Technology in Education* (2007) further highlights that there is a trend in collaborative learning and sharing knowledge in cyber-connected communities, especially in many advanced economies like Hong Kong. This peer-to-peer collaboration can encourage learners to share their knowledge and to deepen the understanding of the subjects they are interested in (2007).

A number of studies (e.g. Netteland, Wasson, & Mørch, 2007) reveal that utilization of ICT can empower the peer-to-peer strategy for both communication and learning among participants, rather than being simply a common space for information sharing. Such utilization has a positive impact on a learning environment by improving the limitations of classroom learning and decreasing the constraints of diverse learning proficiencies. Researchers have also suggested that the use of an online system to support active learning by providing forums for feedback and reflection has been shown to promote greater depth of explanations by students of varying abilities (National Research Council, 2000). The DCP aimed to encourage the sharing of knowledge and information through technology, which plays an important role in communication and information transfer (Zhang, 2006). The DCP provided primary school students with opportunities to become familiar with an e-learning environment and technological application, and develop good practice for interacting with university students and their classmates. The online platform created the sense of equal opportunities to voice their opinions and to learn from others. Students of different educational levels can learn from the university students and from their peers.

SOCIOCOGNITIVE APPROACH: ACTIVITY THEORY AND CONSTRUCTIVISM

The DCP adopted the sociocognitive approach and activity theory to explain how learners' interactions on the online platform in DCP facilitated learners' knowledge acquisition. As Mitchell AND Myles (1998) mention in following the sociocognitive approach, the learning process is seen as social (interpersonal) and individual (intrapersonal), and learners are seen as active constructors of their own learning environment. Educational researchers and scholars have advocated that interaction and dialogue facilitate learners' knowledge acquisition. Meaning arises and evolves during interactions that are influenced by the social relations within a community of practice, and dialogue plays an important role in shaping conceptual development (Ravenscroft, 2001).

The online virtual community created by the KM*S+ system enabled the participating students to build relationships with persons outside their age group. The online platform blurs the boundaries between students with different learning abilities, as everyone shares equal opportunities to voice and to read others' views. The participating students were encouraged to construct knowledge together by voicing their opinions and responding to others' based on others' points of views. Through social interaction and dialogue, knowledge is constructed and transferred. At the same time, this kind of interaction enables the construction of learners' identities (e.g., one of the members in the class, a tutor). Activity Theory (Engeström, Miettinen, & Punamäki-Gitai, 1999) recognizes this interaction and its implications for transformation.

In addition to Activity Theory, Constructivism helps frame the institutionalization and communication of reality construction. It can be used as a lens for understanding the importance of language and action to knowledge construction (Engeström et al., 1999). Participants were able to contribute and construct new knowledge through historical continuity and situated contingency. Persons interacted not only with their learning partners but also the environment, and as a result they can develop conceptual frameworks to explain these interactions and assist in negotiating future interactions (Newhouse, 2002). In other words, the learning environment is crucial for learners' knowledge acquisition.

The need for e-learning technology is crucial. The application of ICT in education can facilitate knowledge transfer and knowledge acquisition across different students' prior knowledge levels. ICT not only facilitates learners going through cognitive learning processes, but also creates a learner-centered environment. This was accomplished in the DCP with the creation of an online virtual community where knowledge is built up and transferred across the online platform, which promotes equal voices.

PROGRAM STRUCTURE

The DCP model shows the interaction of different stakeholders and the key elements of the project. Service-learning, technical support, and resources all played important roles in supporting the project. The Digital

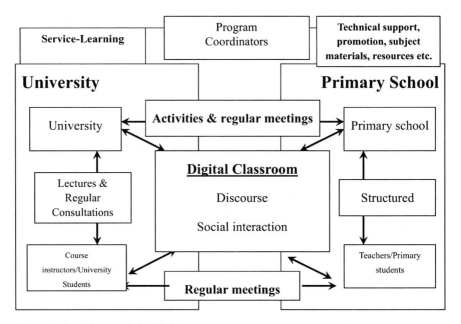

Figure 6.1.   The model of DCP.

Classroom utilized KM*S+ with elements of social interaction and discourse exchange. Cognitive and conceptual development was ongoing with frequent online discussion and idea exchange on this platform. In Figure 6.1, arrows indicate the interactions between different stakeholders in the project. The interactions between teachers and students in both university and primary school are not confined by structured classes and regular meetings, but rather also happen in the digital classroom which enhances cross-generational interactions.

The project included training workshops, reading periods, online discussions, activities and a closing ceremony. Before the start of online discussion, both university and primary school students received training on the functions of the online platform at the beginning of the semester. Meanwhile, they were required to read the books for online discussion. Two books related to personal growth and civic education were selected for each class (except for Primary Four). All of the books were in Chinese except for one in English for Primary Six students in each semester. The books were selected by the primary school teachers according to availability, students' capabilities, and the level of difficulty of the books. The content of the books served as a stimulus for students' thinking and discussion, especially in the areas of civic education and self-responsibilities.

Table 6.1. Roles and Major Tasks of Participating University Students and Primary School Students for the Project

Participant	University Students	Primary School Students		
Number of participants	24	204		
2007	4	35	-	-
2008	8	33	38	-
2009	12	25	35	38
School year	Year 2 & Year 3	Primary 4	Primary 5	Primary 6
Roles	• Peer tutor • Reading companion	• Respondent • Activity participant		
Major tasks	• Intensive reading (two books with the theme of personal growth and civic values, expect for Primary Four students)			
	• Encouraging primary school students to share their reading experiences • Expressing personal opinions • Assisting teachers in supervising and facilitating online discussion • Arranging and designing reading activities • Applying their soft skills and classroom knowledge into activity design and other assignments	• Replying to questions, expressing personal opinions and engaging in discussion on the online forum • Participating actively in discussion • Completing worksheet and related readings • Participating actively in related activities organized by university students		

Library lessons were arranged for primary school students for online discussion every week. They could access the online platform to voice their opinions and to raise questions directly to the teachers whenever they had problems with the online discussions. Primary school students and university students were able to go online anytime outside of the library lessons. There were at least three activities each semester planned by the university students to let primary school students understand the values and messages conveyed in the books and to give the different students more of an opportunity to build relationships. The last session was a closing ceremony, which served as a symbol for the conclusion of the program. University students organized activities and the prize presentation in order to recognize primary school student participants' efforts and to encourage them to do better later. In this project, one university student and one primary school student would be selected by the teachers to be the best mentor and the most outstanding student from each class.

METHODS

Participants

Twenty-four Lingnan University students joined this project voluntarily. They represented three different courses with service-learning: Society and Social Change, Science, Technology and Society, and Work and Occupation (Description of each course and the linkage between course and SL project is in Appendix 1). DCP was their service-learning project for these courses. Six classes of primary school students were chosen according to their class schedule, including one Primary Four class in 2007-2008; one Primary Four and one Primary Five class in 2008-2009; and one Primary Four, one Primary Five and one Primary Six class in 2009-2010. Most of the students were the same for Primary 4 in 2007, Primary 5 in 2008 and Primary 6 in 2009 and Primary 4 in 2008 and Primary 5 in 2009. The primary school students were trained with basic Chinese character input skills and ICT skills to facilitate their participation in this project.

Data Collection

Quantitative and qualitative methods were used to collect data. A questionnaire was designed with mostly closed-ended questions to measure students' learning outcomes. Because the DCP is modified to fit into Lingnan University's Service-Learning Research Scheme (SLRS), the questions were based on the six domains of this scheme, which were rated on a 10-point scale: (a) subject-related knowledge; (b) communication skills; (c) organizational skills; (d) social competence; (e) problem solving skills, and (f) research skills. Questions exploring the impact of students' reading habits and utilization of internet habits were also included for primary school students. Eight open-ended questions (see Appendix 2) were included in the posttest questionnaire to collect feedback on their opinions for the project's improvement, their self-evaluation of their learning, and their feeling after the completion of the program. For university students, a 10-point scale was used on the questionnaire with six open-ended questions (see Appendix 2) in the posttest questionnaire to collect comments and determine the impact of doing service. All participating students, both university students and primary school students, were invited to complete the pretest and posttest questionnaires.

Qualitative methods were used to explore students' learning and experiences of participating in this project, as well as the future development of the project. These methods included focus groups and a content analysis of university students' reflective essays. For the focus groups, participating students and the teachers of the primary school were invited to talk about the their observations of primary school students' learning and their own learning. For the reflective essay, university students wrote a reflective essay about their learning process, feeling, application of subject related knowledge, and recommendation to the program as a final assignment.

RESULTS

Two different sets of data from both university students and primary school students and the responses of the focus groups were analyzed.

Learning Outcomes of University Students

Students rated their ability in the six core SLRS domains (1 = *lowest*, 10 = *highest*) and responded to the open-ended questions. Table 6.2 shows the pretest results and upon the completion (posttest) of the program. Improvement in all aspects were statistically significant using a dependent *t* test.

Among the six SLRS domains, the communication skills domain had the highest increase between the pre- and posttest, followed by problem solving skills. The improvement in these two areas could have been due to the regular communication of university students with the service-learning coordinator, primary school teachers, primary school students, and their group mates for program updates and arrangements. University students also learned how to solve different technical and communication problems while using the online platform, thus training their problem solving skills.

University students' average ratings for organizational skills and subject-related knowledge both increased, which makes sense as students needed to organize the entire project and integrate what they have learned in the classroom into the service-learning project. Though the average rating for social competence and research skills had only a moderate increases, students still felt socially competent to communicate with students and teachers at the school and understood how to do research as they were all involved in organizing the pre- and posttest questionnaires.

Apart from the quantitative data, the qualitative feedback from university students revealed that this program enhanced their understanding of their subject knowledge, their interpersonal skills, problem solving skills, and strengthened their intergenerational relationships. As one student

Table 6.2.   Average Scores of the Constituent Questions

Question	Average Score		Dependent t Test (df = 23)
	Pretest	Posttest	
Subject-Related Knowledge			
1. I understand about the subject-related knowledge.	6.37	6.95	3.72**
Communication Skills			
2. I am tense and nervous while participating in group discussions with peers / agencies / instructors / coordinators	5.83	6.96	5.98***
3. Generally, I am comfortable while participating in a discussion with peers / agencies / instructors / coordinators			
4. Presentation in front of peers / agencies / instructors/ coordinators usually makes me uncomfortable			
5. I feel relaxed while talking with others			
Organizational skills			
6. I will evaluate myself when an activity is completed	6.31	6.72	3.12**
7. I have good time management skills			
8. I can work independently on case work			
9. I know how to allocate tasks to group members			
10. Generally speaking, I know how to take a leadership role in organizing a mass activity			
Social Competence			
11. I cooperate successfully with other students in a variety of situations	6.55	6.91	2.52*
12. I remain calm when problems arises			
13. I am confident in my abilities			
14. I am more aware of social happenings in the community			
15. I am dynamic and adapt easily to new environments			
Problem-Solving Skills			
16. When faced with a hard problem, I believe that, if I try, I will be able to solve it on my own	6.50	7.48	7.74***
17. Before I solve a problem, I gather as many facts about the problem as I can			
18. I know how to design innovative methods to solve social issues			
19. I go through the problem-solving process again when my first option fails			
20. I used my imagination in designing my SLRS / school project			
Research Skills			
21. I know the major research methodologies in social sciences / business studies	5.90	6.23	4.53***
22. I know how to collect data for different research projects			
23. I know how to write up a research proposal			
24. I know the process of doing both qualitative and quantitative researches			
25. I know how to write up a research practicum report			

Note: $*p < .05$. $**p < .01$. $***p < .001$.

from the Society and Social Change course expressed, "I think it is a chance for me to contact with different people in the society, we can learn from each other and it can let me know more about the society." The program also helped the university students address social issues related to technology and motivated them to reflect on the impact of technology in their daily lives, as one student from the Science, Technology, and Society course stated:

> I learned a lot from this program. The one that I have the deepest reflection is the low computer ownership rate of the student that hindered them from logging on to the web page and leave messages at home. It makes me think that when we emphasize the importance of integrating IT in education, there are still a number of people who may not get enough support or ready to face the changes.

Another student from the Work and Occupation course expressed the common desire of service-learning participants to care more about social issues after participating in the program:

> One of the things I learned from this program is that there are people in this world who are not as well-off. You should help them to improve their living quality.... I don't mind. If the teacher really wants to find someone to tutor this kids who can't afford private tutors.... Although I will start my work soon, I don't mind (volunteering as tutors).

Apart from the skills and knowledge learned, nearly all of the students wanted to continue with the service in the primary school and the program aroused their interest in doing service and serving the community in the future.

Learning Outcomes of Primary School Students

Eight learning outcomes were examined: (a) reading habits; (b) internet utilization habits; (c) subject-related knowledge; (d) communication skills; (e) organizational skills; (f) social competence; (g) problem solving skills, and (h) research skills. The quantitative findings revealed that there was a change in primary school students' internet utilization habits, particularly in their frequency of expressing opinions of books online. Primary school students' self-evaluation in their performance in the areas of communication skills and social competence also showed an increase. The most significant increase was seen in research skills, which the skill of researching required information for their assignments and readings.

The qualitative feedback from primary school students was, however, far more positive than   the quantitative results. The primary school students stated that their reading habits had changed significantly after this program. Communicating with university students helped them to improve their communication skills and manners. Some primary school students even expressed their hope to enter university so that they could become university students in this program. The following are details of the findings and analysis of the eight learning outcomes of primary school students and other achievements of the program.

Reading Habits. Based on the data for reading habits, the project aroused students' interest in reading ("To what extent I like reading"). Students also visited the school library more frequently than before, around twice per week. When compared to the previous semester, they tended to read more books. Sometimes, they also shared books with friends and classmates. As all of the selected books were storybooks, students' interest in storybooks was enhanced and they read more in this domain.

Apart from the quantitative data, the responses in focus group interviews also supported that the students were getting increasingly interested

Table 6.3.   Average Scores of the Constituent Questions in the Reading Habit Category of Primary School Students (N = 204)

Question	Average Score		Dependent t-test (df = 203)
	Pretest	*Posttest*	
Average number of visit(s) to school library for book-borrowing (1 = 0 *time*, 2 = *1 time*, 3 = *2 times*, 4 = *3 times*, 5 = *4 or more times*)	2.64	2.75	2.19*
Average number of visit(s) to public library for book-borrowing (1 = 0 *time*, 2 = *1 time*, 3 = *2 times*, 4 = *3 times*, 5 = *4 or more times*)			
To what extend I like reading (1 = *not interested*, 2 = *somewhat not interested*, 3 = *neutral*, 4 = *somewhat interested*, 5 = *very interested*)			
Frequency of sharing book with friend or classmates (1 = *never*, 2 = *seldom*, 3 = *sometimes*, 4 = *frequently*, 5 = *always*)			
Comparing to last semester, I think the number of books I read has been read (1 = *largely reduced*, 2 = *reduced*, 3 = *unchanged*, 4 = *increased*, 5 = *largely increased*)			

Note: *$p < .05$.

Table 6.4.   The Most Frequent Type of Reading Among the Primary School Students (N = 204)

Question	Number of Student (Pretest)	Number of Student (Posttest)	Percent Increase
1. The most frequent type of reading/story (Choices: story, jokes, biography, comics, sciences)	94	110	17%

in reading, as one student shared: "I used to read a book in 2 weeks, but I read four to five books in a week now." Many primary school students expressed their increased interest in reading after the program, and a few primary school students reflected that they liked to read books with more words, rather than simple ones with a lot of pictures.

The qualitative responses revealed that this program had a positive influence on primary school students' attitude toward reading. Developing primary school students' interest in reading and introducing students to multiple ways of interpretation are vital to the program. A few primary school students reflected in focus group interviews that requiring them to finish the selected books could help them finish the whole book and discover the real fun of the book. They also claimed that they understood more about the content of the books.

Internet Utilization Habits. As shown in Table 6.5, the scores of primary school students' internet utilization in reading-related activities increased from pretest to posttest. This is apparently the result of students getting more used to using the internet as a tool for sharing their opinions of the books and is a manifestation of the effect of incorporating technology into reading class and education.

Question 10, which was designed to determine the frequency that primary school students expressed their opinions of the books online, showed an increase between pretest and posttest, meaning the primary school students were spending more time expressing their opinions online as the project progressed. At the same time, Question 7 showed that students went online more for doing homework, probably because they had to share their feelings online after reading the books. They also used more written language, as they were required to use it during online discussion.

Subject-Related Knowledge. The questions in the subject-related knowledge domain included primary school students' understanding of the content and the vocabulary of the selected books as well as their ability to manipulate the computer and the internet. Primary school students'

**Table 6.5.   Average Scores of the Constituent Questions
in the Internet Utilization Habit Category
of Primary School Students (*N* = 204)**

| | Average Score | | Dependent t Test |
Question	Pretest	Posttest	(df = 203)
7. The time that I usually spend online (1 = 0 hour, 2 = 1–7 hours, 3 = 8-14 hours, 4 = 15-21 hours, 5 = more than 22 hours)	2.44	2.64	3.57***
10. Frequency of expressing the opinion on the books online			

Note: ***p < .001.

**Table 6.6.   Number of Students Increase
for the Constituent Questions of the Internet Utilization
Habit Category of Primary School Students (*N* = 204)**

Question	Number of Student (Pretest)	Number of Student (Post-test)	Percent Increase
7. I usually go online for doing home work	90	102	13.33%
9. The language I usually use when I am online (written language) (1 = never, 2 = seldom, 3 = sometimes, 4 = frequently, 5 = always)	85	91	7.06%

subject-related knowledge increased over the course of the project as shown in Table 6.7.

Chinese is one of the two subjects being investigated in this project. One of the learning objectives for primary school students is to improve their formal written Chinese proficiency and their ability to express their ideas. It was widely believed that the overuse of instant messenger, weblogs, and short message services (SMS) had hindered the development of language ability, especially of Chinese due to the use of colloquial Chinese and incorrect grammar in such communications. According to Table 6.7, the average scores increased, which represents primary school students' ability to understand and handle the content of books better as the project continued. For Primary 6 students, an English book was used and simple English questions were included in the online discussion.

**Table 6.7.   Average Scores of the Constituent Questions
in the Subject-Related Knowledge Category
of Primary School Students (N = 204)**

	Average Score		Dependent t Test
Question	Pretest	Posttest	(df = 203)
11. I think I can handle the content of the books.	3.97	4.16	3.43**
12. I think I can learn more vocabulary through reading.			
13. I have no difficulties in operating computers.			
14. I have no difficulties in using the Internet.			

Note: **$p < .01$.

The reasons for the improvement in subject related areas could be that the online discussion enabled primary school students to raise questions concerning the books and respond to others' answers. Others' responses encouraged thinking concerning the theme and the content of the books. One of the primary school students in the focus group interview reflected her improvement in understanding the content of the books when compared to traditional reading lessons: "We didn't just write [our feelings] onto papers after reading the books. People can't reply to you if you just write [onto papers], but they can ask you questions if you type it out online."

In addition, university students acted as role models in responding to ideas, which created a model for primary school students to follow. University students occasionally suggested better ways a sentence or an expression could be constructed in formal written Chinese or English for Primary 6 students. Primary school students imitated the ways and learned the vocabulary expressed by the university students on the discussion forum. One primary school student reported such changes with his experience in the focus group interview:

In the past, I would just answer "good, good, your answer is good." But one of the big brothers [the university peers] told me I should say "I think your answer is very good.", but not reversing the words in the sentence, which would make it spoken Chinese. So I think my organizational ability (in language) has improved.

A few primary school students even expressed that they were able to learn more vocabulary through interacting with university students on the online discussion forum in this program. As one student stated, "the questions they ask [the university students] are deeper, and the vocabulary are more sophisticated. They [the university students] use a lot of idioms."

**Table 6.8.   Average Scores of the Constituent Questions
in the Communication Skills Category
of Primary School Students (N = 203)**

Question	Average Score		Dependent *t* Test *(df = 202)*
	Pretest	*Posttest*	
15. I like to discuss books with others	3.00	3.26	3.46**
16. I think I can effectively express my ideas			
17. I feel nervous and uneasy when participating in group discussions			
18. I feel nervous and uneasy when giving presentations in class			
19. I like to share the content of the books or my opinions face-to-face with classmates, friends, and teachers			
20. I like to share the content of the books or my opinions online with classmates, friends, and teachers			

Note: **$p < .01$.

Communication Skills and Social Competence. Changes in primary school students' performance and self-evaluation of communication skills and social competence were positive. The program aimed to encourage primary school students to share thoughts and enlarge their social circle. It was expected that an intergenerational friendship between university students and primary school students could be established with this program. Primary school students learned ways to express themselves better, thus enhancing their communication skills.

Table 6.8 shows that there was a slight increase in communication skills. The results of the questionnaire revealed that primary school students had more confidence in expressing their ideas effectively.

Primary school students' qualitative feedback collected echoed the quantitative increases in the communication skills domain. When asking primary school students to list what they learned throughout the whole program, more than half of the primary school students mentioned that they learned how to communicate with others effectively and they were happy to interact with university students. Some primary school students specified that they learned how to communicate with others and share their feelings on books using the online discussion platform. Primary school students' responses in the focus group interviews further revealed the positive effect, particularly on their communication skills when faced with disagreement from others. One primary school student recalled she did not easily get irritated when her classmates had differ-ent points of view:

> I learned that even if other people make comments that I don't agree with, or I think it is wrong, I won't walk up to him in reality and scold him. Rather, I would reply him online, saying that "I don't really agree with your idea, because ..." In the past, if someone says something wrong, I won't be so polite and would go up to him and scream: you are wrong!

Online discussions created a buffer through time and space for partici-pants to express their ideas and disagree with others. University students also acted as role models of how to express their disagreement in a polite way. Thus, primary school students were self-aware of their improvement in communicating their disagreement with others.

The quantitative findings in the social competence domain indicated slight change as shown in Table 6.9. However, primary school students' qualitative responses in focus group interviews were positive for social competence. Some primary school students recalled that they enjoyed this program very much because they could meet new friends from the university. They never thought that they could have friends from the uni-versity. For some of them, they still remembered and missed the university students. A few primary school students further reflected that they were keener to meet new friends after joining this program, as one student

**Table 8.9.   Average Scores of the Constituent Questions
in the Social Competence Category
of Primary School Students (N = 204)**

Question	Average Score		Dependent t Test (df = 203)
	Pretest	Posttest	
26. I can cooperate with other classmates / team members.	3.78	3.94	2.43*
27. I like to make new friends			
28. I like to make new friends through the Internet			
29. I like to make new friends of different age and background background.			
30. I have many friends of different age and back-ground (e.g. from other primary / secondary schools / universities / people older than I am)			
31. I think I can easily adapt to new environment or learn new things			

Note: *p < .05.

Table 6.10. Average Scores of the Constituent Questions in the Organizational Skills Category of primary School Students (N = 203)

	Average Score		Dependent t Test
Question	Pretest	Posttest	(df = 202)
21. I feel I can use time wisely	3.57	3.77	3.49**
22. I can promptly finish reading-related assignments given by the teacher			
23. I am usually the group leader or in charge of distributing duties when doing projects			
24. I can effectively use my resources when doing projects			
25. I would do a self-evaluation after I finish an assignment or a project			

Note: **p < .01.

Table 6.11. Average Scores of the Constituent Questions in the Problem-Solving Skills Category of Primary School Students (N = 203)

	Average Score		Dependent t Test
Question	Pretest	Posttest	(df = 202)
32. When I face something I do not understand, I will actively ask questions	3.64	3.77	1.99*
33. I would actively reply to questions posted by classmates / teachers / friends			
34. I am confident that I can deal with problems in learning or reading			
35. When I face problems in learning or reading, I would actively seek help from classmates / teachers / others			
36. I am not afraid of difficulties			
37. If my solution is not effective, I would evaluate the method I used			

Note: *p < .05.

stated "I used to be timid and dare not voice my opinion, but now I would speak out."

Organizational Skills, Problem-Solving Skills, and Research Skills. Primary school students improved their organizational skills (Table 6.10), problem-solving skills (Table 6.11), and research skills (Table 6.12). The

Table 6.12. Average Scores of the Constituent Questions in the Research Skills Category of Primary School Students (N = 201)

	Average Score		Dependent *t* Test
Question	Pretest	Posttest	(df = 200)
38. I would use computer and the Internet to search for required information when reading	3.74	4.09	4.22***
39. I would use computer and the Internet to search for required information when doing projects and assignments			
40. I think I know how to search for required information in the process of learning			

Note: ***p < .001.

quantitative results revealed that this program had a positive influence on students' organizational skills. Although the change in the problem-solving skills domain was small, the change in the Research Skills domain was quite remarkable.

In the focus group, students reflected that the program enhanced their problem-solving skills as they learned not to give up when they did not know how to type the words. A few students also mentioned that they learned how to give organized answers when responding to questions. They also became more active and took a leadership role when doing group work. Further, they were more prone to use computers and the internet to search for information.

Other Learning Outcomes and Achievements

In addition to the eight learning outcomes, other learning outcomes achieved by students through their responses in focus groups and open-ended questions were examined.

Intergenerational Relationships and Partnerships. This program provided an opportunity for primary school students to develop relationships with university students. The relationship between the teachers and the primary school students was also enhanced through this program.

According to the primary school students, making friends with someone not in their age group, particularly university students seemed to be an unattainable myth. Two primary school students further expressed in the focus group interview that they never imagined meeting university students or discussing with university students certain topics before this program. Primary school students, teachers, and university students responded positively concerning establishing intergenerational relationships through this program. Primary school students expressed that they felt more comfortable talking to university students and they were more willing to share their problems with university students involved in this program. Two primary school students further stated in the interviews that they were inspired to get into universities as their future goals. The responses from primary school students echoed the objectives of this program: hoping that university students can help primary school students to build a positive value and life goal.

In addition, teachers reflected that the relationship with the primary school students was improved over the course of this program. This program created a "talking point" for teachers to chat with primary school students. Teachers reminded and encouraged primary school students to engage in the program and online discussion; in addition, more casual communication between teachers and primary school students took place as they had the program as a common experience. The more communication, the better their relationship developed.

Internet Etiquette and the Internet Utilization Habits. Through focus group interviews, teachers' observation, and primary school students' feedback and postings, primary school students learned internet etiquette and the culture of using the internet to express their ideas about the program.

Internet etiquette was introduced implicitly to primary school students in this program. Primary school students in the focus group interviews suggested that they learned how to express themselves in a better way on the internet, especially when pointing out the mistakes and disagreeing with others. This was learned from the university students, who also taught them the manner and expressions to discuss online.

Besides, primary school students learned that they can have other online activities besides playing online games or connecting through Facebook. As one participating primary school student mentioned in the focus group interview, after the completion of this program, he no longer limited his online activity to online games. Teachers also believed that this program can help primary school students learn more about internet-related culture. The trend of using the internet and discussion forum is inevitable; however, it is not included in the formal school curriculum. Teachers all agreed that this program provided important online learning experiences to primary school students through mentoring relationships formed with university students.

Civic and Moral Value from the Books. Although the messages from the books were not included in the questionnaire for evaluating primary school students' understanding about the values conveyed, students'

Table 6.13.   Average Scores of the Constituent Questions in the Expectation Category of Primary School Students (*N* = 203)

Question	Average Score		Dependent *t* Test (*df* = 202)
	Pretest	*Posttest*	
41. On the whole, I expect the Digital Classroom Program to be interesting	3.84	4.21	4.54***
42. On the whole, I expect the Digital Classroom Program to raise my interest in reading			

Note: ***$p < .001$.

responses were reflected in the focus groups. A few of them responded that they could still remember the messages in the books through the activities organized by the university students.

Other Social Skills. Apart from the skills included in the questionnaire, primary school students also reflected that they learned about the importance of team work. This is because they needed to cooperate with classmates when participating in the activities. In the focus groups, students could clearly point out the specific activity in which they had the opportunity to practice their teamwork.

Primary School Students' Expectation. Primary school students responded positively in the expectation domain, reflecting that they found the program interesting and reporting that it increased their interest in reading (Table 6.13). Their qualitative feedback and discussion in the focus group interviews also reflected their interest in the program. Nearly half of the class expressed their desire to join this program in the coming semesters. Some requested that longer, more challenging books should be selected as the reading material in this program.

DISCUSSION AND RECOMMENDATIONS

Based on the feedback from the questionnaires and focus groups, the following recommendations are proposed that could enhance students' learning and improve the future development of the similar online mentoring programs.

Longer Duration of the Program

The primary school students and teachers expressed that the duration of the program, one semester, was too short. The program was ending just as the participating students developed more solid relationships. Even though the relationships between the primary school students and the university students were nurtured and the internet utilization and reading habits had been developed, it is not known if the relationships and the developed skills could be prolonged with such a limited period of interaction. According to the primary school students and teachers interviewed, the program should be extended to 6 months or even a whole year. The longer duration would allow for more interactions and thus stronger relationships between university and primary school students. This might enable a more solid and enduring impact of the program overall.

The Number and Level of Selected Books for the Program

Focusing on one or two books can allow the participating primary school students to get into intensive reading. Both the librarian and classroom teacher shared a similar view that intensive reading can develop students' patience for close reading of the text, rather than just scanning books for quantity. However, it is difficult to keep students interested in just one or two books over a few months, especially as the more capable students may find reading one or two books less challenging. Some of the primary school students requested more books with more words, and some students wanted to read English books. To keep up students' passion in discussing one or two books throughout the semester, the participating university students should continue to post various types of questions with varying levels of difficulty as the program progresses.

More Guidance and Relevant Activities

In addition to posing questions in Chinese, questions in English were also included in the online discussion for Primary Six students. It did not seem too difficult for the students, but both teachers and university students found that the responses rate was much lower when the questions were in English. It would be better for the university students to give more guidance (e.g. defining vocabulary, tips for sentence structure) to the primary school students in the online discussion or during the activities to encourage more participation.

Implications for Future Research

The research demonstrated that service-learning and ICT were associated with student learning in various areas, especially on communication skills and program- solving skills for university students and the reading habits of primary school students. It has provided an important baseline from which future research can explore the impact on the primary school students who joined the program for more than 3 years and university students who joined the program for more than a semester. Focus groups should be conducted with these students in order to get more qualitative feedback on their learning progress. It would be interesting to develop the following questions in the future research.

- Are there other learning outcomes for program participants beyond the preset domains?
- In what ways does the nature of the mentoring relationship between university and primary school students contribute to learning outcomes?
- How do the interactive activities contribute to learning for both university and primary school students?
- What are the longer-term outcomes of the program for both university and primary school students?
- Does involvement in this type of program during the primary years lead to future enrollment in the university?

APPENDIX 1: THE DESCRIPTION OF COURSES AND THE LINKAGE BETWEEN COURSE AND S-L PROJECT

Course Name	Course description	Linkage With DCP (the S-L Project)
SOC204 Society and Social Change	The course let students understand one of the most important concerns of time: social change. It introduces the nature of social change and fundamental concepts related to social change, illustrated by real-life case examples in the Hong Kong context, mainland China, and the region in general.	Throughout the program, students compared how the primary school was different from what they studied before, especially the class size, school facilities, and teaching method. They could realize the social change in the education arena.
SOC334 Science, Technology and Society	The course let students examine and reflect on science and technology's impact on the global village economically, politically, socially and environmentally. It introduces science and technology and their impacts on contemporary society, especially on international relations, social institutions, social groups, and on technology in human civilization.	Through online discussion platform, university students experienced how technology could create impacts on the learning of primary school students and the interaction and communicate between university and primary school students.

| SOC324 Work and Occupation | The course let students explore some of the issues surrounding the nature of work, work ethics, the impact of technology on work and the organization of work in modern workplaces and societies, which enhanced students' understanding of the local and global situation. | By participating in the program, students acted as teachers in the primary school to supervise students on reading and related discussions. They experienced the work of teachers, the organization of a primary school, and the impact of technology on teaching. |

APPENDIX 2: OPEN-ENDED QUESTIONS INCLUDED IN THE PROGRAM EVALUATION QUESTIONNAIRE:

Primary School Students:

"What did you learn from the program?"

"Which part do you like most in the program?"

"Which part do you think that have to be improved in this program?"

"Do you like this learning mode? Why?"

"In what subjects do you want to use this learning model? Why?"

"What is the greatest difficulty that you have faced in the program?"

"What do you think of your performance in the program?"

"What is your learning experience and feeling after completing the program?"

University Students:

"What have you learned through joining the service-learning program?"

"How do you rate your overall performance?"

"Do you plan to continue the services with the agency?"

"Do you intend to serve the community in the future?"

"Did the participation in the service practicum enhance your understanding of the course material?"

"Did the Service-Learning components meet your expectations?"

"Do you have any suggestions for program improvement in the next semester?"

REFERENCES

Bringle, R. G., & Hatcher, J. A. (1995). A service learning curriculum for faculty. *Michigan Journal of Community Service Learning*, 2(1), 112-122.

Chan, A. C., Ma, C. K. H., & Fong, F. M. S. (2006). *Service learning and research scheme: The Lingnan model*. Hong Kong, China: Office of Service Learning (OSL), Lingnan University.

Curriculum Development Council. (2001). *Learning to learn: The way forward in curriculum development: Consultation document*. Hong Kong, China: Curriculum Development Council, Hong Kong Special Administrative Region of the People's Republic of China.

Education Bureau. (2007). *Right technology at the right time for the right task: Consultation document on the third strategy on information technology in education*. Retrieved June 19, 2009, from http://www.edb.gov.hk/FileManager/EN/Content_6177/emb_eng_e.pdf

Engeström, Y., Miettinen, R., & Punamäki-Gitai, R. (Eds.). (1999). *Perspectives on activity theory*. Cambridge, England: Cambridge University Press.

Mitchell, R., & Myles, F. (1998). *Second language learning theories*. London, England: Arnold.

National Research Council. (2000). *How people learn: Brain, mind, experience, and school*. Washington, DC: National Academy Press.

Netteland, G., Wasson, B., & Mørch, A. I. (2007). E learning in a large organization: A study of the critical role of information sharing. *Journal of Workplace Learning, 19*(6), 392-411.

Newhouse, C. P. (2002). Literature review: Impact of ICT on learning and teaching. *The Department of Education*. Retrieved from http://www.det.wa.edu.au/ http://www.det.wa.edu.au/education/cmis/eval/downloads/pd/impactreview.pdf

Ravenscroft, A. (2001). Designing e-learning interactions in the 21st Century: Revisiting and rethinking the role of theory. *European Journal of Education, 36*(2), 133-156.

Zhang, C. Y. (2006). *The evaluation of information system implemented based on concept of communicable medium on knowledge management—A case study of an elementary school in MiaoLi county*. Retrieved from http://www.kms.tw/InfoFiles/info/122/094YDU00396015.pdf

PART III

DISCIPLINARY CONTEXTS FOR RESEARCH AND PRACTICE

CHAPTER 7

CROSSING BOUNDARIES IN SERVICE-LEARNING PROFESSIONAL DEVELOPMENT

Preservice and Inservice Teachers Learning Together

Marjori M. Krebs

ABSTRACT

This chapter summarizes survey research conducted over a 3-year period, with both teacher candidates and their inservice cooperating teachers who participated in a series of 3 professional development workshops to plan and implement high-quality service-learning. Each series of workshops were offered over the span of an entire school year. The research was designed to understand motivations to attend such professional development opportunities with a teaching partner and motivations to implement service-learning in classrooms. The highest motivators for attendance and implementation were the participants' interests in service-learning, no charge for the workshop, attendance with a teaching partner, receipt of free classroom materials, reimbursement for substitutes, attendance during the school day, and observations of academic and personal gains of their students.

Understanding Service-Learning and Community Engagement:
Crossing Boundaries Through Research, pp. 129–156
129

A conversation in a teacher preparation methods class:

> Teacher Candidate 1: How can I motivate my students to learn?
>
> Teacher Candidate 2: What do I need to do to get my students to care about school?
>
> Teacher Candidate 3: What do I say when my students ask, "Why do I need to know this?"
>
> Teacher Education Faculty Member: Implement service-learning in your classroom!
>
> Teacher Candidates 1, 2, & 3: Okay, but my cooperating teacher doesn't know what it is and won't let me.

As a teacher educator who has participated in these discussions for far too many semesters, my question to myself became: "So, how do I train my teacher candidates in this pedagogy so that their cooperating teachers in the field will also understand the processes of service-learning and the many benefits it has for students?" Thanks to a grant from the New Mexico Commission on Community Volunteerism, year-long service-learning professional development workshops were conducted for 3 years for teacher candidates and their cooperating teachers together. This article explains the professional development series and the research conducted in conjunction with this professional development program. Throughout this article, *inservice cooperating teacher* refers to the classroom teachers who are currently teaching; *teacher candidate* refers to the university-level student teacher; and *student* refers to the K-12 child in the classroom.

THE LITERATURE: SERVICE-LEARNING AND PROFESSIONAL DEVELOPMENT

The benefits students derive from service-learning are well-documented. Researchers report that students attain personal, interpersonal, social, and academic benefits from participation in service-learning (Aquila & Dodd, 2003; Eyler & Giles, 2002; Melchior & Bailis, 2002; Scales, Blyth, Berkas, & Kielsmeier, 2000; Scales & Roehlkepartain, 2004; Search Institute, 2000). In the area their of own personal development, students report increases in self-confidence, self-esteem, leadership skills, and personal decision-making skills (Aquila & Dodd, 2003). In addition, students report career benefits and spiritual growth (Eyler & Giles, 1999) from their participation in service-learning. Socially, students who participate in service-learning report a positive impact on their social responsibility (Scales et al., 2000), civic attitudes, and volunteerism (Brandeis University, 1999). As a result of participation in service-learning, students also see themselves as valuable resources for their organizations and their communities (Eyler & Giles, 1999; Search Institute, 2000).

Connections Between Service-Learning and Teacher Education

Not only students, but teacher candidates too, have benefited from participation in service-learning as part of their teacher preparation programs. Researchers have indicated that infusing service-learning into teacher preparation can be a powerful tool, especially in the area of engagement, not only for the teacher candidates in their teacher education programs but also for the children in their field experience classrooms.

According to Zekpke and Leach (2010), there is a definite need for this type of learning in higher education. In their review of 93 research studies from around the world regarding improving student engagement in higher education, the authors name ten proposals for action that relate directly to the importance of creating opportunities for student engagement. These areas of student engagement include intrinsic motivation, engagement of students with each other and with their teachers, support from the institution, and creating opportunities to challenge social beliefs. There is a clear alignment between these ten proposals for action and implementing service-learning for both teacher candidates and the students in their classrooms. The ten proposals for action to increase student engagement in higher education include

1. enhancing students' self-belief;
2. enabling students to work autonomously, enjoy learning relationships with others, and feel they are competent to achieve their own objectives;
3. recognizing that teaching and teachers are central to engagement;
4. creating learning that is active, collaborative, and fosters learning relationships;
5. creating educational experiences for students that are challenging, enriching, and extend their academic abilities;
6. ensuring institutional culture is welcoming to students from diverse backgrounds;

7.   investing in a variety of support services;

8.   adapting to changing student expectations;

9.   enabling students to become active citizens; and

10. enabling students to develop their social and cultural capital (p. 169).

High-quality service-learning is one strategy to meet these proposals for action to increase engagement in student learning in higher education. Anderson (1998) concurs: "Service-learning appears to have considerable potential as a method to achieve important goals of both K-12 education and teacher preparation ... service-learning can be a worthwhile and powerful learning experience" (p. 3).

In a study conducted by Todd (2010), teacher candidates participated in action research and service-learning projects in their field experience schools. He concluded that students learned more about citizenship by their involvement in addressing real issues in the schools. They were not just observers, but partners inside the building contributing to the quality of learning in the school. Service-learning pedagogy shifts attention away from an exclusive preoccupation with education as a private gain and seeks to balance that concern with a focus on the common good. Can teacher preparation programs develop an ethic of service among candidates? In this case, the answer is yes (p. 10).

Along with the many benefits service-learning provides to teacher candidates, there are also important challenges that should be addressed in order for service-learning to be successfully implemented in teacher education programs. Those areas of concern include an already overburdened curriculum that must be taught in a relatively short period of undergraduate education, the lack of connections students in higher education have with the local communities to arrange successful service-learning sites, and the difficulty of connecting service-learning activities to accrediting agencies that create standards for teacher preparation programs (Anderson, 1998).

Even with these challenges, there are benefits to continuing to work to implement service-learning in teacher education. Wasserman (2010) explored the benefits of integrating service-learning into a reading and language arts methods course. She uncovered five key themes expressed in the teacher candidates' journal entries regarding service-learning and their teacher preparation programs: authentic assessment, stronger vocabulary development, increased comprehension and writing skills, integration of reading and writing standards in different content areas, and visualizing themselves as being successful in working in diverse student environments.

When teacher candidates learn these powerful lessons early, they carry these practices throughout their careers. To meet one of the challenges pointed out by Anderson (1998), an overcrowded curriculum in teacher education, this research project used the professional development training model to train teacher candidates in high-quality service-learning. In addition, in the case of this study, the teacher candidates participated in the professional development in service-learning alongside their inservice cooperating teachers, creating another layer of support and a safety net for trying these new strategies with students. However, this model does not come without its own struggles in implementation.

Through the New Mexico Service-Learning Legacy Project, preservice teachers participate along with inservice cooperating teachers, in a three-part workshop series to learn how to implement high-quality service-learning with their own students in their field experience classrooms. Though researchers have documented the effects of preservice teacher participation in service-learning during their teacher preparation programs (Anderson, 1998; Todd, 2010; Wasserman, 2010), there is little evidence of research conducted regarding training teacher candidates to implement high-quality service-learning projects in their field experience classrooms through professional development, and additionally, in partnership with their cooperating teachers.

Professional Development for Teachers

Even though there is little research in this area of training teacher candidates to implement service-learning in their own classrooms through the professional development model, there is research available on professional development for inservice teachers. *Education Week* published a special report, *Professional Development: Sorting Through the Jumble to Achieve Success* (Sawchuk, 2010). The author defined professional development as "ongoing training investments in the teaching force" (p. S2). The goal of professional development is identified as the process to "ensure that teachers have opportunities to improve their craft and are given tools with which to do so and that the school systems have a way of determining whether students learn more as a result" (p. S2). Sawchuk concludes that the current state of educational professional development is "mediocre, scattershot training, apart from doing little to help students, is a burden for teachers" (p. S2).

In spite of this negative view of educational professional development, researchers have identified best practices in professional development, and reported their findings in *Professional Learning in the Learning Profession: A Status Report on Teacher Development in the United States and Abroad.*

The researchers outlined four key components of effective professional development: (a) student achievement is related to sustained and intensive professional development, (b) substantial professional development (approximately 50 hours) is necessary to improve skills and student learning, (c) collaboration is important in professional learning, and (d) there is a need to provide support for new teachers (Darling-Hammond, Wei, Andree, Richardson, & Orphanos, 2009).

Not only is providing effective, sustainable professional development a complex process involving many factors, as indicated above, but also professional development for teachers is expensive. Estimates of annual district expenditures on inservice days and training for teachers' professional development range from $6,000 to $8,000 per teacher. Many districts have difficulty even putting a dollar figure on the cost of their professional development because most professional development opportunities are supported by a variety of different budget areas: grants, substitute costs, materials, facilitators and trainers, facilities, and other areas. One area of concern, as pointed out by Sawchuk, is that "because districts tend to characterize professional development as programming, they typically underestimate other investments in teachers' knowledge and skills" (2010, p. S4). In these difficult financial times, school districts are carefully analyzing every budget line item. In order to successfully train teachers in high-quality service-learning strategies, professional development programs must be of high quality while also being delivered in a cost-effective manner.

MOTIVATIONS TO PARTICIPATE IN SERVICE-LEARNING

In order for teachers to gain the most knowledge and skills from their professional development experiences, as indicated by Sawchuk (2010) as an area of concern in professional development, teachers should first be motivated to attend the professional development experience. In this case, teachers must be motivated to learn about service-learning in order to reap the greatest benefits from their participation. For those studies that have been conducted on higher education faculty motivation to participate in service-learning, the majority attributed their motivation to the desire to find benefits for their students and their students' learning (McKay & Rozee, 2004). In a qualitative study conducted with K-12 teachers investigating their motivations to implement service-learning, the most important motivator was the variety of connections that the teachers made. When implementing service-learning projects, K-12 teachers reported the importance of connections with a variety of constituencies: students, other teachers, parents, administrators, the community, and the curriculum. Being able to connect with these different groups motivated these teachers to initiate and to continue to implement service-learning projects with their students (Krebs, 2008).

This research is designed to identify motivators for teacher candidates and their inservice teachers to implement high-quality service-learning pedagogy with their students. One common connecting point that was built into the model was for cooperating teachers and their teacher candidates to attend the professional development series together. The professional development design relies on the importance of the connection and interaction between teachers (teacher candidate and cooperating teacher) as one factor contributing to their motivation to implement service-learning.

The New Mexico Service-Learning Legacy Project

In order to design a high-quality service-learning professional development model, the organizers of the New Mexico Service-Learning Legacy Project (NMSLLP) designed this professional development experience for teachers to follow the professional development framework recommended by Darling-Hammond et al. (2009). This framework highlights the need for professional development to be intensive, substantial, involve collaboration with teaching partners, and supportive of the teacher candidates and their novice levels of experience. In addition, the design for the NMSLLP included training both teacher candidates and their inservice cooperating teachers together to meet the criteria of cost-effectiveness (Sawchuk, 2010) and the importance of connecting and interacting with other teachers (Krebs, 2008).

The New Mexico Service-Learning Legacy Project began as part of a grant received by Partnerships Make a Difference from the State of New Mexico Coalition for Community Volunteerism. Partnerships Make a Difference is a nonprofit service-learning professional development group that conducts service-learning workshops and graduate courses across the United States. This group of current and former K-12 educators and higher education faculty members are experienced in conducting service-learning workshops to train participants to implement high-quality service-learning with their students in grades K-12.

METHODS

Participants attended a series of three workshops focused on planning and implementing high-quality service-learning pedagogy in K-12 classrooms, with the majority of participants recruited from elementary classrooms. These workshops were held in October, February, and April for 3 years with five different groups of participants in both rural and urban settings. The aim of this research was to determine if providing training to teacher candidates and their and inservice cooperating teachers *together* over time, using specified themes and strategies, increased motivation and/or sustainability for implementing service-learning pedagogy in their classrooms.

Session Modules

In Session I, participants were introduced to the *What and Why of Service-learning* through video examples of high-quality curriculum-based service-learning as an instructional strategy in K-12 classrooms. Participants also explored the key themes that were woven throughout the workshop series: (a) understanding the concept of *legacy;* (b) identifying and demonstrating *gifts, fascinations, and positive character traits;* (c) understanding and becoming part of a *community;* (d) taking *action* on something that matters; (e) engaging in *reflection* to explore what difference was made; and (f) envisioning the *future*, to know that we can change our lives and the lives of others. After participating in activities that introduced each of these themes, participants examined existing service-learning projects through a step-by-step process for project planning. Their assignment until the next session was to explore possibilities of service-learning projects in which they were interested, and to begin to use the project planning model to think through project implementation.

In Session II, held 3 months later, participants focused on the importance of reflection and learned about a variety of reflection models in which they could implement with their students. They also participated in a mini-service-learning project in which they learned about the issues facing foster children through statistics (investigation), heard two former foster children speak about their experiences (preparation), created no-sew blankets to be distributed to foster children (action), wrote poems about their participation (reflection), and presented the blankets to a representative from an association that works with foster children (celebration). Finally, participants were given time to plan and set goals for their own service-learning projects.

Two months later in the final session, Session III, participants shared multimedia presentations of the service-learning projects they had planned or implemented with their students and gathered feedback from the facilitators and other participants. Participants evaluated the content of each session at its conclusion, ranking various categories of each session from 0-4 (0 = *not helpful*; 4 = *very helpful*). In reviewing the ratings from all three sessions, participants rated each session with an average 3.95 rating (*very helpful*).

Participants

Over the 3-year period, a total of 128 teacher candidates and inservice cooperating teachers participated in professional development workshops; 69 were inservice teachers, 56 were teacher candidates, and 3 held other roles. Overall, 96 participants taught in urban areas and 32 participants taught in rural areas, with 32 teacher candidates and their inservice cooperating teachers participating in pairs. The remaining participants were individual teachers and teacher candidates who were interested in service-learning and attended individually.

In terms of teaching experience, 45.7% of the participants had less than 1 year of teaching experience, mainly because of the number of teacher candidate participants. Of the inservice teachers, the largest number had between 2 to 5 years of teaching experience (59%) (see Table 7.1).

The workshops were originally targeted for elementary-level teachers and teacher candidates, so the vast majority (67.9%) of the participants taught kindergarten through fifth grade. In addition, 27.2% of participants taught in middle schools (Grades 6 through 8), and a small minority (1.2%) taught in high schools (Grades 9 through 12).

In terms of teaching styles, it is not surprising that 96% of participants *agreed* or *strongly agreed* that their teaching styles as *hands-on* and *flexible*. Similarly, 96% *agreed* or *strongly agreed* that they identified themselves as *facilitators of learning*, focusing on *students' self-discovery of knowledge,* and described themselves as *okay when things don't go as planned.* In terms of their teaching beliefs, 100% of participants *agreed* or *strongly agreed* that *rapport with students is important* and students need to *discover their own passion and purpose in their lives.* Again, not surprising given their voluntary

Table 7.1. Years of Teaching Experience of Inservice Cooperating Teacher Participants

Years of Teaching Experience	Percent of Inservice Cooperating Teacher Participants
2-5 years	58
6-9 years	18.5
10-17 years	8.7
18 years or more	14.8
Total	100

participation in this workshop series focused on service-learning, 100% of participants believe that *it is important to connect their students to their communities*.

Data Collection

Each participant completed three separate surveys administered at the end of each of the three professional development workshops (i.e., initial survey, midpoint survey, completion survey), which included both qualitative and quantitative items. (See Appendices A, B, and C.) Qualitative data were coded for emerging themes. Participants' quotes were used as examples of appropriate themes and findings.

RESULTS

In the analyses, no significant differences existed between the responses of the teacher candidates and the inservice cooperating teachers. As a result of quantitative and qualitative data, several important themes emerged regarding motivations to plan and implement service-learning, the impact of participating in service-learning, and the importance of planning and implementing service-learning projects with a teaching partner.

Motivators for Participants to Attend

When participants were asked what motivated them to attend the NMSLLP professional development workshop series, 97.5% responded that their own "personal interest in service-learning" was *very* or *somewhat important*. Following in a close second was that the "workshop series was free" (88.9%). Just as important (82.7%) was the "opportunity to attend with a teaching partner." Other motivators for attendance for over 70% of the participants were the "opportunity to receive free classroom materials," "funds provided to pay for a substitute," and "workshops were offered during the school day." Other important motivators, as indicated in Table 7.2, were "having prior experience with service-learning and/or community service," and having the "support from the building principal to attend."

Important from the university perspective is the fact that only 12.3% of participants indicated that the "opportunity to earn graduate credit" was a motivating factor to attend the professional development workshop series. This included the responses of the teacher candidates, who in their

**Table 7.2.   Motivator to Attend Service-Learning
Professional Development Workshops**

Motivator	Percent of Participants Indicating Extremely Important or Important
Personal interest in service-learning	97.5
Workshop series was free	88.9
Opportunity to attend with a teaching partner	82.7
Opportunity to receive free classroom materials	74.1
Some funds provided to pay for classroom substitute	71.6
Workshops were offered during the school day	71.6
Prior experience in service-learning and/or community service	65.4
Support from building principal to attend	58.0
Opportunity to earn graduate credit	12.3

last semester of undergraduate work were eligible to take courses for graduate credit.

Impressions of Attending and Planning

Participants responded favorably to having the opportunity to attend this professional development workshop with a teaching partner. Participants indicated that they *agreed* or *strongly agreed* that the opportunity to attend the workshop series with a teaching partner "helped me implement ideas from the workshop" (92.5%). In addition, participants believed that it was "easier to implement service-learning projects when my teaching partner and I have received the same training" (89.3%), and also attending with a teaching partner included "helped me remember ideas we discussed in the workshop" (88.4%).

In their responses to open-ended questions regarding planning and implementing service-learning projects with their teaching partners, participants indicated that working with their teaching partners was a positive experience in their working relationships. One inservice cooperating teacher said, "We remind and encourage each other every day." Another explained, "I couldn't do this project without her." Others indicated that working with a partner made both of them more creative, able to focus on the details, and increased the working relationship between the inservice cooperating teacher and the teacher candidate. For example, "I believe that working with a partner makes the planning for curriculum more creative and purposeful toward student learning." "We dream up extensions every day—two people working together is great!" "We could split the lessons according to our strengths in the different areas." "I believe that working with a partner makes the planning for curriculum more creative and purposeful toward student learning." "I like doing this alongside somebody else and not by myself."

Impressions of the Impact of Service-Learning on Students

Regarding the impact of service-learning on their students, participants were asked at two different times during the workshop series what their reasons were for either their willingness to continue to plan or implement service-learning (midpoint survey) or their observations following implementation of service-learning (completion survey). One hundred percent (100%) of participants indicated they were willing to continue to plan and implement service-learning because of observing "greater empathy" in their students. Following implementation, participants observed "greater depth of thinking" (100%) and "authentic learning" (100%) in their students. In addition, over 90% of participants also observed "visible improvement in writing" and "academic growth" in their students (see Table 7.3).

With regard to the impact of service-learning on their students, one participant commented that, "Lessons like this will stay with them for the next 30 years." Another participant observed that, "The students are very enthusiastic and motivated," and that they "see them looking beyond themselves to the community around them."

Impressions of the Impact of Service-Learning on Teachers

As indicated, teachers must be motivated to implement service-learning in order for students to benefit from their participation in service-learning. With regard to the impact of service-learning on the inservice

Table 7.3.   Impact of Service-Learning on Students

Area of Impact for Students	Percent of Participants Indicating Extremely Important or Important	
	Midpoint Survey	Completion Survey
Greater depth of thinking	97	100
Authentic learning	65.5	100
Greater empathy	100	97.7
Visible improvement in writing	97	89.4
Academic growth	96.9	92.8

cooperating teachers and the teacher candidates themselves, participants were very positive about their own experiences with planning and implementing service-learning. Participants were asked at both the midpoint and completion of the workshop series about different reasons for either their willingness to continue to plan or implement service-learning or their observations following implementation of service-learning, specifically focusing on their teaching. One hundred percent (100%) of participants indicated that "making meaningful connections with students" was *very* or *somewhat important* in both their willingness to continue to plan and implement service-learning projects and was also observed following implementation. Participants also indicated at a rate of 94% or above the following areas of impact service-learning had on their teaching: "ability to build and create rapport," "learning more information," "bringing meaning and purpose to teaching," "energizing," "seeing gratifying results," and "opportunities to integrate subject areas" (see Table 7.4).

Participants gave several examples of their positive experiences implementing service-learning with their students. One inservice cooperating teacher commented, "Service-learning makes me do what I believe in but don't always include in my curriculum." Other participants commented, "I know I am bringing meaning to education and learning," and "The meaning will come when they remember these projects years from now, but also the gratification I receive from knowing how many people we have helped."

Impressions of the Impact of Service-Learning on Professional Connections

Participants were asked at the midpoint and completion of the workshop series to respond to the impact of service-learning on their profes-

Table 7.4. Impact of Service-learning on Teachers

Area of Impact Observed on Teachers	Percent of Participants Indicating Extremely Important or Important	
	Midpoint Survey	*Completion Survey*
Meaningful connections with students	100	100
Ability to build and create rapport	100	95.3
Learning more information	100	97.7
Bringing meaning and purpose to teaching	97	100
Energizing	96.9	100
Seeing gratifying results	93.9	100
Opportunities to integrate subject areas	97	97

Table 7.5.   Impact of Service-Learning on Professional Connections

	Percent of Participants Indicating Extremely Important or Important	
Area of Impact Observed in Professional	Mid-Point Survey	Completion Survey
Connections with local businesses and organizations	96.8	88.3
Support of administrators	96.7	79.1
Sharing project implementation with a partner	89.5	93
Communication and connection with building/district administrators	87.4	67.5
Communication and connection with parents	84.8	86.1

sional connections. As a result of implementing service-learning, the greatest area of impact was on the participants' "connections with local businesses and organizations" with 96.8% indicating this as an *important* reason for their willingness to continue to plan and implement service-learning and 88.3% saw this as *very* or *somewhat important* following implementation. The impact of "sharing project implementation with a partner" was also *important* to participants, especially following implementation (93%).

Interestingly, at the midpoint, 96.7% of participants said that the "support of administrators" was *important* in their willingness to continue to plan and implement service-learning, but at the completion stage, only 79.1% indicated this as an area of importance following implementation. Of lesser importance to participants when planning and implementing service-learning were professional connections participants made with administrators, with 87.4% of participants indicating this as an area of importance. Even more interesting is that following implementation of service-learning projects, only 67.5% of participants indicated communication and connection with administrators as an area of importance (see Table 7.5).

Other Impressions of the Impact of Service-Learning

Participants responded to additional survey questions regarding other areas of impact on their willingness to continue to plan and implement service-learning projects following their participation on the workshops

Table 7.6. Impact of Service-Learning on Other Areas

	Percent of Participants Indicating Extremely Important or Important	
Area of Impact Observed in Other Areas	Midpoint Survey	Completion Survey
Grant funds available	100	66.8
Media and/or public exposure	65.5	48.9

series. In the area of "media and/or public exposure" two thirds of participants (65.5%) at the midpoint indicated this as an area of importance in their willingness to continue to plan and implement service-learning projects, and at the conclusion less than half (48.9%) named media as an area of importance. Additionally, at the midpoint, 100% of participants indicated the importance of "grant funds available" in their willingness to continue to plan or implement service-learning, but at the conclusion, only 66.8% indicated this as an area of importance following implementation (see Table 7.6).

PARTICIPANTS' NEXT STEPS
IN IMPLEMENTATION OF SERVICE-LEARNING

Finally, participants were asked to rate their probability of the next steps they would take with regard to service-learning in their classrooms. In the area of "implementation of a service-learning project next year," 97% of participants indicated they would *very likely* or *probably* implement a service-learning project. Likewise, 97% indicated they would *very likely* or *probably* "encourage other teachers to attend the workshop," and 97% would "encourage other teachers to implement service-learning projects in their own classrooms."

Implications for Practice

In this study, teacher candidates and their inservice cooperating teachers shared their thoughts on a variety of areas related to service-learning and its implications in their classrooms. Students in K-12 classrooms are not able to realize the many academic and personal benefits of service-learning unless their teachers are motivated to work with students in their classrooms to implement service-learning. In order for teachers to implement high-quality service-learning projects, they must first be motivated to do so, and second, be professionally trained in this process. Administrators and service-learning facilitators must understand what factors bring teachers to the table of service-learning professional development—when by doing so takes them away from their students and their classrooms to learn about this type of pedagogy, especially in this era of high-stakes testing and increasing costs for substitutes. There are important motivators to encourage participants to attend service-learning professional development experiences, and also motivators to plan and implement service-learning projects in their classrooms. In contrast, there are areas that are not motivational for participants to learn about or implement service-learning experiences.

Motivation to Attend Service-Learning Professional Development Experiences

The prominence of personal interest indicates that inviting teachers to attend professional development trainings in their particular areas of interest is obvious, but this is not always the case. Thus, principals would get much stronger responses and perhaps better follow-through in implementing various teaching strategies from their teachers if they knew the areas of interest of their teachers and matched those with professional development opportunities.

Second, the importance of attending with their teaching partners can also influence future professional development programs. When administrators are faced with scarce resources in the area of professional development, they should consider sending more than one teacher to a service-learning professional development experience. With two or more attending, as indicated in the comments from the participants, there is a greater likelihood that they will indeed implement service-learning.

Finally, those offering service-learning professional development experiences should consider these additional motivating factors that were salient to participants: (a) a personal interest in service-learning, (b) no charge for the series of workshops, (c) free classroom materials, (d) funds were provided to pay for classroom substitutes, and (e) that the workshops were offered during the school day.

Motivation to Plan and Implement Service-Learning Projects

In order to make professional development opportunities effective, participants must not only be motivated to attend, but also motivated to implement service-learning projects in their classrooms. With regard to service-learning, the areas that had the most impact on their willingness to implement or to continue to implement service-learning were those most closely connected to observations they made of their own students. Because the teachers observed greater depth of thinking, authentic learning, greater empathy, improvement in writing, and academic growth, the participants were motivated to continue to implement service-learning with their students. In addition, participants saw personal and professional benefits for themselves, including making meaningful connections with students and parents, building and creating rapport with students, learning more information themselves, bringing meaning and purpose to their teaching, being energized, seeing gratifying results, having opportunities to integrate subject areas, and making connections with local businesses and organizations.

In order for teachers to realize the benefits for their students of participating in service-learning, teachers must be afforded the time to reflect on their own experiences in implementing service-learning. District administrators will realize an even greater return on their investment in service-learning professional development if they offer informal reflection and sharing sessions with teachers who have implemented service-learning in their classrooms. In these sessions teachers would have the time to think about the effects service-learning has had on their students and themselves. When teachers identify such experiences as observing academic growth and greater depth of thinking in their students in combination with being energized and bringing meaning and purpose to their teaching, then the principals know the experience has been a positive one for all involved.

Nonmotivators for Attendance, Planning, and Implementation of Service-learning

Just as important in these findings regarding motivations are areas that were *not* motivating factors in attending service-learning professional development workshops and planning and implementing service-learning projects. Receiving graduate credit for attending the training was *not* a motivator for professional development workshop attendance for the majority of participants. In addition, media and public relations exposure for their activities was *not* a motivator for planning and implementing service-learning. Providing graduate credit for professional development takes a great deal of coordination and administrative time. Understanding that teachers are not motivated to attend service-learning professional development experiences because of graduate credit is offered may save those at the district level both time and energy.

Interestingly there were two areas teachers initially thought were important for their willingness to continue to plan and implement service-learning projects at the midpoint were not as important at the completion of their projects. Those areas included (a) communication and connection with the building administrator, and (b) the availability of grant funds. Participants initially believed that having the blessing of the building administrator would be important, along with grant funding to help finance their projects, but once teacher candidates and cooperating teachers implemented their projects, they saw that these two areas were not as important as they had originally indicated. These results do not suggest that either of these two areas inhibit the implementation of service-learning, but they may not need as much attention as service-learning practitioners have previously thought.

Implications for Further Service-Learning Research

As indicated above, several important questions remain. First, because cooperating teachers and teacher candidates attended these professional development experiences together, a longitudinal study to determine how many participants are still implementing service-learning projects would indicate the continued effectiveness of this professional development experience. Second, because of the findings regarding motivation and implementation, a replication of the study with a larger participant pool would give researchers more information on several key areas, especially (a) the lack of importance of graduate credit opportunities, (b) the importance of the relationships between teachers and their administrators for implementing service-learning projects, (c) the importance of media and public relations exposure, (d) availability of grant funding, and (e) the frequency with which teacher candidates implement service-learning when becoming employed and teaching in their own classrooms. In a brief e-mail follow-up survey conducted, every teacher candidate respondent who had been hired as a full-time teacher had implemented a service-learning project with students in their first year of teaching, which suggests very favorable outcomes.

CONCLUDING COMMENTS

With scarce professional development dollars available, the results of this research suggest that encouraging teachers to attend in pairs or teams seems to have a positive effect on the possibility of implementation of service-learning projects with teacher candidates. All too often, districts use the strategy of sending one "building representative" to a training or workshop with the desired goal in mind that these representatives return to their schools to lead other teachers in whatever skill or strategy was learned. Information from this research indicates that sending more than one person from each building can result in greater implementation.

In addition, the results of this study suggest that district administrators should explore the levels of personal interest in service prior to selecting participants, and find or offer service-learning workshops that (a) are free of charge, (b) provide free classroom materials, (c) are held during the school day and (d) provide substitutes for participating teachers, in order to gain the greatest benefit for their time and money. As one teacher candidate indicated, it is important to include teacher candidates in research and professional development experiences such as the NMSLLP, for in reality, in a matter of months, these teacher candidates of today become inservice teachers in the classrooms of tomorrow.

APPENDIX A: NEW MEXICO SERVICE-LEARNING LEGACY PROJECT—SESSION 1 QUESTIONNAIRE

1. Please enter your code name for this study: _____

2. Indicate your role: __ Teacher Candidate __ Cooperating Teacher

3. Years of teaching experience: ___0-1 ___2-5 ___6-9 ___10-13 ___14-17 ___18 or more

4. Current Grade Level: ___K-2 ___3-5

5. Did you attend Session 1 of the New Mexico Service-Learning Legacy Project with your Cooperating Teacher or Teacher Candidate as a partner? ___Yes ___No

6. Rate the importance of each item below with regard to **your motivation to participate** in the New Mexico Service-Learning Legacy Project (4 = Extremely Important; 3= Important; 2= Somewhat Important; 1= Not Important):

a.	Cooperating Teachers Only: (Teacher Candidates skip to question b.)				
	Opportunity to earn graduate credit.	4	3	2	1
b.	Opportunity to receive free classroom materials	4	3	2	1
c.	Support from building principal to attend	4	3	2	1
d.	Opportunity to attend with your teaching partner	4	3	2	1

e. Some funds provided to pay for classroom substitute	4	3	2	1
f. Personal interest in service-learning	4	3	2	1
g. Prior experience with service-learning and/or community service	4	3	2	1
h. Workshop series was free	4	3	2	1
i. Opportunity for professional development	4	3	2	1
j. Workshops were offered during the school day	4	3	2	1

Other motivating factors:

7. Indicate your level of **understanding of the following concepts** upon completing Session 1 (4 = Very clear understanding; 3 = Clear understanding; 2 = Somewhat clear understanding; 1= Unclear understanding

a. Characteristics of high quality curriculum-based service-learning	4	3	2	1
b. Importance of collaborating effectively with community partners	4	3	2	1
c. Introduction to a suggested planning model for designing and conducting high quality service-learning projects aligned with state standards	4	3	2	1
d. Introduction to *Everyday People Make a Difference* materials as a classroom resource	4	3	2	1
e. Introduction to *Celebrating Everyday Heroes* activity kit as a classroom resource	4	3	2	1
f. The theme of "legacy" and related activities	4	3	2	1
g. The theme of "gifts" and related activities	4	3	2	1
h. The theme of "community" and related activities	4	3	2	1
i. The theme of "taking action that matters" and related activities	4	3	2	1
j. The theme of "reflection" and related activities	4	3	2	1
k. The theme of "envisioning the future and creating a legacy" and related activities	4	3	2	1

8. Rank the degree of **effectiveness of the following teaching strategies and methods** used as part of this workshop (4= Extremely effective; 3 = Effective; 2= Somewhat effective; 1 = Ineffective):

a. Video clips used to demonstrate key concepts	4	3	2	1
b. Legacy activities: role models, "legacy quilt," etc.	4	3	2	1
c. Gifts activities: multiple intelligences flowers, verb list, etc.	4	3	2	1
d. Dreamtown activity	4	3	2	1

e. Project planning demonstration	4	3	2	1
f. Overview of *Everyday People Make a Difference* materials	4	3	2	1

9. Based on the suggestions/guidelines provided by the facilitators, what "next steps" and strategies do you plan to implement with your students prior to Session 2 in February?

10. How do you foresee your teaching partner and yourself working together on these strategies prior to Session 2?

11. What questions/concerns do you still have regarding implementing a service-learning project in your classroom? Remember that Session 1 is just a beginning, and we will be helping you build further skills and confidence throughout the year.

APPENDIX B: NEW MEXICO SERVICE-LEARNING LEGACY PROJECT—SESSION 2 QUESTIONNAIRE

1. Please enter your code name for this study: _____

2. Indicate your role: __ Teacher Candidate __ Cooperating Teacher

3. Did you attend Session 2 of the New Mexico Service-Learning Legacy Project with your Cooperating Teacher or Teacher Candidate as a partner? ___Yes ___No

4. Rate the importance of each item below with regard to **your willingness to continue to implement or to plan to implement a service-learning project** in conjunction with the workshops provided by the New Mexico Service-Learning Legacy Project (4 = Extremely Important; 3 = Important; 2 = Slightly Important; 1 = Not Important):

a. Meaningful connections made with students through the project or the planning of a project	4	3	2	1
b. Meaningful connection with my partner teacher (either Master Teacher or Student Teacher)	4	3	2	1
c. Opportunity to communicate and connect with parents	4	3	2	1
d. Opportunity to communicate and connect with building and/or district administrators	4	3	2	1
e. Opportunity to connect with local business(es) or service organization(s)	4	3	2	1
f. Media and/or public relations exposure	4	3	2	1
g. See authentic learning taking place from my students	4	3	2	1

h. Opportunity to integrate subject areas	4	3	2	1
i. Visible improvement in student writing abilities	4	3	2	1
j. I see gratifying results in my teaching efforts when implementing or planning to implement service-learning	4	3	2	1
k. Implementing or planning to implement service-learning brings meaning and purpose to my teaching	4	3	2	1
l. Observation of academic growth in students	4	3	2	1
m. Observation of greater depth of thinking in my students	4	3	2	1
n. Observation of greater empathy in my students	4	3	2	1
o. My ability to build greater rapport with my students	4	3	2	1
p. I have learned new information through this project	4	3	2	1
q. Implementing or planning to implement a service-learning project is energizing	4	3	2	1
r. Ability to share project implementation with my teaching partner	4	3	2	1

5. Other reasons you are interested in and motivated to implement or plan to implement your service-learning project: _____

6. Please rate your level of agreement or disagreement with each item below (4 = Strongly Agree; 3 = Agree; 2 = Disagree; 1 = Strongly Disagree):

a. I would describe my teaching style as "hands-on."	4	3	2	1
b. I would describe my teaching style as "flexible."	4	3	2	1
c. I see myself as a "facilitator of learning."	4	3	2	1
d. I believe rapport with students is important.	4	3	2	1
e. I am okay when things don't work out exactly as I have planned them in my classroom.	4	3	2	1
f. I try to allow students to participate in "self-discovery" as they learn.	4	3	2	1
g. I believe it is important to connect students to their community.	4	3	2	1
h. It is important for me to help students discover their passion and purpose.	4	3	2	1
i. My teaching partner has helped me remember ideas we discussed in the first workshop session.	4	3	2	1
j. Participating in this workshop with my teaching partner has helped me implement ideas from the workshop sessions.	4	3	2	1

k. I might have planned and/or implemented my service-learning project differently had I attended alone.   4   3   2   1

l. It is easier to implement service-learning when my teaching partner and I have received the same training.   4   3   2   1

m. The *Everyday People Make a Difference* materials are effective to use with my students.   4   3   2   1

n. My students enjoy their work using the *Everyday People Make a Difference materials*.   4   3   2   1

7. Indicate your level of understanding of the following concepts discussed in Session 2 (4 = Very clear understanding; 3 = Clear understanding; 2 = Somewhat clear understanding; 1 = Unclear understanding):

a. Characteristics of high quality curriculum-based service-learning   4   3   2   1

b. Importance of collaborating effectively with community partners   4   3   2   1

c. Strategies for designing and conducting high quality service-learning projects aligned with state standards   4   3   2   1

d. Assessing service-learning projects   4   3   2   1

e. Using *Everyday People Make a Difference* materials as classroom resources   4   3   2   1

f. Using *Celebrating Everyday Heroes* program materials as a classroom resource   4   3   2   1

g. The theme of "legacy" and related activities   4   3   2   1

h. The theme of "gifts" and related activities   4   3   2   1

i. The theme of "community" and related activities   4   3   2   1

j. The theme of "taking action that matters" and related activities   4   3   2   1

k. The theme of "reflection" and related activities   4   3   2   1

l. The theme of "envisioning the future and creating a legacy" and related activities   4   3   2   1

8. Rank the degree of effectiveness of the following teaching strategies and methods used in Session 2: Note: Questions will be included in this section such as (4 = Extremely effective; 3 = Effective; 2 = Somewhat effective; 1 = Ineffective)

a. Video clips used to demonstrate key concepts   4   3   2   1

b. Legacy activities   4   3   2   1

c. Community-building activities   4   3   2   1

d. Brain-based learning activities   4   3   2   1

9. What ideas did you learn from Session 2 that you plan to implement with your students between now and our next workshop in May?

10. How do you foresee your teaching partner and yourself working together on between now and our next workshop in May?

11. What concepts are you most excited to pursue with your students?

12. What parts of project planning and/or implementation have you completed thus far?

13. What has been the most rewarding part of this process?

14. What has been the most frustrating part of this process?

15. What concerns do you still have regarding implementing a service-learning project in your classroom?

16. What ideas, concepts, roadblocks, etc. would you like to see addressed in the final workshop of this series?

17. How would you describe your working relationship with your teaching partner in planning and implementing service-learning in your classroom thus far?

APPENDIX C: NEW MEXICO SERVICE-LEARNING LEGACY PROJECT—SESSION 3 QUESTIONNAIRE

1. Please enter your code name for this study: _____

2. Indicate your role: __ Teacher Candidate __ Cooperating Teacher

3. Did you attend Session 3 of the New Mexico Service-Learning Legacy Project with your Cooperating Teacher or Teacher Candidate as a partner? ___Yes ___No

4. Describe the service-learning project you implemented with your students:

5. Rate the importance of each item below with regard to **the implementation of your service-learning project** in conjunction with the workshops provided by the New Mexico Service-Learning Legacy Project: (4 = Extremely Important; 3 = Important; 2 = Slightly Important; 1 = Not Important):

    a. Meaningful connections made with students through   4   3   2   1
        the project or the planning of a project

    b. Meaningful connection with my partner teacher   4   3   2   1
        (either Master Teacher or Student Teacher)

c.	Opportunity to communicate and connect with parents	4	3	2	1
d.	Opportunity to communicate and connect with building and/or district administrator(s)	4	3	2	1
e.	Support and encouragement from building and/or district administrator(s)	4	3	2	1
f.	Opportunity to connect with local business(es) or service organization(s)	4	3	2	1
g.	Media and/or public relations exposure	4	3	2	1
h.	Seeing authentic learning taking place from my students	4	3	2	1
i.	Opportunity to integrate subject areas	4	3	2	1
j.	Visible improvement in student writing abilities	4	3	2	1
k.	Seeing gratifying results in my teaching efforts when implementing or planning to implement service-learning	4	3	2	1
l.	Implementing or planning to implement service-learning brings meaning and purpose to my teaching	4	3	2	1
m.	Observation of academic growth in students	4	3	2	1
n.	Observation of greater depth of thinking in my students	4	3	2	1
o.	Observation of greater empathy in my students	4	3	2	1
p.	My ability to build greater rapport with my students	4	3	2	1
q.	I have learned new information through this project	4	3	2	1
r.	Implementing or planning to implement a service-learning project is energizing	4	3	2	1
s.	Ability to share project implementation with my teaching partner	4	3	2	1
t.	Grant funds are available to me to assist in implementing my service-learning project	4	3	2	1

6. Other reasons you were interested in and motivated to plan and/or implement your service-learning project:

7. Indicate your level of **understanding of the following concepts** discussed in Session 3 (4= Very clear understanding; 3= Clear understanding; 2 = Somewhat clear understanding; 1= Unclear understanding):

a.	Characteristics of high quality curriculum-based service-learning	4	3	2	1
b.	Importance of collaborating with community partners	4	3	2	1

c. Strategies for designing and conducting high quality service-learning projects aligned with state standards	4	3	2	1
d. Assessing service-learning projects	4	3	2	1
e. Using *Everyday People Make a Difference* materials as a classroom resource	4	3	2	1
f. Using *Celebrating Everyday Heroes* program materials as a classroom resource	4	3	2	1
g. The theme of "legacy" and related activities	4	3	2	1
h. The theme of "gifts" and related activities	4	3	2	1
i. The theme of "community" and related activities	4	3	2	1
j. The theme of "taking action that matters" and related activities	4	3	2	1
k. The theme of "reflection" and related activities	4	3	2	1
l. The theme of "envisioning the future and creating a legacy" and related activities	4	3	2	1

8. Rank the **degree of effectiveness of the following teaching strategies and methods** used in Session 3 (4 = Extremely effective; 3 = Effective; 2 = Somewhat effective; 1 = Ineffective):

a. *Paper Clips* video used to demonstrate key concepts	4	3	2	1
b. Service-learning Elements Check-list	4	3	2	1
c. "Your Pledge" Activity	4	3	2	1
d. Mosaic Activity	4	3	2	1
e. Sharing of service-learning projects implemented by workshop participants:	4	3	2	1

9. What ideas did you learn from Session 3 that you plan to implement with your students?

10. How would you describe your working relationship with your teaching partner in planning and implementing service-learning in your classroom thus far?

11. Describe ways you and your Teaching Partner have shared the responsibility of implementing your service-learning project.

12. Has working together on this project improved your working relationship with your Teaching Partner? Why or why not?

13. Describe your working relationship with your Teaching Partner over the last several months in implementing your service-learning project.

14. What, if any, concepts have you enjoyed teaching and working with your students?

15. What has been the most rewarding part of this process?

16. What has been the most frustrating part of this process?

17. What concerns do you still have regarding implementing a service-learning project in your classroom?

18. What suggestions do you have regarding changes to this workshop series to better prepare you to implement service-learning in your classroom?

19. Please rate your answers to the following questions using this scale (4 = Very likely; 3 = Probably; 2 = Unlikely; 1 = Definitely not):

    a. How likely are you to implement a service-learning project with your students next year? 4 3 2 1

    b. How likely are you to encourage other teachers to attend this workshop in the future? 4 3 2 1

    c. How likely are you to encourage other teachers to implement service-learning projects with their students in the future? 4 3 2 1

20. Please add any other comments, suggestions, or feedback on this workshop or any of the workshops in this series:.

REFERENCES

Anderson, J. (1998). *Service-learning and teacher education*. Washington, DC: ERIC Clearinghouse on Teaching and Teacher Education. [ED421481]

Aquila, F. D., & Dodd, J. M. (2003). *Learn and serve Ohio: Annual evaluation report*. Cleveland, OH: Cleveland State University.

Brandeis University. Center for Human Resources. (1999). *Summary report: National evaluation of learn and serve America*. Waltham, MA: Author.

Darling-Hammond, L., Wei, R. C., Andree, A., Richardson, N. L., & Orphanos, S. (2009). *Professional learning on the learning profession: A status report on teacher development in the United States and abroad*. Dallas, TX: National Staff Development Council.

Eyler, J. S., & Giles, D. E. (1999). *Where's the learning in service-learning?* San Francisco, CA: Jossey-Bass.

Eyler, J. S., & Giles, D. E. (2002). Beyond surveys: Using the problem solving interview to assess the impact of service-learning on understanding and critical thinking. In A. Furco & S. H. Billig (Eds.) *Service-learning: The essence of pedagogy* (pp. 147-159). Greenwich, CT: Information Age.

Krebs, M. M. (2008). Sustainability of service-learning: What do K-12 teachers say? In M. Bowdon, S. Billig, & B. Holland (Eds.), *Scholarship for sustaining ser-*

vice-learning and civic engagement (pp. 85-109). Charlotte, NC: Information Age.

McKay, V., & Rozee, P. D. (2004). Characteristics of faculty who adopt community service-learning pedagogy. *Michigan Journal of Community Service-learning, 10*(2), 21-33.

Melchior, A. & Bailis, L. N. (2002). Impact of service-learning on civic attitudes and behaviors of middle school and high school youth: Findings from three national evaluations. In A. Furco & S. H. Billig (Eds.), *Service-learning: The essence of pedagogy* (pp. 201-222). Greenwich, CT: Information Age.

Sawchuck, S. (2010, November 10). Professional development: Sorting through the jumble to achieve success. *Education Week: A Special Report on Teacher Learning.* Retrieved from www.edweek.org/go/pdreport

Scales, P. C., Blyth, D. A., Berkas, T. H., Kielsmeier, J. C. (2000). The effects of service-learning on middle school students' social responsibility and academic success. *Journal of Early Adolescence, 20,* 332-358.

Scales, P. C., & Roehlkepartain, E. C. (2004). *Community service and service-learning in U.S. public schools, 2004: Findings from a national survey.* Minneapolis, MN: National Youth Leadership Council.

Search Institute (2000). *An asset builder's guide to service-learning.* Minneapolis, MN: Author.

Todd, R. H. (2010). Can we develop a professional ethic of service in education? *Journal of Research on Service-Learning and Teacher Education, 1*(1), 1-11.

Wasserman, K. (2010). Highly structured service-learning: Positive impacts on the teacher candidates, cooperating teachers, and fourth graders. *Journal of Research on Service- Learning and Teacher Education, 1*(1), 1-16.

Zepke, N., & Leach, L. (2010). Improving student engagement: Ten proposals for action. *Active Learning in Higher Education, 11*(3), 167-177.

CHAPTER 8

SERVICE-LEARNING AND THE NONTRADITIONAL STUDENT

What's Age Got to Do With It?

**Helen Rosenberg, Susan Reed,
Anne Statham, and Howard Rosing**

ABSTRACT

The increasing presence of "nontraditional" students in higher education can complicate efforts to use service-learning methodologies. Analysis of data from 919 undergraduate students at 3 universities suggests that students with nontraditional characteristics have different perceptions of the value of service-learning for different intended outcomes. In examining student views of whether the service-learning experiences helped them (a) understand what they learned in class, (b) develop personal skills, (c) develop career plans, and (d) enhance their level of civic engagement, results showed that older students felt that service-learning enhanced the content of their courses but significantly less so than younger students, especially first generation students. Working students were less enthusiastic about the value of service-learning for the development of their personal skills than others. The implications of these findings for the support of non-

Understanding Service-Learning and Community Engagement:
Crossing Boundaries Through Research, pp. 157–178

traditional students as well as the opportunities suggested for further involvement of first generation and activist students are discussed.

Institutions of higher education have embraced the opportunity to promote an active citizenry through the proliferation of service-learning courses that are assumed to help develop personal and political skills, provide career preparation, and promote the value of community involvement (Coalition of Urban Serving Universities, 2010). However, the effort has not targeted growing numbers of nontraditional students on campus, who are expected to increase 19% in the undergraduate student population between 2006 and 2017, compared to a projected 10% growth for traditional students (U.S. Department of Education, 2009). These students are likely to be drawn to such courses because of their practical approach to learning (Kassworm, Polson, & Fishback, 2002; Schuetze & Slowey, 2002) and, for older students, their developmental need to share their skills and knowledge with others (Snyder & Clary, 2003). In order to design programming that meets the needs of nontraditional students, it is important to understand how they respond to service-learning courses, and if they believe they achieve the outcomes from these that we intend.

The definition of "nontraditional," is complicated because the term has been used to refer to working students, older students, single parents and, sometimes, first generation college students. Nontraditional students are generally defined as those undergraduates who fall into one or more of these categories: (a) older than 24 or 25 years of age (39% of undergraduates are 25+ years old according to U.S. Department of Education, 2009); (b) part-time students (48% of undergraduates according to U.S. Department of Education, 2002); (c) employed (39% of undergraduates work full time according to U.S. Department of Education, 2002); (d) have dependents other than a spouse (27% of undergraduates according to U.S. Department of Education, 2002). Sometimes, being the first member of their families to attend college is also included in the definition of nontraditional students, and forty-seven percent of beginning undergraduates meet this criterion (U.S. Department of Education, 2001).

Which of these characteristics is most likely to influence the perceived value of service-learning outcomes for nontraditional students? Determining this is further complicated by the fact that the potential components of nontraditional are interrelated, making it difficult to disentangle their impact. For example, 82% of undergraduates who are 24 years and above are working; adult undergraduates who work make up one third of total undergraduates (U.S. Department of Education, 2003). Forty-nine percent of nontraditional students who have dependents are single parents (U.S. Department of Education, 2002); 27% of all undergraduates have dependents and 13% are single parents. Of those beginning under-graduates whose parents have no college experience, 31% are 24 years of age and above.

LITERATURE REVIEW AND THEORETICAL MODEL

The literature on adult learning suggests that nontraditional students, and perhaps especially older students, may respond to service-learning experiences differently than more traditional students. Although principles of effective learning hold true for students of all ages, most adult learning theorists contend that the social context of adults' lives and their developmental stages are different enough from younger students that they lead to different outcomes for the two groups of students, warranting special attention when designing learning events (Reed & Marienau, 2008). MacKeracher (2004) identified the following characteristics of adult learners: adults negotiate multiple roles and responsibilities; differences between individuals become more distinctive with age; adults prefer to learn from real life situations; adults have a wealth of prior learning upon which they build new learning; adults prefer to be involved in decisions regarding learning; and adults learn in dialogue with others.

Although this literature focuses on characteristics of adults as learners, other scholarship suggests that because of older students' psychosocial development they are particularly likely to be attracted to opportunities to serve others while learning. At the stage of adult development called "generativity" (Erikson, 1959), individuals experience the desire to nurture future generations, usually fulfilled in midlife. Snyder and Clary (2003) used the Loyola Generativity scale to examine the role of generativity in adult motivation to volunteer and found a correlation. Bureau of Labor Statistics (2010) and other research confirmed that adults are most likely to volunteer between the ages of 35-44, closely followed by those 45-54 years of age.

Principles that have directed the development of service-learning courses build upon many of the same principles that have also directed the development of adult learning theory: the value of experiential learning (Kolb, 1984), the benefit of focusing on specific problems while learning (Keeton, Sheckley, & Griggs, 2002), the social nature of learning (Fenwick, 2003), and the importance of reflection upon experience (Eyler, 2001; Jarvis, 2006). Combining insights from both the adult learning and service-learning literatures suggests that learning style and background differences between traditional and nontraditional students must be taken into consideration when designing a service-learning program (O'Connell, 2002).

The service-learning literature has begun to address similarities and differences between traditional and nontraditional students including, for example, that adult and working students participated in and valued service-learning as much as other students (Holland & Robinson, 2008; Sather, Reed-Bouley, & Fair, 2008). Holland and Robinson (2008) report on two studies. A survey of students in the California State University system, and another at Occidental College found that students who worked reported higher levels of participation in service-learning courses. Sather, Reed-Bouley, and Fair (2008) surveyed undergraduates enrolled in two institutions in Omaha. Although they found some differences between working and nonworking students' perceptions of the value of service-learning for their learning and professional development, they concluded overall that working students did not find service-learning to be too time consuming and they rated the experience positively.

There is some evidence, however, that adults may be less satisfied with their service-learning experiences than younger students (Rosenberg, Reed, Statham, & Rosing, 2008), unless adults' prior learning and skills are recognized both in community placements and reflection upon their placement (Largent & Horinek, 2008). Largent and Horinek (2008) found that a redesign of a service-learning program at a community college not only improved the satisfaction of adult students but increased the satisfaction of students of all ages with their service-learning courses. The study tracked changes in the perceptions of older students that service-learning experiences were enhancing their development. Initially, the older students were less likely to report enhanced development than younger students; after follow-up interviews with a few adult students, administrators concluded that older students would benefit from more reflection upon their own prior experiences in the community and from projects in which their knowledge and skills were taken into consideration in the design of their involvement and training. After faculty and community partners made the suggested changes, surveys showed no age difference in perceived outcomes, and the mean score of student satisfaction increased for all.

Understanding and responding to these differences may be crucial as institutions seek to retain newer, less traditional students. Compared to traditional students, older and working students are less likely to persist in their education (Jacobs & Hundley, 2005). Of those older students who identified themselves as workers first and students second, 62% were no longer enrolled and had not completed their degrees after 6 years (U.S. Department of Education, 2003). Wlodowski and Kassworm (2003) found that, among adult students, the primary reasons cited for leaving college related to conflicts across school, work, and home. On the other hand, adult students have been found to do as well or better than their younger counterparts, to feel generally accepted in mixed age classrooms, and to be as satisfied or more so with their educational experiences than younger students (Kassworm, 2010).

Although research on age is more extensive than research on other characteristics of nontraditional students, evidence suggests that changes in curriculum that benefit older learners are likely to engage all types of nontraditional students by addressing conflicting aspects of their lives in the learning process (Jacobs & Hundley, 2010). Service-learning is a methodology with demonstrated success in developing personal skills, as well as in higher rates of degree completion (Eyler, Giles, Stenson & Gray, 2001). However, more research is needed to determine whether these same outcomes are found with all types of nontraditional students (Smith, 2008). An answer to that question would contribute to efforts by faculty and administrators to design service-learning courses and other community based programming that promotes learning and retention of the nontraditional student.

THEORETICAL MODEL AND HYPOTHESES

Integrating insights from the above literature, three themes were developed to drive the analysis of factors that may be associated with differences between traditional and nontraditional students: (a) the value of experiences conditioned by opportunity for acquiring valued skills and expertise, (b) instances that reinforce highly valued aspects of life, and (c) the need to resolve conflicts between various spheres of life. In terms of opportunity, older and working students were expected to have had more employment experiences that have enhanced personal and professional abilities than traditional age or nonworking students. Therefore, traditional students were expected to value the benefits of service-learning opportunities more highly. Likewise, first generation college students were expected to be more appreciative of service-learning opportunities because of possibly constrained (rather than enhanced) opportunities for skill development.

An opposite thrust may come from students who find that their service-learning experiences reinforce highly valued predispositions or orientations, in this case increasing rather than lowering the benefits they perceive. Older students' developmental inclination to support others as well as their predilection for experience-based learning were expected to be associated with more positive perceptions of the benefit of service-learning as well as the value of community involvement, especially when their service-learning experiences connected with and reinforced their own personal expertise. Students who came into these experiences with a predisposition to be civically engaged were expected to react more positively.

The third theme, the need to resolve conflicts, suggested that service-learning experiences that reduce rather than intensify students' attempts to fill the myriad roles they play at work, school, and home would be experienced more positively. Thus, service-learning courses that allow flexibility in timing and type of participation were expected to generate more positive responses by the students who are participating.

The research explored the first two themes, by examining the impact of age, employment, and first generation to complete college on student perceptions. Older students and those who were employed were expected to perceive fewer benefits in some areas, given their enhanced opportunities for experiences elsewhere. First generation college students were expected to perceive more benefits in some areas, given their lack of certain experiences or resources. The following perceptions of traditional and nontraditional students about service-learning were examined: the degree to which service-learning helped them (a) understand what they learned in class, (b) develop personal skills, (c) develop career plans, and (d) enhance their level of civic engagement. The analysis allowed examining the impact of age, employment, and first generation college completion as characteristics of nontraditional students, while controlling for gender, race, class standing, volunteer experience, and the university attended.

Controlling for university attended accounted for differences between the types of courses students took that were influenced by institutional culture or practice, as well as for characteristics of the institutions themselves. For example, regional comprehensive public universities have a higher percentage of adult students than main campuses or private universities (Holland, 2005) and private for profit universities are now serving a majority of older students who delayed attending college (U.S. Department of Education, 2002). About a third of the undergraduates in both public and private 4-year universities are older undergraduates or those working full-time, but students at public 2-year schools are most likely to be working full time.

METHODS AND ANALYSIS

Methods

Service-learning administrators at the three Midwestern campuses—the University of Southern Indiana (USI), the University of Wisconsin-Parkside (UW-Parkside) and DePaul University in Chicago—agreed to administer surveys with identical questions in spring 2009 to undergraduate students enrolled in service-learning courses on those campuses. There were 18 common statements in each survey in the form of an ordinal scale ranging from *strongly disagree* (1) to *strongly agree* (4) that measured perceptions of service-learning. These 18 statements are listed in the Appendix. A factor analysis of all items showed that students reacted to their service-learning experiences in four distinct areas, whether these experiences helped them to (a) understand what they were learning in the class, (b) develop personal skills such as communication and problem solving, (c) develop or pursue career plans, and (d) enhance their level of civic engagement. As these factors had theoretical coherency and represent distinct types of outcomes treated in the existing literature on service-learning, four scales were computed as dependent variables.

Surveys included nine independent predictors of service-learning that have been identified in previous research. First, three measures of nontraditional student status: age (dichotomized as traditional—25 and younger and nontraditional—26 and older, as commonly available in the three sets of data); employment (hours worked coded as an ordinal variable across the three sets of data); if either parent had a college degree. Data were not collected on whether or not students were supporting dependent family members. Other variables controlled for included: race (dichotomized as white and students of color), class standing, gender, previous volunteer experience, credits enrolled (dichotomized as 12 or fewer and 13 or greater), and the school (campus) attended (with DePaul used as the reference category and the other campuses represented by two dummy variables coded as 1).

Nine hundred nineteen surveys were completed from undergraduate students across all three universities for spring 2009. Each campus used a slightly different method for data collection. USI staff solicited students to participate in the survey who were in service-learning classes; most of the surveys were distributed in person at the end of the semester, but some students responded online. At UW-Parkside, surveys were distributed in person to students in service-learning courses at the end of the semester; none were completed online. At DePaul, all undergraduate service-learning students were asked to complete an online survey separate from their end-of-term service-learning evaluation. The online survey had statements common to those of the two other campuses.

Data Analysis

A principal components factor analysis was performed on the 18 items measuring views about service-learning, producing four factors that represented 56% of the variance among all 18 statements, resulting in four scales or types of outcomes: (a) connecting classroom learning to community projects, (b) development of personal skills, (c) career preparation, and (d) community involvement. Factor loadings were strongest for connecting classroom learning to community projects and development of personal skills and weakest for career preparation. Despite differences in the strength of factors in this model, Cronbach's alpha coefficients indicate good consistency among items within factors. Scales for each factor were created by multiplying the factor loadings for each item in the scale and then summing across items. Ranges for scales are dependent upon the value of the factors that comprise the scale. Although the factors for career preparation and community involvement are both comprised of two items, the range of these scales differs because the factors loadings for community involvement are stronger than those for the scale for career development. Factor loadings, reliability coefficients, the ranges for each scale and the mean scores for each factor are reported in Table 8.1. The relatively high means show that students rated their experiences with service-learning favorably overall.

Table 8.2 provides correlations among the independent variables. Correlations are statistically significant between most independent variables, although the value of each correlation is not strong enough to be concerned about multicollinearity effects. Thinking of the various indicators of nontraditional status, we see that age and hours worked were significantly positively correlated with each other but only hours worked is significantly negatively correlated with whether a parent had a degree. Thus, older students tended to work more hours, but students whose parents had a college degree tended to work fewer hours.

School, age, gender, race, credits earned, if either parent had a degree, and previous volunteer experience were dummy coded and entered into the analysis with the ordinal level variables, class standing, and employment (hours worked). Each ordinal level variable had four levels and was entered as interval level data. Older students, women, whites, students with 13+ credits, those with at least one degreed parent, and those with previous volunteer experience were coded as 1.

Students at USI tended to be younger, while those at UW-Parkside were older. USI had more white students than the other campuses. UW-Parkside students worked more hours than those at other campuses, and there were more women students at USI than the other campuses. A greater percentage of students at UW-Parkside had higher class standing than the students at the other campuses, but they took fewer credits than students from other campuses. Students from DePaul reported that at least one parent has a college degree more often than students on other campuses. Fewer percentages of students from UW-Parkside had previous volunteer experience than other campuses. Thus, there were differences among the

Table 8.1.   Factor Loadings, Reliability Coefficients, Scale Ranges and Means Across Factors

Factors	Loadings	Chronbach Alpha	Scale Range	Means
Factor 1: Connecting learning to community		.82	2-9	6.92
The community project aspect of this course helped me to understand the subject matter and how it can be used in everyday life.	.744			
The community project helped me to better understand the course lectures and readings.	.737			
I understood the purpose of this community project in relation to the subject matter being taught in class.	.715			
Factor 2: Development of personal skills		.84	3-12	9.11
The community project helped me to become aware of my personal strengths and weaknesses.	.758			
The community project enhanced my ability to communicate with others in a 'real world' setting.	.781			
The community project helped me to develop my problem-solving skills.	.706			
This project helped me to see how I can contribute to my community.	.744			
Factor 3: Career Preparation		.72	.5-3	1.94
This community project helped me gain professional contacts for future employment.	.333			
The community project in this course assisted me in clarifying my career plans.	.397			
Factor 4: Community Involvement		.85	1-5	3.73
After college I will volunteer/participate in the community.	.596			
I think it is very important to be actively involved in the community.	.547			

campuses with regard to composition of the student body and those who engaged in service-learning, so it is important to control for campus.

Students 26 years and older were more likely to be male, persons of color, and upper class. They were also more likely to work more hours, take fewer credits, and were less likely to have volunteered before, compared to students 25 and under. Persons who worked more hours tend to be older, male, persons of color, upper class, and take fewer credits; like older students they were less likely to have volunteered before. Students

Table 8.2. Correlations Among Independent Predictors (N = 919)

Correlation	UW-P	USI	DePaul	Age	Gender	Race	Credits	Class Standing	Hours Worked	Parent has Degree	Volunteered Before
Independent predictors											
UW-P	1.0	-.72*	-.30*	.17*	-.35*	-.13*	-.21*	.26*	.35*	-.12*	-.14*
USI		1.0	-.54*	-.13*	.34*	.28*	.07*	-.23*	-.25*	.01	.14*
DePaul			1.0	-.04	-.03	-.21*	.15*	-.02	-.10*	.15*	-.01
Age				1.0	-.10*	-.10*	-.23*	.14*	.12*	-.06	-.07*
Gender					1.0	.04	.15*	-.17*	-.22*	.01	.10*
Race						1.0	.08*	-.11*	-.07*	-.00	.00
Credits							1.0	-.10*	-.23*	.03	.11*
Class standing								1.0	.22*	-.11*	-.07*
Hours worked									1.0	-.09*	-.12*
Parent has degree										1.0	.12*
Volunteered before											1.0

Table 8.3. Correlations Among Dependent Factors (N = 919)

	Connecting Learning to Community	Development of Personal Skills	Career Preparation	Community Involvement
Connecting learning to community	1.0	.70*	.53*	.45*
Development of personal skills		1.0	.52*	.64*
Career preparation			1.0	.41*
Community involvement				1.0

*Note: *p < .05.*

whose parents had not earned a college degree worked more hours, were persons of color, took fewer credits, and were less likely to have previously volunteered. However, they were no more likely than other students to be older or male.

Correlations among dependent variables or scales (Table 8.3) showed that while these factors were all related, and hence in the same general domain, they were also fairly distinct. The strongest correlation was between connecting classroom learning to service experiences and the development of personal skills. This suggests that students whose learning increased as a result of their service-learning experiences were also very likely to benefit personally in terms of enhanced problem solving skills and recognizing their own strengths and weaknesses. The correlations among the other scales were lower though still substantial. These correlations suggest that there seemed to be a distinction between the extent to which service-learning is related to personal as opposed to professional competencies and community commitment. Yet, all the dependent factors in this study were significantly positively related suggesting that service-learning benefits contribute to overall student development in multiple areas, albeit to different extents.

Campus Context

In general, the three institutions support service-learning courses for both traditional and nontraditional students in similar ways by employing an academic-based model that integrates service experiences with classroom learning and related assignments. With the exception of DePaul, which hosts a specialized curriculum for nontraditional students through its School for New Learning, there is no formal curricular distinction made between traditional and nontraditional students as it relates to curriculum development and, more specifically, service-learning practice. In the case of DePaul, many nontraditional students also enroll in the traditional undergraduate degree programs rather than the School for New Learning (students from The School for New Learning were not surveyed for this study). At UW-Parkside, there is a weekend college program that is tailored to working students, but enrollment in this program is low; USI offers a degree completion program but, like DePaul, many traditional undergraduates enroll in these programs along with nontraditional students.

Although the service-learning programs at each institution were administered in a similar manner, there were several differences that distinguish the institutions from one another. USI is a public regional university with 11,000 students enrolled across 66 majors and 11 graduate degree programs. It serves a regional, rural tri-state area including more than 20 counties in Indiana, Illinois, and Kentucky. Among the undergraduate students surveyed, 94% categorized themselves as white and 84% were female. Seventy percent said they had volunteered previously, reflecting a very high rate of volunteerism among the local population in general. UW-Parkside is a public undergraduate institution serving 5,000 students in 34 majors and two master's degree programs. Ninety-four percent of students come from Kenosha or Racine Counties in Wisconsin or from Northeastern Illinois. In contrast to the two public institutions, DePaul is a 4-year private Catholic University in Chicago that enrolls 25,000 students in 275 undergraduate and graduate degree programs. The university has two main campuses located in a dense urban environment and draws students from diverse backgrounds and communities. Although DePaul is the only one of the three institutions that hosts a specialized program for adult students, students in this program were not sampled for this study. Both traditional and nontraditional students were surveyed from the general undergraduate population.

Table 8.4 describes the population of students at each university and the sample of students who completed surveys after their service-learning projects. Demographic descriptions of students in service-learning generally reflect each university's population in relation to the variables discussed above. The indicators of nontraditionality measured here—age, hours worked, and having a parent with a college degree—varied by institution. UW-Parkside had the largest percentages of students in service-learning classes who were 26 years of age and older, with twice as many older students (22%) in these courses compared to both USI and DePaul. About 60% of UW-Parkside students in service-learning courses worked 21 or more hours per week, while DePaul students worked fewer hours and over 60% had at least one parent who graduated from college, much higher than the percentages on the other two campuses.

Table 8.4. Demographic Description Comparing Three University Undergraduate Populations With Students who Participated in Community Based Service-Learning, Spring, 2009

Demographic Descriptor	University of Southern Indiana		University of Wisconsin-Parkside		DePaul University	
	Undergraduates	CBL Students	Undergraduates	CBL Students	Undergraduates	CBL Students
	n = 8,438	n = 480	n = 4,337	n = 293	n = 14,236	n = 146
	%	%	%	%	%	%
26 and older	16.3	9.4	19.2	21.8	17.0	10.3
Female	59.0	84.2	54.3	45.7	54.7	66.4
White	90.0	93.5	73.4	76.8	57.8	65.8
13+ credits	62.0	77.9	51.8	57.7		78.8
Class Standing						
Freshman	30.3	13.5	26.4	1.4	14.9	7.5
Sophomore	21.9	11.5	22.2	3.4	21.3	15.8
Junior	21.1	35.4	21.0	32.4	22.1	29.5
Senior	27.7	39.6	30.5	62.8	41.6	47.3
Hours Worked						
0		28.3		4.4		24.0
1-15		28.5		20.5		37.0
16-20		16.0		17.1		12.3
21+		27.1		58.0		26.7
Parents have degree		45.4		36.2		62.3
Volunteered before		70.0		53.6		62.3

One additional difference, this in terms of approaches to service-learning, is that DePaul encourages service-learning course enrollment for upper classmen through its core liberal studies program that requires all undergraduates to complete an experiential learning course in their third year. Enrolling in an approved service-learning course is one of four ways to complete this requirement. The other two campuses have no such requirement.

RESULTS

Table 8.5 presents the results of the regression analysis for the independent effects of each variable on each of the four factors. In addition, interaction effects for each of the significant predictors for each campus were included in the analysis, but none was statistically significant. Table 8.5 displays the b coefficients (unstanderdized refression coefficients) and overall variance explained for each factor.

Results by Outcome Measure

Each outcome factor was related to independent predictors in unique ways, further supporting the inference that each factor taps a separate domain of student outcomes for service-learning. The extent to which students connected classroom learning to community experience was related to age, whether a parent holds a degree, class standing, and the campus. Younger students had a more positive reaction, as did upper classmen,

Table 8.5.   Significant Predictors for Undergraduate Populations for Four Factors: b Coefficients

	Connecting Classroom Learning	Developing Personal Skills	Career Preparation	Community Involvement
Constant	6.19	8.88	1.67	3.52
UW-Parkside	.38*	.39	.22*	-.13
USI	.24	.46*	.26*	-.03
Female	.09	.04	.07	.23*
White	-.07	-.32	.01	-.10
26+	-.30*	-.28	-.08	.07
Parent has degree	-.20*	-.22	-.03	-.11*
Class standing	.18*	.12	.04	-.01
13+ credits	-.03	-.03	-.06	.08
Weekly hours worked	-.02	-.14*	-.03	-.02
Volunteered before	.18	.16	.05	.36*
R^2	.04*	.03*	.06*	.11*

Note: *$p < .05$.

and first generation college students. Students at UW-Parkside also had more positive reactions, which was independent of these other factors.

Developing personal skills through service-learning was significantly related to hours worked and campus. Students who worked fewer hours were more likely to report that their personal skills were developed as a result of their service-learning experiences, and students at USI were also more positive. Career preparation was not related to characteristics of the students, but there is an overall effect for campus, with students at both USI and UW-Parkside having a more positive reaction on this outcome, perhaps suggesting that these campuses placed a different emphasis on this possibility or on developing this competency. Finally, community involvement was not related to campus, but was related to gender, whether a parent had a college degree, and previous volunteer experience. Women, students with previous volunteer experience, and first generation college students were more likely to report that their civic involvement was enhanced as the result of these experiences.

Trends

First, each of the dependent measures had different sets of significant predictors, suggesting that the separate domains were distinct. Second, the campuses differed in terms of the positive nature of students' reactions to their service-learning programs. Overall, students from both public universities, UW-Parkside and USI, felt they derived greater benefits from their service-learning experiences than did students from DePaul.

Also, the different aspects of nontraditionality had differential patterns. Age was one of the strongest predictors of perceived learning (with younger students more often reporting enhanced learning), but was not significant for the other outcome measures. Whether a student has a parent with a college degree was important for the perception that community projects enhanced learning and community involvement, with first generation students feeling they gained more on both dimensions. Hours worked was important for perceived gains in personal skills, with students working fewer hours feeling they gained more from their experiences than students who worked more hours. For most outcomes, more traditional students felt they gained more; the exception being first generation students, where nontraditional students felt they gained more from these experiences.

Apart from these trends, students with lower class standing less often reported connecting what they learn in their classes with their service-learning experiences, and students who reported enhanced community involvement as a result of their service-learning experiences tended to be women, those students for whom neither parent has achieved a college degree, and those who have previously volunteered.

DISCUSSION

Implications for Model and Hypotheses

These findings yielded partial support for the hypotheses and model. As predicted, lack of prior experience might increase the value of certain possible outcomes for some groups more than others. Older students were less enthusiastic about the value of service-learning to their learning (not hypothesized), but, as expected, first generation students were more so. As expected, students who worked fewer hours reported greater gains on the development of personal skills. None of the measures of nontraditionality were related to career preparation. Finally, older and working students did not differ from other students in their value of community involvement, but first generation students were particularly appreciative of this outcome, suggesting that service-learning may be a particularly important aspect of programming designed to retain such students. Overall, then, it does seem that the principle that gaining new experiences will enhance perceived benefits of service-learning may be operating here.

There was some support for the expectation that reinforcement of strongly held beliefs or values would be related to positive perceptions. Students with previous volunteer experience were more likely to report enhanced community involvement, as were women who are traditionally more engaged in community building activities. This might explain some of the campus differences found, which could be attributed in part to the higher rates of community embeddedness and connection often found in more rural areas.

Implications for Practice

Differences in students' prior opportunities for experiences that promote skills and expertise were related to their perceptions of the benefit of service-learning. Students who had not been in the workforce welcomed the opportunity to develop skills in the community while going to school. For this student population, community-based projects to address community issues were promoting their competence in the areas of communication and teamwork. As suggested by the literature, however, older and working students may not experience community-based work as advancing significant growth unless it is consciously designed to draw upon preexisting knowledge and skills in both classroom discussion and project design as Largent and Horinek (2008) had found. Based on their research that changing practice enhanced older students' experiences, service-learning practitioners in the classroom as well as the community are more likely to reach the nontraditional student if they learn as much as they can about the prior experiences of each student at the beginning of the term and work with each individual to design a project that will develop competence in new areas. We know from years of service-learning research that students value service-learning most if they feel that they made a meaningful contribution to the community (Eyler et al., 2001). Nontraditional students demonstrating a higher level of expertise are not likely to be satisfied unless they are given the opportunity to employ their capabilities in service to the community.

First generation college students are a subsample of working students who were particularly appreciative of the benefit of service-learning opportunities for the enhancement of their classroom experience and expressed strong support for the value of community involvement. Many institutions are designing programs in order to retain this particular population of students that include first year cohorts and career preparation workshops with the purpose of creating a college environment that is welcoming and that relates future goals to course work (Gullatt & Jan, 2003). Given the findings in the current research that first generation students recognized the value of learning while engaged with community issues, service-learning courses could enhance first year and career exploration programming.

Second, students who reported that their service-learning experiences reinforced highly valued predispositions or orientations were more likely to feel that service-learning would sustain their community involvement. Students who reported having volunteered before taking the service-learning course, particularly women, were advocates for community-based projects in their courses and expressed commitment to continuing community involvement. These students were not more likely to be older students, despite the statistics showing that older people volunteer more and the research on generativity, which suggests that older students would be more inclined. Perhaps the question on the survey, "Did you volunteer in the community before taking this course?" does not connote for older students the range of community work in which they are involved daily at their churches, children's schools, and political organizations. In any event, service-learning has the potential to build upon adults' inclinations and experiences to develop citizens who engage with those from different cultures and recognize interdependence; that is, adults living lives of commitment (Parks Daloz, Keen, Keen, & Daloz Parks, 1996). In order to engage older, working students in community-based activities, institutions of higher education need to help resolve conflicts between various spheres of life for these students.

Although this analysis did not address this concern for nontraditional students, service-learning courses are often organized around placements or projects that require students to be in the community during the day, when full-time working adults are otherwise employed. Holland and Robinson (2008) explain the sometimes frustrating resistance of universities with growing numbers of nontraditional students when they say, "...much more than community colleges, 4-year colleges and universities are challenged by historical expectations and stereotypes about university student behavior, especially the notion that students should put their studies paramount in organizing their lives" (p. 23). Community-based projects can be designed so that students accomplish goals set by partner organizations on their own schedule rather than needing to be present during business hours. Older students can even build upon already existing relationships in their communities, taking the opportunity to expand their level of involvement.

Implications for Future Research

The results of this study suggest the need for further research in order to identify effective practices that further engage nontraditional students in service-learning in order to enhance learning, skill development, career preparation, and ongoing community involvement. Future studies will want to reconfirm these outcome domains by refining them and developing common measures that can be used consistently in the analysis of student experience so that results from different populations can be compared in meta-analysis.

In order to advance knowledge about the experiences of nontraditional students, most surveys of service-learning students will need to add questions about age, hours working, and whether a parent has a degree. In addition, having information about single parenthood, a characteristic of nontraditional students that could have a significant impact on student engagement in service-learning as well as our practice with this population, warrants further study. Community-based projects could be designed for entire families to enable parents to participate fully. With standard measures of nontraditionality, future studies of service-learning could assess the relative impact of these four characteristics on students as well as communities. Students who bring a wealth of experience and skill might build stronger relationships in communities and be appreciated for skills of self-direction, communication, and collaboration.

One of the limitations of this research was the inability to control for quality of the service-learning course that each student took. Furthermore, there was not sufficient information about variation among the three institutions to account for significant differences in the experiences of students beyond attributes of the students themselves. Do service-learning experiences vary significantly between public and private institutions, perhaps with state universities emphasizing career preparation? Do community-based projects in large urban areas differ from those in rural communities? This suggests that further examination is needed of how institutional practice, regional differences, and urban concentration may be related to nontraditional students' service-learning outcomes.

APPENDIX: COMMON STATEMENTS ON SERVICE LEARNING

1. The community project aspect of this course helped me to understand the subject matter and how it can be used in everyday life.
2. The community project helped me to better understand the course lectures and readings.
3. Community projects should be a part of more classes at this university.
4. I felt that the community project I did through this course benefited the community.
5. I felt comfortable working with the community organization.
6. I worked directly with a community partner and/or faculty member through this course.
7. This community project helped me gain professional contacts for future employment.
8. I understood the purpose of this community project in relation to the subject matter being taught in class.
9. The community project helped me to become aware of my personal strengths and weaknesses.
10. The community project in this course assisted me in clarifying my career plans.
11. The community work involved in this project made me more aware of my own biases and prejudices.
12. The community project enhanced my ability to communicate in a "real world" setting.
13. The community project helped me to develop my problem-solving skills.

14. The syllabus provided for this course outlined the objectives of the community project in relation to course objectives.

15. The other students in this class did not play an important role in my learning.

16. This project helped me see how I can contribute to my community.

17. After college I will volunteer/participate in the community.

18. I think it is very important to be actively involved in my community.

REFERENCES

Bureau of Labor Statistics. (2010). *Volunteering in the U.S.* Washington, DC: U.S. Department of Labor.

Coalition of Urban Serving Universities. (2010). *Urban universities: Anchors generating prosperity for America's cities.* Retrieved from http://www.usucoalition.org/downloads/part6/USU_White_Paper_Report_2010

Erikson, E. H. (1959). *Identity and the life cycle.* New York, NY: Norton.

Eyler, J. (2001, Summer). Creating your reflection map. *New Directions for Higher Education, 114,* 35-43.

Eyler, J. S., Giles, D. E., Stenson, C. M., & Gray, C. (2001). *At a glance: What we know about the effects of service-learning on college students, faculty, institutions and communities, 1993-2000* (3rd ed.). Washington, DC: Learn and Serve America, Corporation for National and Community Service.

Fenwick, T. J. (2003). *Learning through experience: Troubling orthodoxies and intersecting questions.* Malabar, FL: Krieger Press.

Gullatt, Y., & Jan, W. (2003). *How do pre-collegiate academic outreach programs impact college-going among underrepresented students?* Washington, DC: Pathways to College Network Clearinghouse.

Holland, B. A. (2005). Institutional differences in pursuing the public good. In A. J. Kezar, T. C. Chambers, & J. C. Burkhardt (Eds.), *Higher education for the public good* (pp. 235-260). San Francisco, CA: Jossey-Bass.

Holland, B. A., & Robinson, G. (2008, Summer). Community based learning with adults: Bridging efforts in multiple sectors. In S. Reed & C. Marienau (Eds.), *Linking adults with community: Promoting civic engagement through community-based learning New directions in adult and continuing education* (No. 118, pp. 17-30). San Francisco, CA: Jossey-Bass.

Jacobs, F., & Hundley, S. P. (2010). *Understanding and supporting adult learners: A guide for colleges and universities.* San Francisco, CA: Jossey-Bass.

Jarvis, P. (2006). *Towards a comprehensive theory of human learning.* New York, NY: Routledge.

Kassworm, C. E. (2010). Adult learners in a research university: Negotiating undergraduate student identity. *Adult Education Quarterly, 60*(2), 143-160.

Kassworm, C., Polson, C., & Fishback, S. (2002). *Responding to adult learners in higher education*. Malabar, FL: Krieger Press.

Keeton, M., Sheckley, B., & Griggs, J. (2002). *Effectiveness and efficiency in higher education for adults: A guide for fostering learning*. Dubuque, IO: Kendall/Hunt Press.

Kolb, D. (1984). *Experiential learning: Experience as the source of learning and development*. Upper Saddle River, NJ: Prentice Hall.

Largent, L., & Horinek, J. (2008, Summer). Community colleges and adult service learners: Evaluating a first year program to improve implementation. In S. Reed & C. Marienau (Eds.), *Linking adults with community: Promoting civic engagement through community based learning*. New Directions in Adult and Continuing Education, (No. 118, pp. 37-47). San Francisco, CA: Jossey-Bass.

MacKeracher, D. (2004). *Making sense of adult learning*. Toronto, Canada: University of Toronto Press.

Marienau, C., & Reed, S. C. (2008). Educator as designer: Balancing multiple teaching perspectives in the design of community based learning. In S. Reed & C. Marienau (Eds.), *Linking adults with community: Promoting civic engagement through community based learning. New Directions in Adult and Continuing Education* (No. 118, pp.61-74). San Francisco, CA: Jossey-Bass.

O'Connell, T. (2002). A matter of experience: Service-learning and the adult student. In E. Zlotkowski (Ed.), *Service-Learning and the first-year experience: Preparing students for personal success and civic responsibility* (Monograph No. 34, pp. 39-50). Columbia, SC: University of South Carolina, National Resource Center for the First-Year Experience and Students in Transition.

Parks Daloz, L. A., Keen, C. H., Keen, J. P., & Daloz Parks, S. (1996) *Common fire: Leading lives of commitment in a complex world*. Boston, MA: Beacon Press

Reed, S. C., & Marienau, C. (Eds.). (2008, Summer). Linking adults with community: Promoting civic engagement through community based learning. *New Directions in Adult and Continuing Education* (No. 118, pp. 1-107). San Francisco, CA : Jossey-Bass.

Sather, P., Reed-Bouley, J., & Fair, M. (2008, October). *The impact of employment on student engagement in service-learning*. Paper presented at the 8th annual conference of the International Association for Research on Service-Learning and Community Engagement, New Orleans, LA.

Schuetze, H. G., & Slowey, M. (2002). Participation and exclusion: A comparative analysis of non-traditional students and lifelong learners in higher education. *Higher Education, 44*, 309-327.

Smith, M. C. (2008). Does service-learning promote adult development? Theoretical perspectives and directions for research. In S. Reed & C. Marienau (Eds.), *Linking adults with community: Promoting civic engagement through community based learning. New Directions in Adult and Continuing Education* (No. 118, pp.5-15). San Francisco, CA: Jossey-Bass.

Snyder, M., & Clary, E. G. (2003) Volunteerism and the generative society. In E. de St. Aubin, D. McAdams, & T. Kim (Eds.), *The generative society: Caring for future generations* (pp. 221-237). Washington, DC: American Psychological Association.

U.S. Department of Education, National Center for Education Statistics. (2001). *Students whose parents did not go to college: Postsecondary access, persistence, and attainment* (NCES 2001–126). Retrieved from http://nces.ed.gov/das/epubs/ 2005171/references.asp

U.S. Department of Education, National Center for Education Statistics. (2002). *Special analysis: Nontraditional undergraduates* (NCES 2002-012). Retrieved from http://nces.ed.gov/search/?output=xml_no_dtd&site=nces&client= nces&q=2002%2D0

U.S. Department of Education, National Center for Education Statistics. (2003). *Work first, study second: Adult undergraduates who combine employment and post secondary enrollment* (NCES 2003-267). Retrieved from http://nces.ed.gov/ pubs2003/2003167.pdf

U.S. Department of Education, National Center for Education Statistics. (2009). *Digest of education statistics, 2008* (NCES 2009-020). Retrieved from http:// nces.ed.gov/pubsearch/pubsinfo.asp?pubid=2009020

Wlodowski, R. J., & Kassworm, C. E. (Eds.) (2003). Accelerated learning for adults: The promise and practice of intensive educational formats. *New Directions for Adult and Continuing Education*. San Francisco, CA: Jossey-Bass.

CHAPTER 9

A CIVICALLY ENGAGED RECIPROCAL LEARNING PROCESS IN DENTAL EDUCATION

**Stuart M. Schrader, Abbe B. Shapiro,
David A. Zahl, Susan L. Zunt, and Emily Deering**

ABSTRACT

Numerous oral health complications face people living with cancer (PLWC). Data show that increasing access to oral health care prior to, during, and after cancer treatment leads to a decrease in oral health complications. Nevertheless, few newly diagnosed cancer patients or dental health professionals understand the critical connection between oral and systemic health as it relates specifically to cancer. To ensure that more dental providers understand this connection before entering the practice community, each student at the Indiana University School of Dentistry must successfully complete an Objective Structured Clinical Examination (OSCE) with PLWC prior to graduation. A constructivist grounded theory thematic analysis of student and simulated patient (SP) responses to questions about the OSCE was conducted; both SPs and dental students reported mutually and reciprocally benefitting from participating. These findings suggest that it is important that dental education involve SP's as real patients as there are benefits to both student learning and patient learning.

Understanding Service-Learning and Community Engagement:
Crossing Boundaries Through Research, pp. 179–198

NEED FOR BECOMING CIVICALLY ENGAGED
IN THE ORAL HEALTH CARE OF CANCER PATIENTS

According to the National Cancer Institute (2010), 11.4 million Americans are living with cancer and 1.4 million new cases of cancer are diagnosed annually. Cancer is the leading cause of death worldwide (World Health Organization, 2010). Oral disease and conditions resulting from cancer treatments can impact people living with cancer's (PLWC) quality of life, lead to serious life-threatening systemic infections, and affect their ability to complete planned cancer treatment, thereby, compromising a successful treatment outcome (U.S. Department of Health and Human Services National Institute of Health (NIH), 2009).

Oral complications or considerations occur in nearly 100% of PLWC receiving radiation for head and neck malignancies and nearly 40% of patients receiving chemotherapy (NIH, 2009). PLWC encounter numerous specific oral health care complications, including mucositis (mouth sores), xerostomia (dry mouth), oral bleeding, and increased caries (cavities) (Trotti et al., 2003). While some of these complications occur only during treatment, some can persist for years. Associated with these oral complications are increased pain, difficulty communicating, increased risk for infection, and possible hemorrhage (McGuire, 2003).

Oral health-related Quality of Life (OHRQoL) measures have been used in several studies (Linsen, Schmidt-Beer, Fimmers, Grüner, & Koeck, 2009; Baker, Pankhurst & Robinson, 2006) with cancer patients to assess the impact of oral complications on a PLWC's ability to perform common activities. OHRQoL measures assess one's ability to perform activities such as eating and enjoying food, speaking and pronouncing words properly, oral hygiene, sleeping, relaxing, smiling, and willingness to show one's teeth without embarrassment. Baker et al. (2006) found the most prevalent OHRQoL issues to be "functional limitations (speech, taste), psychological discomfort (self-consciousness, tenseness) and physical pain (aching, eating) and, to a lesser extent, psychological disability (difficulty relaxing, embarrassment)" (p. 358). Mouth sores resulting from head and neck radiation are reported as a particularly painful complication (Ohrn, Wahlin, & Sjoden, 2001) which reduces an individual's quality of life and willingness to continue such therapies, thereby, compromising the possibility for a successful outcome (Barker, Epstein, Williams, Gorsky & Raber-Durlacher, 2005). Treatment of oral complications adds an additional, often significant, financial burden to the substantial costs already associated with cancer treatment (Elting et al., 2003).

Rationale for Civic Education: Identifying Public Concerns

NIH (2009) acknowledged the need for PLWC to be seen regularly for a dental assessment and proper education on oral hygiene techniques. Appropriate health literacy and access to dental care can influence a PLWC's general and oral health quality of life, thereby, possibly reducing incidence of oral complications. Despite increased knowledge and national recommendations that oral health care become an integral feature of cancer treatment, oral care has yet to be systematically paired with other traditional oncology treatment modalities. Inclusion of a dental professional with an oncology team is relatively rare (McGuire, 2003), few dental schools formally educate future dental professionals regarding cancer and health literacy (Cannick et al., 2007), and state board of dental or medical examiners do not require applicants to demonstrate proficiency in early detection of oral cancer (Kerr, Cangrani, Gany, & Cruz, 2004).

Most medical and dental schools are not adequately preparing future health professionals with comprehensive cancer-related curricula (Burzynski, Rankin, Silverman, Scheetz, & Jones, 2002; Cannick et al., 2007). When clinical educators and practicing health professionals have limited access to educational opportunities about oral health care for cancer patients, it is not surprising that future dental providers lack adequate training and subsequently PLWC in dental offices are then infrequently provided effective educational materials on this topic (Zakrzewska, Leeson, Mcliskey, & Vickers, 1997). However, when a dental provider as part of an integrative oncology team provides oral health care prior to, during, and postradiation, the risk of serious oral complications is significantly reduced (NIH, 2009).

Despite the strengths of diverse oral health care regimes and practices, and the growing range of knowledge that exists among health professionals serving PLWC, a barrier that limits these strengths is the lack of standardized curriculum for future health professionals. There is little standardization within dental higher education regarding training about oral health care for cancer patients (Cannick et al., 2007) and licensure requirements vary from state to state (American Dental Association, 2010). As a result, in part, little progress has been made in decreasing the high incidents of cancer-related oral health complications.

Civic Engagement With People Living with Cancer

According to the American Psychological Association (n.d.), civic engagement involves, "individual and collective actions designed to identify and address issues of public concern" (para 2). Following the recommendations of the American Dental Education Association Presidential Commission Report (Haden et al.,2003) on improving the oral health status of all Americans, the Indiana University School of Dentistry (IUSD) developed relationships with PLWC and community organizations serving this specific patient population in order to begin addressing this public concern. IUSD is providing educational training for future dental providers through an Objective Structured Clinical Exam (OSCE) with PLWC, while also acting as a community resource in providing low-cost high-quality oral health care for local PLWC.

An OSCE is a timed formative or summative performance based examination method based on objective testing and direct observation of planned simulated clinical encounters between students and either *standardized patients* or *simulated patients* (Wallace, Rao, & Haslam, 2002). Typically, individuals are hired to fulfill this role in clinic-based education. Vu & Barrow's (1994) definition of standardized patients includes people who are trained to re-present a clinical problem (e.g., depression, substance abuse, diabetes, obesity and nutritional concerns, financial barriers in accessing care). More traditionally, medical and dental schools have used trained actors, who have years of theatrical and performance training, to portray standardized patients (Watson et al., 2004). A standardized patient is one who is well-trained to simulate a specific illness or character-story in a standard way.

A simulated patient (SP) on the other hand is an actual patient who is well-trained to present an illness in a standardized manner (Austin, Gregory, & Tabak, 2006). SPs are now used in a variety of disciplines such as psychology, psychiatry, medical education, nursing, pharmacy, social work, and speech language pathology (Kaslow et al., 2009; Watson et al., 2004; Wakefield, Cook, & Boggis, 2003; Wallace et al., 2002; Zraick, Allen, & Johnson, 2003). Using SPs in teaching programs is recommended for teaching collaborative patient centered communication skills in which the patient is a mutual partner in all health care decision making (Epstein, et al., 2005). Some of these skills include such factors as empathy, mutuality, clinical decision making, problem solving, diagnosing, and interpersonal communication skills (Epstein & Hundert, 2002).

Benefits of Using "Real" Simulated Patients in an OSCE

IUSD utilizes both standardized and simulated patients, depending on the focus of the OSCE. Each OSCE provides a teaching and learning setting prior to students beginning their clinical experiences, and both standardized and simulated patients grade dental students on their interpersonal/relational (e.g., empathy) and communication skills (e.g., appropriate use of verbal and nonverbal cues). One of the central reasons that OSCE has been so successful has been the use of real SPs. In OSCEs that utilize SPs, students are also graded on their ability to complete specific clinical objectives (i.e., completion of a salivary flow test). Use of actual patients gives students the opportunity to see oral health complications associated with a given condition, be it cancer, HIV/AIDS, or developmental disabilities. Furthermore, the use of real SPs also gives students the opportunity to engage with members of the community who are traditionally underserved by health providers and who have not historically had an opportunity to give sufficient voice to the biological, social and psychological considerations of their illness.

IUSD acknowledges the crucial need to educate future dentists to be adequately prepared to play an active role in increasing patient access to oral health care. Students' participation in this civic engagement OSCE assists them in recognizing and appreciating human diversity and commonality, in learning about access to care issues facing patients, and in developing empathy, and a sense of social responsibility for medically and psycho-socially complex patients.

Program Design

The OSCE was developed using Yoder's (2006) 10-step *framework for service-learning in dental education* to provide a structure for planning, implementing, and evaluating the learning experiences. As such, we first identified an appropriate "academic link" (p. 116) between our school and local cancer facilities or agencies. Second, we successfully developed "sustained community partnerships" (p. 117) with the local National Cancer Institute designated Indiana University Simon Cancer Center which helped to recruit SPs for the OSCE. IUSD also collaborated to develop interorganizational partnerships with community agencies such as Camp Bluebird (the first U.S. adult cancer camp with locations throughout the country, www.campbluebird.com) and the local Support of People with Head and Neck Cancer (www.spohnc.org) support group. By working with these groups, IUSD was able to connect with persons who had experienced cancer related oral complications and who had a desire to use their personal experiences to help educate dental students.

Third, through collaboration between faculty and the community partnerships, we articulated "civic engagement objectives" (Yoder, 2006, p.118) for our students' and for the SPs. The objectives aligned with the national Commission on Dental Accreditation standards in expecting that students will meet or exceed competencies in the effective use of patient-centered interpersonal communication and behavioral management skills in promoting, improving, and maintaining a patient's oral health. Fourth, we provided SPs and students with "broad preparation" (p.119) for this OSCE.

One of the first steps for preparation included the development of the patient case. IUSD staff explained the OSCE process and connections between oral health and systemic health to the newly hired SPs. Next, the SPs shared their oral health habits and comprehensive medical, social, and medical histories. The commonalities, categories, and themes that emerged were then used to develop a standard character story that each SP later performed during the OSCEs. Additionally, prior to participation in the OSCE, each SP was given a thorough intraoral screening and a salivary flow test by a licensed dental faculty at IUSD. This allowed IUSD to screen for any possible serious oral lesions and/or opportunistic infections and to provide necessary oral health care. Intraoral photos and a dental and medical history that was taken during this process assisted IUSD in further developing the simulated patient case.

Once the development of the simulated patient case was finalized, SPs completed a comprehensive training process. SPs were asked to memorize specific medical, medication, dental, social, cultural and general psychosocial conditions of the case. Training PLWC to be SPs also involved having them watch video recordings of previous SP encounters, review relevant cultural communication skills and feedback evaluation forms, discuss oral health care articles and related materials given to students prior to the OSCE encounter, and engage in role-playing of the entire encounter. During the review of previous OSCE videos and role-playing exercises, SPs used the feedback forms and practiced scoring dental student's clinical interviewing skills. This process was vital to increasing interrater reliability among SPs.

In addition, another component of preparation involved training for the experience. Prior to entering the exam room for the OSCE, both students and SPs participated in various preencounter training. In class, students received direct training on how to complete the clinical aspects of the OSCE, and attended lectures on various aspects of cancer and oral health, which included how to work with medically and dentally complex patients. On-line, students were provided with explicit OSCE protocols, evidence-based reading materials related to oral complications of cancer treatments and socioeconomic factors which may impede a PLWC's access to care, a detailed SP patient chart, and a standardized OSCE evaluation checklist.

Fifth, we incorporated "sustained engagement" (Yoder, 2006, p. 119). This learning experience is purposefully presented to second-year dental students immediately prior to entering into clinic so that students may apply the knowledge gained from this simulated clinical experience. The second-year dental students initial preclinical exposure to the sociocultural barriers and considerations in accessing oral health care is intended as the only first step in having students appreciate their social responsibilities in assisting this patient population. From this activity students are provided with an educational context for future volunteering opportunities in years three and four of their clinical education (e.g., oral cancer screening opportunities in conjunction with other local agencies such as the Little Red Door or with units at the IU Simon Cancer Centers).

Sixth, we prepared our SP and student encounter based on the principle of "reciprocal learning" (Yoder, 2006, p.119). Working with such a medically-complex patient population affords our students a rare opportunity for reflective practice in critiquing how to effectively manage this type of clinical interview and how best to conduct a test for dry mouth, while also providing an educational opportunity for the SPs to learn more about oral health.

Seventh, we have remained committed to the principle of "guided reflection" (Yoder, 2006, p. 119). Over the course of 2009 and 2010, each of 194 second-year dental students participated in one 12-minute OSCE with one of 15 local cancer survivors acting as a SP. Specific clinical objectives were outlined for students with the expectation that they complete them during the first 10 minutes while the final 2 minutes of the encounter allowed the SP to provide oral feedback to the student about their communication and clinical skills. Once the OSCE concluded each day, the SPs participated in a round-table discussion to evaluate and debrief their personal experiences.

The OSCE protocol utilized 4 forms of written evaluation and feedback. Two were completed by SPs and two by dental students. At the conclusion of each OSCE encounter the SP completed a standardized feedback rating form. The feedback form included two open-ended questions focused on identification of the student's strengths and weaknesses and 15 yes/no questions that gauged the student's clinical interviewing, interpersonal, and problem-solving skills, which figured into the student's cumulative OSCE grade. Both SPs and students completed a written assessment of their personal experience once the OSCE was completed. Additionally, a peer-review was completed of each student's videoed encounter which utilized a standardized feedback form, the same as that used by the SPs. This presented an additional reciprocal learning opportunity for students to observe the interaction of their peers with a PLWC.

The eighth step of Yoder's (2006) framework involves "community engagement" (p. 120). Enactment of this process provided us an opportunity to collaborate with the local cancer community so as to increase the outreach of our OSCE program goals through these informal social networks. Ninth, IUSD faculty and students are continually involved in "ongoing evaluation and improvement" (p. 120) of the OSCEs program. Both student and SP evaluations are used in identification of programmatic improvements. Finally, IUSD seeks "opportunities for community-engaged scholarship" (p. 121) which provides further evidence of our commitment to publicly address the oral health needs of PLWC.

In this paper we present the results of 2 years (2009, 2010) of data gathered from dental students and community participants living with cancer who participated in the OSCEs. We conducted a retrospective study of educational data about how students and simulated patients viewed working together other during a community-engaged, experiential learning OSCE. The purpose of this study is to explore a reciprocal experiential learning experience between persons living with cancer as simulated patients and second-year dental students involved in an OSCE.

METHODS

Fifteen SPs and 194 second-year dental students participated in a cancer related OSCE during the spring semesters of 2009 ($n = 99$) and 2010 ($n = 95$). Students and simulated patients replied in writing to the following questions: Students: (a) What did you like about this SP encounter? (b) How could this SP activity be improved in the future? (c) What did you learn that can be helpful in your future dental practice? Simulated Patients: (a) What did you like about working on this SP encounter? (b) How could this SP encounter be improved upon in the future? (c) What did you learn that could be helpful in your future visits to dentists? In this chapter, we explore the findings from the two post-OSCE assessments.

Analysis of Post-OSCE Assessments

Naturalistic, contructivist, grounded theory approach was used in designing and developing categorized themes (Charmaz, 2002) of each OSCE assessment. Reflective consideration was given to not only the role of the researchers in gathering the data but also analyzing the subtleties of their meaning. Emerging themes were first identified by one researcher who isolated themes or common semantic issues, concerns, and phrases that emerged within and across responses. These themes were then independently reviewed and verified by two other researchers (Holsti, 1969). Themes continued to emerge until it was determined that conceptual saturation was reached (Flick, 2002). Such saturation occurred after three criteria were used to evaluate the themes: (a) recurrence (i.e., same meaning yet different words), (b) repetition (i.e., same wording), and (c) forcefulness (i.e., powerfulness of particular words or phrases in expressing a key idea) (Owen, 1984). Themes were finally categorized based on the underpinning of the relevant literature (Strauss & Corbin, 1990).

RESULTS

The categories generated by the analysis of answers to open-ended questions are nondiscrete, as many respondents provided multiple answers to each question. The results are reported for students and simulated patients.

Student Assessments

Students were first asked: "What did you like about the SP encounter?" Many student statements highlight the *realism* involved in working with actual cancer patients. One student reported:

> I liked the experience with the *real* patient. The patient gave me good feedback to improve on and also gave me a more realistic feeling of how it will be like to deal with a real cancer patient.

Nearly 70% of the dental students appreciated the authentic experiences and stories PLWC had to offer. Approximately 40% of the dental students appreciated the opportunity to actually complete real clinical procedures. They reported that doing so enhanced their understanding of the relationship between oral health care and cancer therapies. Sixteen percent (16%) of dental students noted that conversation flowed better and feedback was more meaningful in OSCEs with SPs (PLWC) compared with standardized patients (professional actors). This connection to simulated patients may have also been grounded in students reporting that they liked the SP's personality (41%).

We next asked the students, "What did you learn from the feedback given to you by the simulated patient?" This question is a modified version of one originally asked in 2009 to enhance student's critical reflection. Therefore, we are only reporting the students' 2010 responses to this question (n=95). Many students reported that SPs provided very useful specific feedback. For example one student stated: "I learned that I should be more comfortable about my strengths and not undermine the knowledge I possess. Also, I learned to pay attention to detail regarding sterility." The following are the four most frequent responses as specifically identified by the students to this question. First, 25% of the students expressed the need to continue to improve their communication skills. Specific areas of improvement included: decreased use of medical or dental jargon, increased explanation of the necessity of dental procedures, and ensuring a patient understood the material by asking for confirmation. Second, one of the main objectives of an OSCE is to provide students with a structured educational setting to practice communication and rapport building skills in a simulated clinical setting prior to seeing patients in a clinic. The need is evidenced by reports of SPs stating that the students need more self-confidence (21%) and rapport building skills (8%) before entering a clinical setting. Third, when working with immuno-compromised patients, following universal precautions are of increased importance for the dentist. In this OSCE, as with all clinical matters, students were expected to wash their hands prior to engaging in any physical contact with the SP and to wear a mask when conducting any clinical procedures. Students reported that SPs stated that the majority of students did follow proper procedures and that some (12%) dental students did not either wash their hands and/or wear their masks when conducting certain clinical tests.

The third question asked, "How could this simulated patient activity be improved in the future?" Students overall would have liked more time to develop a personal connection with the patient. There were three main themes of responses from students on ways to improve upon this clinical experience. First, some students (30%) suggested more time for the encounter (30%) whereas others (23%) wanted more time and/or fewer objectives for the encounter. Second, a number of logistical suggestions were given, such as "have materials separated for each test", "small size gloves needed in operatory", and "more time warnings" needed to be provided. These minor logistical procedural matters are presently being improved upon for future OSCEs. Finally, approximately 10% of the students would have liked an orientation of the actual exam room prior to the OSCE encounter to familiarize themselves with the location of materials needed for conducting a particular oral health test and the spatial layout of the room.

The final question the students were asked was: "What did you learn today that can be helpful in your future dental practice?" One student's response demonstrated the usefulness of the OSCE for clinical training and the value of utilizing actual PLWC as simulated patients during the encounter. This student responded, "I learned how to appropriately do the Schirmer test and feel well-prepared for clinicals. I also increased my ability to speak to patients with complex medical histories." Although many students valued the authenticity of the experience in working specifically with PLWC, the students recognized that skills gained from this exercise would, in most cases, be transferrable to other patient populations. The students reported four main areas for how their experience was transferable for future clinical practice. First, interpersonal skills are vital in developing a strong personal connection in doctor/patient relationship. Twenty-five percent (25%) of the students recognized the importance of establishing rapport with a patient in their future dental practice. Second, a specific clinical skills set is needed to effectively treat a medically complex patient. Twenty percent (20%) of the students specified that they now have an increased ability to treat PLWC, having gained an awareness of oral health complications specific to cancer, appropriate related treatments, palliative care needs, the importance of developing collaborative working relationships with oncology physicians, and specific clinical practices necessary when working with this patient population. Third, nearly 14% of the students acknowledged the importance of continuing to work on time management in a dental practice. Finally, in a broader sense, 11% of the students reported a need to continue gaining skills that will assist them in communicating more effectively with their patients.

Simulated Patient Assessments

There were three similar questions asked of the SPs regarding their experiences in the OSCE. The first question asked: "What did you like about working on this SP encounter?" One SP wrote: "[I liked] learning more about dry mouth and its effects [and] assisting, even in a small way, students to become more confident and capable in interacting with patients/clients." This response exemplified the reciprocal learning component of the OSCE process. The following were the most frequent responses provided by all the SPs. All respondents (100%) liked the opportunity to be helpful or useful in the educational process of future dental providers. Approximately 53% of the SPs commented that they were appreciative of receiving a dental education during the OSCE process. Thirty-three percent (33%) of the SPs remarked that collaborating with other PLWC was an additional benefit of their OSCE participation.

Second, SPs were asked, "How could this simulated patient activity be improved in the future?" One SP responded: "A little more time for the patient and dentist to get to know each other and to relax." Nearly three-fourths of the SPs (73%) desired more time for this encounter for increased rapport building and dental education, the student/SP oral feedback session, and/or generally for the encounter. The dental students had a similar response in requesting more time or fewer objectives for this OSCE.

The third question asked of SPs was: "What did you learn that can be helpful in your future visits with dentists?" SPs in general remarked about how useful this OSCE was in helping cancer survivors in the future and how as PLWC they will likely become more active participants in their own health care. One SP summarized well this sentiment when stating, "How they should approach me, what questions should be asked pertaining to medicines and family history. What I should be asking upfront if uncertain." The most frequent SP responses addressing these issues were that 60% of the SPs reported having increased expectations of their dentists or identified a communicative dental style or approach they now prefer after participating in the OSCE. Forty-seven percent of the SPs stated they have become more confident and capable dental consumers in how they will select dental providers in the future. Finally, 47% of the SPs reported that they appreciated gaining specific suggestions from the students about how to care for dry mouth, a common side effect of various cancer treatments.

DISCUSSION

Overall, this OSCE provides a valuable reciprocal learning experience for both students and SPs. Both PLWC SPs and dental students reported benefitting from participation in the OSCE encounter. For the dental students the benefits of participating were threefold: (a) Having an opportunity to interact with a real patient with actual oral health symptoms, (b) gaining an awareness of how to better diagnose and treat oral health complications related to cancer, and (c) learning to provide better patient centered care for PLWC. For PLWC, the main patient benefits were fourfold: (a) achieving an increased sense of usefulness by educating future dental providers, (b) gaining skills in becoming more confident dental consumers, (c) gaining an understanding of specific oral health complications facing cancer patients, and (d) receiving an overall education about oral health prevention and maintenance.

Reflections on Reciprocal Learning: Students and SPs Teaching Each Other

Students reported an appreciation for the "authentic experience" and SPs liked the opportunity because it was "helpful or useful in the educational process of future dentists." Previous studies found that students deeply valued the authenticity of simulated clinical encounters with *real* patients (Bokken et al., 2009) and that such experiences deepened student's understandings, provided constructive feedback, reduced anxiety, increased confidence, influenced attitudes and behaviors, increased respect for patients, and increased acquisition of skills by placing learning in a *real* context (Wykurz & Kelly, 2002). The authenticity and positive educational outcomes our students experienced are, perhaps unlikely without the educational impact of engaging with *real* SPs who are community members living with cancer. Regardless of discipline (e.g., nursing, medicine, psychology, social work, pharmacy), students are likely to appreciate working with *real* biological, psychological, social, and cultural issues facing a variety of health care consumers.

The possible reason why SPs may have reported the importance of their role in the simulated *realism* of the OSCE as being *helpful and useful* could be due to feelings of empowerment in teaching students about the oral complications associated with the treatment of their disease (Wykurz & Kelly, 2002). Another empowering process in this OSCE for SPs is, in part, related to SPs reporting that they were "appreciative for having received dental education" from the students while they themselves also acted as educators for students. Patients like our SPs who feel empowered by their ability to teach health practitioners and their mutual receptiveness in being taught about health care information are generally viewed as active and equal collaborators in the management of their own health care. These types of patients then typically report greater patient satisfaction which can thereby lead to better health outcomes (Greenfield, Kaplan, Ware Jr., Martin, & Frank, 1988). The prevailing opinion among scholars engaged in shared health care communication decision making research is that patient education is a significant motivator in patients feeling empowered to collaborate with health care providers about health decisions (Mok, 2001). Presumably, the educational impact this OSCE had on its SPs may have empowered them to become active collaborators in their own oral health care. Becoming both educators and learners may also empower them to advocate for the oral health care of other PLWC by sharing their experiences and knowledge of managing oral complications associated with their therapies. SPs in OSCEs across disciplines could likely feel a sense of personal satisfaction in the reciprocity of teaching and learning, thereby, enabling them to become more knowledgeable, confident and capable health care consumers.

Lastly, students reported they "appreciated the meaningful feedback provided by SPs" about their OSCE performance. Students specifically stated that the SPs provided feedback on how to improve their communication skills in the areas of use of technical jargon, checking and clarifying information, and explaining clinical procedures. Because SPs do not have the years of medical/dental training of their standardized patient counterparts, they must rely more on their personal experiences with health professionals to provide feedback to students about their communicative and interpersonal skills. SP-specific communicative feedback was meaningful not necessarily for its sophisticated assessment, but because it was delivered by *real* PLWC based on their *real* interactions with their health professionals. This finding is congruent with other studies (Bokken et al, 2009) which suggest that even though SPs deliver a higher quantity and quality of feedback, students still find the experience of simulated patients highly instructive and valuable to their education. Students from a variety of disciplines (e.g., law, physical therapy, education counseling) could realize the potential in working with SPs to enhance their communication skills and contribute to the learning of others.

Students' and SPs' Reflections on How to Improve the OSCE Experience

Both students and SPs suggested they wanted more time for making a personal connection and/or building rapport with each other. Building effective rapport is part of the relationship-centered and patient-centered care (Epstein et al., 2005) curriculum at IUSD throughout the first 2 years of dental education. This key principle of finding common ground is heavily emphasized within lectures/discussions, problem-based learning cases, exercises and other didactic course work. All students who participated in the OSCE were expected to engage their patients in rapport building by shaking the patients hand, asking what the patient would like to be called, introducing themselves, making eye-contact, and engaging in social, nonmedical small talk. Students may have fulfilled their expectation of actively engaging in the greeting portion of rapport building; however, they and the SPs may have recognized that there was not enough time to find common ground and to form a stronger relational personal connection based on mutual personal narratives (e.g., both persons originating from the east side of town). Students across disciplines in a timed experiential learning experience for the first time are likely to feel the need for more time to make a personal connection with a SP. Students are likely to benefit in educational experiences in which they begin to recognize the importance of relational connections, mutuality, trust, and common ground as communicative actions essential for delivering health care services.

Effective rapport building between patients and health care providers is essential in developing patient-provider trust (Mainous, Kerse, Brock, Hughes, & Pruitt, 2003). The limited time for social, nonmedical discussions may have impaired developing trust between the student and the SP.

Teaching students about the importance of building rapport and trust during this reflective learning exercise is important (Pearson & Raeke, 2000; Safran et al., 1998) and health professionals who cultivate trusting doctor-patient relationships see more positive health outcomes for their patients. Specifically, PLWC who are engaged in trusting relationships with their health providers may see a decrease in medical/dental fear and better treatment adherence (Hillen, de Haes, & Smets, 2010).

Students and SPs Learn from Each Other

The majority of our SPs reported that after participating in the OSCE that they now recognize a communicative dental style or approach they prefer from their dental provider. Many of our SPs reported during our informal debriefing sessions that they liked many of the rapport building skills mentioned previously, as well as some of the communication skills that students reported as being important for future dental providers. Two communication skills in need of further development that were mentioned in particular by both students and SPs included using jargon-free language and checking and clarifying information.

Patient comprehension during medical consultations is associated with greater satisfaction and better adherence to treatment (Ley, 1988); therefore, presumably avoiding complex medical language is vital for comprehension. OSCEs offer future dental providers considerable opportunity to learn how to more effectively use dental and medical language. Appropriate explanations are imperative for understanding dental and medical meanings and to avoid misunderstandings. Health care providers need to learn how to effectively assess their ability to explain health care concepts to their patients (Silverman, Archer, Gillard, Howells, & Benson, 2010). There are specific gender and other cultural differences in how patients understand health care communication; therefore, health care providers need to negotiate these differences. OSCEs are valuable to dental students because they provide them an opportunity to engage with a culturally diverse patient population with various psycho-social demographics, medically-complex conditions, and differing levels of cognitive processing ability.

Additionally, the students reported feeling more confident in their ability to provide care and services to PLWC, and SPs reported that they are more confident and capable consumers of oral health care services because of the mutuality of learning from each other during their OSCE experience. Studies with other medically compromised patient populations suggest that dental students who learn about and from medically compromised populations are more likely to treat these patients in the future (Kuthy, McQuistan, riniker, Heller, & Qian, 2005; Kuthy, Heller, Riniker, McQuistan, & Qian, 2007). Civically engaged OSCEs in other disciplines might yield similar findings in that students may report feeling more confident in providing future care and services for medically complex patients/clients and SPs might report greater confidence in advocating for their own health care.

LIMITATIONS

This study was limited by several factors. First, not all SPs completed the postencounter SP Assessment due to illness-related exhaustion after participation in OSCEs. In the future we will be mindful of the SPs needs to fill out any postencounter forms as soon as any SP has finished the OSCE. Second, not all of the SP's oral feedback given during the group's debriefing sessions about the student's daily performance was effectively captured by SPs on their own assessments. Ultimately, thematic analysis was only conducted on the written SP assessments, and it might be productive in future research to analyze audio recorded and transcribed debriefing sessions. Finally, the analysis of student and SP themes suggested that reciprocal learning and attitudinal shifts occurred during the OSCE experience. Although the thematic analysis and descriptive statistics provided a picture of the student-SP relationship, the changes in knowledge and attitudes were not quantified. The addition of pre- and post-OSCE knowledge and attitudes assessments and subsequent analysis may provide greater insight to the significance of the reciprocal learning and attitudinal shifts.

CONCLUSION

Appropriate management of good oral health throughout all stages of cancer and cancer treatment is essential, and cancer survivors' ability to maintain and improve their oral health is enhanced by including a dental professional on an oncology team. The design, development, and evaluation of OSCEs such as this one are critical in teaching dental students specific clinical and communication skills about dental oncology, as well as stressing to students the value of becoming an involved health care partner with medical oncologists in the care of cancer patients before, during, and after cancer therapies. Students are better able to appreciate various complex issues facing cancer patients in maintaining and enhancing their oral health, while PLWC feel empowered in helping future dental providers better understand their oral health care needs. As future dental providers and cancer survivors become increasingly aware of the oral health implications of cancer treatments, a reduction in serious oral health complications will occur and enhanced quality of life for PLWC is likely.

This OSCE serves as a summative evaluation of dental students' clinical communication, problem solving, and history taking skills with PLWC. After the OSCE students reported that the reciprocal nature of this experiential learning experience increased their appreciation and knowledge about oral health complications connected to various cancer treatments, and it made them feel more clinically and psychosocially prepared to serve PLWC. Meanwhile, SPs reported feeling that they were provided a great opportunity to learn more about oral health care and to have an ability to educate dental students about cancer survivor's oral health needs. The broader impact of this OSCE is that while future dental providers are better equipped to serve this patient population upon joining the practice community, it also had an immediate impact on the local cancer patient community. SPs' recently acquired oral health care knowledge from their OSCE participation can possibly have a positive affect with friends, family, and care givers, by empowering SPs to educate others to better advocate for a cancer survivor's oral health care needs. Similarly, civically engaged OSCEs used in other professional training settings may motivate students to participate in the future care and services of other particular patient or client populations.

REFERENCES

American Dental Association. (2010). *State dental licensure for US dentists*. Retrieved from http:///www.ada.org/492.aspx

American Psychological Association. (n.d.). *Civic engagement*. Retrieved from http://www.apa.org/education/undergrad/civic-engagement.aspx

Austin, Z., Gregory, P., & Tabak, D. (2006). Instructional design and assessment: Simulated patients vs. standardized patients in objective structured clinical examinations. *American Journal of Pharmaceutical Education, 70*(5), 1-7.

Baker, S. R., Pankhurst, C. L., & Robinson, P. G. (2006). Utility of two oral health-related quality-of-life measures in patients with xerostomia. *Community Dentistry and Oral Epidemiology, 34*, 351-362.

Barker, G. J., Epstein, J. B., Williams, K. B., Gorsky, M, & Raber-Durlacher, J. E. (2005). Current practice and knowledge of oral care for cancer patients: A survey of supportive health care providers. *Support Care Cancer, 13*, 32-41.

Bokken, L., Rethans, J. J., van Heurn, L., Duvivier, R., Scherpbier, A., & van der Vleuten, C. (2009). Students' views on the use of real patients and simulated patients in undergraduate medical education. *Academic Medicine, 84*, 958-963.

Burzynski, N. J., Rankin, K. V., Silverman, S., Jr., Scheetz, J. P., & Jones, D. L. (2002). Graduating dental students' perceptions of oral cancer education. *Journal of Cancer Education. 17*, 83-84.

Cannick, G. F., Horowitz, A. M., Garr, D. R., Reed, S. G., Neville, B. W., Day, T. A., Woolson, R. F. & Lackland, D. T. (2007). Oral cancer prevention and early detection: Using the PRECEDE-PROCEED framework to guild the training of health professional students. *Journal of Cancer Education, 22*(4), 250-253.

Charmaz, K. (2002). Grounded theory: Objectivist and constructivist methods. *Handbook of Qualitative Research*. Thousand Oaks, CA: SAGE.

Epstein, R. M., Franks, P., Fiscella, K., Shields, C. G., Meldrum, S. C., Kravitz, R. L., ... Duberstein, P. R. (2005). Measuring patient-centered communication in patient-physician consultations: theoretical and practical issues. *Social Science and Medicine*, 61, 1516-1528.

Epstein, R.M. & Hundert, E.M. (2002). Defining and Assessing Professional Competence. *The Journal of the American Medical Association, 287*(2), 226-235.

Elting, L.S., Cooksley, C., Chambers, M., Cantor, S.B., Manzullo, E., & Rubenstein, E.B. (2003). The burdens of cancer therapy: Clinical and economic outcomes of chemotherapy-induced mucositis. *Cancer, 98*, 1531-1539.

Flick, U. (2002). *An introduction to qualitative research*. Thousand Oaks, CA: Sage Publications.

Greenfield, S., Kaplan, S.H., Ware, J. E., Jr., Martin, E., & Frank, H. (1988). Patients' participation in medical care: Effects on blood sugar control and quality of life in diabetes. *Journal of General Internal Medicine. 3*(5), 448-457.

Haden N. K., Catalanotto, F. A., Alexander, C. J., Bailit, H., Battrell, A., Broussard, ... Valachovic, R. W. (2003). Improving the oral health status of all Americans: Roles and responsibilities of academic dental institutions: A report of the ADEA President's Commission. *Journal of Dental Education, 67*(5), 563-583.

Hillen, M. A., de Haes, H. C., & Smets, E. M. (2010). Cancer patients' trust in their physician—A review. *Psychooncology*. (Advanced electronic publication).

Holsti, O.R. (1969). *Content analysis for the social sciences and humanities*. Reading, MA: Addision-Wesley.

Kaslow, N. Grus, C., Campbell, L., Fouad, A., Hatcher, R., & Rodolfa, E. (2009). Competency assessment toolkit for professional psychology. *Training and Education in Professional Psychology*, 3(4), S27-S45.

Kerr, A. R., Changrani, J. G., Gany, F. M., & Cruz, G. D. (2004). An academic dental center grapples with oral cancer disparities: Current collaboration and future opportunities. *Journal of Dental Education. 68*(5), 531-541.

Kuthy, R. A., McQuistan, M. R., Riniker, K. J., Heller, K. E., & Qian, F. (2005). Students' comfort level in treating vulnerable populations and future willingness to treat: Results prior to extramural participation. *Journal of Dental Education. 69*(12), 1307-1314.

Kuthy, R. A., Heller, K. E., Riniker, K. J., McQuistan, M. R., & Qian, F. (2007). Students' opinions about treating vulnerable populations immediately after completing community-based clinical experiences. *Journal of Dental Education. 71*(5), 646-654.

Ley, P. (1988). Communicating with patients improving communication, satisfaction and compliance. *Psychology and Medicine Series*. New York, NY: Chapman and Hall.

Linsen, S., Schmidt-Beer, J., Fimmers, R., Grüner, M., & Koeck, B. (2009). Cranio-mandibular pain, bite force, and oral health-related quality of life in patients with jaw resection. *Journal of Pain and Symptom Management. 37*(1), 94-106.

McGuire, D.B. (2003). Barriers and strategies in implementation of oral care standards for cancer patients. *Support Care Cancer. 11*, 435-441.

Mainous, A. G., III, Kerse, N., Brock, C. D., Hughes, K., & Pruitt, C. (2003). Doctors developing patient trust: Perspectives from the United States and New Zealand. *New Zeal Fam Physician, 30*, 336-341.

Mok, E. (2001). Empowerment of cancer patients: From a Chinese perspective. *Nurse Ethics, 8*(1), 69-76.

National Cancer Institute. (2010). *SEER stat fact sheets: All sites* [Data file]. Retrieved from http://seer.cancer.gov/statfacts/html/all.html#incidence-mortality

Öhrn, K. E., Wahlin, Y. B., & Sjoden, P. O. (2001). Oral status during radiotherapy and chemotherapy: A descriptive study of patients experiences and the occurrence of oral complications. *Support Care Cancer, 9*, 247-257.

Owen, W. F. (1984). Interpretive themes in relational communication. *Quarterly Journal of Speech, 70*, 274-287.

Pearson, S. D., & Raeke, L. H. (2000). Patients' trust in physicians: Many theories, few measures, and little data. *Journal of General Internal Medicine, 15*(7), 509-513.

Safran, D. G., Taira, D. A., Rogers, W. H., Kosinski, M., Ware, J. E., Jr., & Tarlov, A. R. (1998). Linking primary care performance to outcomes of care. *Journal of Family Practice. 47*, 3.

Silverman, J., Archer, J., Gillard, S., Howells, R., & Benson, J. (2010). Initial evaluation of EPSCALE, a rating scale that assesses the process of explanation and planning in the medical interview. *Patient Education and Counseling*, 1-5.

Strauss, A., & Corbin, J. (1990). Basics of qualitative research. *Techniques and Procedures for Developing Grounded Theory.* Newbury Park, CA: SAGE.

Trotti, A., Bellm, L. A., Epstein, J. B., Frame, D., Fuchs, H. J., Gwede, C. K., ... Zilberberg, M. D. (2003). Mucositis incidence, severity and associated outcomes in patients with head and neck cancer receiving radiotherapy with or without chemotherapy: A systematic literature review. *Radiotherapy Oncology. 66*, 253-262.

U.S. Department of Health and Human Services National Institutes of Health. (2009). *Oral complications of cancer treatment: What the dental team can do* (National Institute of Dental and Craniofacial Research Publication No. 09-4372). Bethesda, MD: National Oral Health Information Clearinghouse.

Vu, N. V., & Barrow, H. S. (1994). Use of standardized patients in clinical assessments: recent developments and measurements findings. *Educational Researcher, 23*, 23-30.

Wakefield, A., Cooke, S., & Boggis, C. (2003). Learning together: Use of simulated patients with nursing and medical students for breaking bad news. *International Journal of Palliative Nursing, 9*(1), 32-38.

Wallace, J., Rao, R., & Haslam, R. (2002). Simulated patients and objective structured clinical examinations: review of their use in medical education. *Advances in Psychiatric Treatment, 8*, 342-342.

Watson, M., Skelton, J., Bond, C., Croft, P., Wiskin, C., Grimshaw, J., & Mollison, J. (2004). Simulated patients in the community pharmacy setting-Using simulated patients to measure practice in the community pharmacy setting. *Pharmacy World & Science, 26*(1), 32-37.

World Health Organization. (2010) *Cancer fact sheet.* Retrieved from http://www .who.int/mediacentre/factsheets/fs297/en/index.html

Wykurz, G., & Kelly, D. (2002). Developing the role of patients as teachers: Literature review. *BMJ, 325,* 818-821.

Yoder, K. (2006). A framework for service-learning in dental education. *Journal of Dental Education, 70*(2), 115-123.

Zakrzewska, J. M., Leeson, R. M. A, Mcliskey, M., & Vickers, M. (1997). The development of patient information leaflets: Care of the mouth after radiotherapy. *Gerontology, 14,* 48-53.

Zraick, R., Allen, R., & Johnson, S. (2003). The use of standardized patients to teach and test interpersonal and communication skills with students in speech-language pathology. *Advances in Health Sciences Education, 8*(3*)*, 237-248.

ABOUT THE AUTHORS

Nancy Blank, PhD, is an associate professor of criminal justice and the coordinator of the Undergraduate Criminal Justice Practicum and Internship Program. Her research focuses on academic-based service-learning, diversity service-learning, and youth court programs.
E-mail: nbblank@widener.edu

Robert G. Bringle, PhD, PhilD, is Chancellor's Professor of Psychology and Philanthropic Studies and executive director of the Center for Service and Learning at Indiana University-Purdue University Indianapolis. His scholarly interests related to service-learning, community service, and civic engagement include student and faculty attitudes and motives, educational outcomes, institutionalization, assessment, and measurement issues.
E-mail: rbringle@iupui.edu

Alfred Chan Cheung-ming, PhD, is currently chair professor of social gerontology, Department of Sociology and Social Policy, member of the council, director of the Asia-Pacific Institute of Ageing Studies, and director of Office of Service Learning at Lingnan University. Professor Chan's research areas focus on social gerontology, health and social care, welfare policy, and program evaluation.
E-mail: sscmchan@ln.edu.hk

Sharon Chan Sin-yui, MPhil, is an assistant teaching fellow in the Department of Sociology and Social Policy at Lingnan University, concurrently working toward a PhD in the Department of Social Work and Social Administration at the University of Hong Kong. She has over 5 years of experience in leading service-learning courses and supervising service-

learning students. She is also experienced in qualitative research methods.
E-mail: sharon@ln.edu.hk

Polly Chiu Yin-nei, BBA, is currently the senior project officer for the Office of Service Learning at Lingnan University. She obtained her undergraduate degree in Business Administration from City University of Hong Kong. She has over 4 years of experience in organizing service-learning courses and leading service-learning groups. She has experience in curriculum design and qualitative and quantitative research and program evaluation.
E-mail: pollychiu@ln.edu.hk

Emily Deering, MA, is a recent graduate of Communication Studies at Indiana University-Purdue University Indianapolis, and she has just started her predoctoral work at the University of Pittsburgh.
E-mail: edeering@umail.iu.edu.

Lawrence Fehr, PhD, is a professor of psychology. His is the author of two books and has written journal articles on topics such as elder abuse, children's cognitive development, and service-learning.
E-mail: lafehr@widener.edu

Elizabeth Goering, PhD, received her PhD in organizational communication from Purdue University, Indiana, and is associate professor in the Department of Communication Studies at Indiana University-Purdue University Indianapolis. Her research focuses primarily on the intersections between culture and communication in a variety of contexts.
E-mail: bgoering@iupui.edu

Julie A. Hatcher, PhD, is an associate professor of philanthropic studies in the School of Liberal Arts at Indiana University-Purdue University Indianapolis. She is the director of Undergraduate Programs and a senior scholar with the Center for Service and Learning. Her research focuses on the role of higher education in civil society, civic learning outcomes in higher education, and the philanthropic motivations of professionals.
E-mail: jhatcher@iupui.edu

Crystal Henderson, MA, received her degree in applied communication studies from Indiana University and is currently an adjunct faculty member in the Department of Communication Studies at Ivy Tech Community College in Indianapolis. Her research interests include civic engagement

among youth and young adults, social movements, and political discourse.
E-mail: clhender@ivytech.edu

Barbara L. Ibrahim, PhD, is founding director of the John D. Gerhart Center for Philanthropy and Civic Engagement at American University in Cairo. The program was launched in 2006 for strengthening Arab philanthropy and civic engagement and is based in Cairo. Prior to that she was regional director for West Asia and North Africa at the Population Council, a position she held since 1991.
E-mail: bibrahim@aucegypt.edu

Marjori M. Krebs, EdD, is an assistant professor at the University of New Mexico in the Department of Teacher Education. She works with teacher candidates and cooperating teachers, along with teaching methods courses for students.
E-mail: mkrebs@unm.edu

Carol Ma Hok-ka, PhD, is an adjunct assistant professor in the Department of Sociology and Social Policy and the assistant director in the Office of Service-Learning in Lingnan University. She has a particular passion for the promotion of intergenerational programs and is an active participant/researcher in both elderly services and youth services.
E-mail: carolma@ln.edu.hk

Tami L. Moore, PhD, is an assistant professor of higher education in the Educational Leadership Program at Oklahoma State University. Her research agenda focuses broadly on the role of higher education institutions in the communities they serve, employing social and critical theory in the reading of community engagement. Her current projects explore issues related to faculty work and community-engaged scholarship, and the relationship between geographic place and community engagement in the United States, the United Kingdom, and Australia.
E-mail: tami.moore@okstate.edu

Michael Q. Patton, PhD, is an independent organizational development and evaluation consultant. He is former president of the American Evaluation Association and author of six evaluation books. He teaches regularly in The Evaluators' Institute, the American Evaluation Association's professional development courses, and The World Bank's *International Program in Development Evaluation Training*.
E-mail: mqpatton@prodigy.net

Jocey Quinn, PhD, is a professor of education at the University of Plymouth. Her key research interest is the interrelationship between education and culture. Her work has focused on lifelong learning and issues of social exclusion and knowledge transformation, exploring changes in what counts for knowledge and who has access to it. Her current work includes coordinating the ESRC seminar series New Perspectives on Education and Culture.
E-mail: jocey.quinn@plymouth.ac.uk

Susan Reed, PhD, is an associate professor at the School for New Learning, DePaul University, where she employs community based learning to teach adults about health care access. Her published books and articles are in both the areas of health disparities and community based learning with adults.
E-mail: sreed@depaul.edu

Helen Rosenberg, PhD, is an associate professor of sociology and faculty director for community-based learning and research at the University of Wisconsin-Parkside. She has taught in the areas of deviance and gerontology, and she has been active in community-based learning projects throughout her twenty year tenure at the university.
E-mail: rosenbeh@uwp.edu.

Howard Rosing, PhD, is the executive director of the Steans Center and an adjunct faculty in community service studies, anthropology, and peace, justice and conflict studies as well as an affiliate faculty in community psychology at DePaul University in Chicago. His research focuses on urban food access, migration, and economic restructuring in the Caribbean and Chicago and community-based research as pedagogy.
E-mail: hrosing@depaul.edu.

Lorilee R. Sandmann, PhD, is a professor in the adult education program, Department of Lifelong Education, Administration, & Policy at the University of Georgia. Her research focuses on leadership and organizational change in higher education with special emphasis on the institutionalization of community engagement, as well as faculty roles and rewards related to engaged scholarship.
E-mail: sandmann@uga.edu.

Stuart M. Schrader, PhD, is a clinical assistant professor of behavioral sciences, Oral Biology Department, Indiana University School of Dentistry and an Adjunct Clinical Assistant Professor, Department of Family Medicine, Indiana University School of Medicine. His research interests

include: Dental and medical education, civic engagement and service-learning, HIV/AIDS care and services, dental oncology and assessments of various forms of OSCEs.
E-mail: sschrade@iupui.edu.

Sandy S. S. Yeung, MA, received her degree in East-West drama at the Chinese University of Hong Kong. She was the project officer in Office of Service Learning, Lingnan University in 2007 and was engaged in the Digital Classroom Project during 2007–2009. She has been actively participating in promoting art and cultural activities among youth.

Abbe B. Shapiro, MSW, received her degree in social work from Indiana University in May of 2011. She is currently a care coordinator for Choices, Inc. in Indianapolis, Indiana.
E-mail: abbeshapiro@gmail.com.

Lori Simons, PhD, is an associate professor of psychology and the coordinator of the Undergraduate Psychology Practicum and Internship Program. Her research focuses on academic-based and cultural-based service-learning and community perceptions of experiential education programs. In addition, *Kevin Barnes, Denise Georganas, & George Manpuram* are undergraduate students in the psychology department at Widener University.
E-mail: lnsimons@mail.widener.edu.

Anne Statham, PhD, is a professor of sociology and director of the Service-learning Program at University of Southern Indiana. She has published books and papers in the fields of women and work, gender studies, women and poverty, environmental studies, social psychology, and engaged scholarship and service-learning.
E-mail: aastatham@usi.edu.

David A. Zahl, M.A., is a curriculum development and clinical skills education specialist in the Office of Academic Affairs at the Indiana University School of Dentistry. He coordinates standardized and simulated patient objective structured clinical exams and manages aspects of the Doctor of Dental Surgery curriculum.
E-mail: dzahl@iupui.edu.

Susan L. Zunt, DDS, MS, is a professor of oral pathology and chair, Oral Pathology, Medicine and Radiology, Indiana University School of Den-

tistry.   Her scholarly interests reside in dental education and in the diagnosis and management of oral disease.
E-mail: szunt@iupui.edu

CPSIA information can be obtained at www.ICGtesting.com
Printed in the USA
LVOW101732191011

251201LV00002B/1/P